AD Biography
Sedaka Nei

P9-DGQ-972

Podolsky, Rich. Neil Sedaka : rock'n'roll
survivor : the inside story of his incredible
comeback   9001080209

DISCARDED BY
MEAD PUBLIC LIBRARY

NEIL SEDAKA

ROCK'N'ROLL SURVIVOR

ROCK'N'ROLL SURVIVOR

NEIL SEDAKA

THE INSIDE STORY OF HIS INCREDIBLE COMEBACK

Rich Podolsky

Foreword by
ELTON JOHN

NEIL SEDAKA: Rock'n'Roll Survivor
THE INSIDE STORY OF HIS INCREDIBLE COMEBACK
by Rich Podolsky

A Jawbone Book
First Edition 2013
Published in the UK and the USA by Jawbone Press
2a Union Court,
20–22 Union Road,
London SW4 6JP,
England
www.jawbonepress.com

ISBN 978-1-908279-42-2

Volume copyright © 2013 Outline Press Ltd. Text copyright © Rich Podolsky.
All rights reserved. No part of this book covered by the copyrights hereon may
be reproduced or copied in any manner whatsoever without written
permission, except in the case of brief quotations embodied in articles or
reviews where the source should be made clear. For more information contact
the publishers.

EDITOR Tom Seabrook
DESIGN Paul Cooper

Printed by Regent Publishing Services Limited, China

1 2 3 4 5 17 16 15 14 13

CONTENTS

9001080209

FOREWORD BY **ELTON JOHN** 7

AUTHOR'S NOTE 10

INTRODUCTION 16

CHAPTER 1: *MY YIDDISHE MOMMA* 19

CHAPTER 2: *IT HURTS TO BE IN LOVE* 41

CHAPTER 3: *THE MONEY STOPS ROLLING IN* 49

CHAPTER 4: *STAR-CROSSED LOVERS* 59

CHAPTER 5: *EMERGENCE* 71

CHAPTER 6: *HEY NEIL, SING EMBRACEABLE YOU* 81

CHAPTER 7: *PHIL CODY, PHIL CODY* 88

CHAPTER 8: *SOLITAIRE* 100

CHAPTER 9: *THE HUNGRY YEARS* 106

CHAPTER 10: *THE TRA-LA DAYS ARE OVER* 116

CHAPTER 11: *ELTON TO THE RESCUE* 125

CHAPTER 12: *LAUGHTER IN THE RAIN* 148

CHAPTER 13: *SEDAKA'S BACK* 157

CHAPTER 14: *LOVE WILL KEEP US TOGETHER* 164

CHAPTER 15: *BREAKING UP IS HARD TO DO (AGAIN)* 172

CHAPTER 16: *YESTERDAY ONCE MORE* 178

CHAPTER 17: *SHOULD'VE NEVER LET YOU GO* 185

CHAPTER 18: *SAYING GOODBYE TO HOWIE* 193

CHAPTER 19: *SEDAKA: AN AMERICAN IDOL* 199

CHAPTER 20: *THE SECRET SAUCE* 209

CHAPTER 21: *WAKING UP IS HARD TO DO* 219

CHAPTER 22: *THE REAL NEIL* 224

EPILOGUE 236

THE TRA-LA DAYS: AN AFTERWORD BY **PHIL CODY** 241

DISCOGRAPHY 243

SELECT LIVE APPEARANCES, 1958–78 256

ENDNOTES 259

BIBLIOGRAPHY & SOURCES 260

INDEX 263

ACKNOWLEDGEMENTS 268

For my father, Morris Podolsky, who loved Frank Sinatra's phrasing, Johnny Mercer's lyrics, and the business of making and selling records.

FOREWORD

by Elton John

I grew up listening to everything that came out of America. 'Oh! Carol' was probably the first song I heard by Neil, quickly followed by 'Calendar Girl' and 'Happy Birthday, Sweet Sixteen.' To begin with, I loved his voice and I loved his songs. Consequently, when I grew older and understood where they came from—the Brill Building—it all made sense.

I was a fan straightaway. He made a lot of records in a row on the RCA label, and I remember buying them all. We only had two or three programs in England where you could hear rock'n'roll music, and it was probably on a Saturday in 1959 when I first heard 'Oh! Carol.'

I used to buy all the music publications, and I saw pictures of Neil. I followed the American charts and the English charts. At that time, English pop music wasn't that great, so we were all inspired by the songwriters and singers coming out of America.

I wasn't aware that Neil had moved to England to try and forge a comeback until the 10cc recordings (*The Tra-La Days Are Over* and *Solitaire*) were made. I didn't know because I was in America when all that was happening. Those recordings re-launched Neil's career sensationally in Britain. Everybody loved those records. I became reacquainted with him then, and for the first time in my life I got to meet him.

I was a huge fan of *The Tra-La Days Are Over*. It was great to see someone who played the piano. I've always been a great lover of people who disappear and then come back because they're genuinely talented, and they have their day in the sun. I hate it when people like that are forgotten about. Neil was swept away by Beatlemania, but great songwriters always re-establish themselves, because they don't stop writing great songs.

Neil had a huge Renaissance. We used to hang out in Britain during that time, and that's when I started my record company, Rocket. I wanted to release his new songs in America, because nobody else would release them there—even after he had three or four hits in Britain. I asked him if we could release his album, and 'Laughter In The Rain' was the first single on Rocket in America. And the rest is history.

I just thought it was an injustice—here was this man who fought for his life, came to England, made his career again by writing great songs, and America was ignoring him. These were great songs and great recordings. It was great to have him on my label. I was so proud. We may have done him a favor by releasing them, but I wanted this record desperately, because I felt it was a great record—a fabulous record.

And then Neil had hits and his career began to soar in America again. It was poetic justice—as it should have been. I'm just glad to have had a part in it, because he deserved it. He's a great writer—he's one of my peers, one of the people I looked up to as a songwriter.

Look at 'Breaking Up Is Hard To Do.' I was blown away by the simplicity of the melody. It's a classic song—a standard. It will always be sung. It's one of the great songs of all time, whether you're singing it fast or whether you're singing it slow. Neil's second attempt was singing it slow, and that's the mark of a great song.

Neil is also a great classical pianist. He could have been a classical pianist, but he realized he wanted to be a pop musician. I could have been a classical pianist, too, but I wanted to be in rock'n'roll. It's more fun.

First and foremost, I'm a songwriter, and I've been influenced by the greats. Neil was and is one of the greats. As a younger performer, I was influenced by Neil, and then to become friends later in life—it's the greatest compliment you could possibly have, because without people like Neil, I wouldn't be here.

Neil is fun. He's great company. He's kind. He's been so supportive to me. We're cut from the same cloth. He's been a great addition to my life. It's great when you meet those people who have been your heroes, and they turn out to be heroes again. And he is. To be given his blessing that you're doing a good thing—it means so much. I'm a huge admirer of his ability to play the piano, write songs, and sing. When we get together we have the biggest laugh. We're just like two old yentas.

ELTON JOHN,
Los Angeles,
February 2013

AUTHOR'S NOTE

When I was growing up in Philadelphia in the 50s, I had two passions: the Philadelphia Phillies and rock'n'roll—not necessarily in that order.

The Phillies were a hard team to love. In 1950, when I was four, they won the National League pennant, but for the rest of the decade they never lived up to that promise. If it weren't for Richie Ashburn, I might have completely turned my back on them.

Ashburn was a fair-haired kid from Tilden, Nebraska, who played centerfield for the Phillies as gracefully as Baryshnikov danced onstage. He could run like the wind and hit with the best of them.

Watching Ashburn play was a joy that I had assumed was a birthright for every Phillies fan. Then, one January morning in 1960, I woke up to some terrible news: the Phillies had made a deal to send Ashburn to the Chicago Cubs for two players who were soon forgotten. I was devastated, and when I opened the *Philadelphia Daily News* that day, I discovered that sports editor Larry Merchant felt the same way. "Who gives a damn in the dead of winter that the Phillies made another move for the future," he wrote. "Richie Ashburn is gone, and I'd like to pay my respects."

When I read that, something happened to me. For the first time, I realized how someone else's written words could affect and move me. That moment was the first time I ever thought about becoming a writer.

Around that same time, my father, who was a record buyer for Sun Ray's chain of stores in Philly, started bringing home 45rpm records. The first batch he brought home, in the fall of '58, included hits like Ricky Nelson's 'Poor Little Fool,' The Everly Brothers' 'Bird Dog,' and The Elegants' classic '(Where Are You) Little Star.'

I would go down to our basement and start fitting those annoying little plastic spindle adapters into the hole in the center of the 45s, since most record players in those days were built to play only 33 and 78rpm music. I would load up the spindle with five or six 45s at a time, watch them drop slowly, and play them over and over until I had most of them memorized.

In January 1959, as I was approaching my 13th birthday, my dad brought home a new batch that included a group of songs that illustrated how diversified rock'n'roll had become by then. Among them were ballads by Tommy Edwards ('It's All In The Game') and country singer Conway Twitty ('It's Only Make Believe'), The Kingston Trio's folk classic '(Hang Down Your Head) Tom Dooley,' and Phil Spector's wonderful 'To Know Him Is To Love Him,' which Spector recorded for $40 with his group The Teddy Bears.

And there was also one more, slow story song: 'The Diary,' by a new kid named Neil Sedaka. I loved it immediately. When Sedaka sang Howie Greenfield's lyrics over his own melody, he told the story of a guy with a crush on a girl, too shy to let her know. He sang it with a shyness of his own that was convincing. In that one song he captured the emotions of probably millions of teenagers—including me—who felt the same way.

When Sedaka sang the song on *American Bandstand*, I was shocked by how young he looked. Instantly likeable, the song rose to number 14 on the charts—an impressive feat for a virtually unknown artist.

(At the time, I didn't know that Neil had written Connie Francis's hit song 'Stupid Cupid' the summer before.)

I made sure to pay attention when my favorite Philly DJs—Joe Niagara at WIBG and Jerry Blavat at WHAT—mentioned Sedaka's name. About six months after 'The Diary' left the charts, Neil was back with a smash called 'Oh! Carol,' and from there his career took off. He quickly followed up with hits like 'Stairway To Heaven,' 'Calendar Girl,' and 'Breaking Up Is Hard To Do,' which reached number one in the summer of '62.

Neil had a great formula for his songs, which everyone seemed to love. He'd begin and end them with a series of "tra-la-las" or "dooby-doos," with the lyrics fitting in between. He called them sandwich songs.

Classically trained at Juilliard, Neil longed to branch out away from the sandwich-song formula, but what none of us knew at the time was that the record executives at RCA had restricted him to using just four chords: C, A minor, D minor, and G. Their attitude was "if it ain't broke, don't fix it." By the time they finally gave in to Neil's request for artistic freedom, it was late 1964, and the British Invasion had put nearly every American pop singer into retirement.

For the next decade, Sedaka would struggle to make a living. These were lean years filled with self-doubt, the humility of having to perform in dives, and the loss of hundreds of thousands of dollars through disreputable management. His decade-long quest for a comeback ran into one roadblock after another. Better men would have given up. Instead, Sedaka moved to Britain, where they still loved his music and were willing to play his new songs on the radio.

In 1974, when Sedaka made his triumphant return to the top of the charts with 'Laughter In The Rain,' I was as thrilled as anyone.

After all he'd been through, here was a great American comeback story—one that would be accentuated when The Captain & Tennille broke through with Neil's 'Love Will Keep Us Together' and inserted their own line at the end of the song as a tribute to him: "Sedaka is back."

Sedaka followed 'Laughter' with another number one song, 'Bad Blood,' and further hits like 'The Immigrant' and 'That's When The Music Takes Me,' and then he took everyone by surprise with his beautiful ballad version of 'Breaking Up Is Hard To Do.' In 1980, he offered yet another surprise when he recorded a duet with his 17-year-old daughter, Dara. Their collaborative ballad, 'Should've Never Let You Go,' reached the top 20 on the pop charts and number one on *Billboard*'s Adult Contemporary charts.

All of those songs made for great memories—not only for me but also for the millions of Sedaka fans around the world. I was a huge fan. So when I was writing my last book, *Don Kirshner: The Man With The Golden Ear,* I was genuinely thrilled to hear Neil's voice on the other end of the phone in response to my request for an interview.

In that book, which was about all the great songwriters Kirshner discovered (including Neil and Carole King), I wrote a story about a fight that ensued between Kirshner and Neil's manager during the recording of 'Next Door To An Angel.' The topic was a little touchy, since Neil's manager had been having an affair with his mother. When the book came out in March 2012, I wasn't sure how Neil would take it. I got my answer a month later, when he was interviewed by the *New York Post* for their regular Sunday feature, 'In My Library.' Neil listed four books among those in his library: biographies of Frank Sinatra, Johnny Mercer, and Paul McCartney, and, to my delighted surprise, *Don Kirshner: The Man With The Golden Ear*. I couldn't believe my good fortune. When he told the interviewer that the book was "a great read," I knew there was no doubt about how he felt.

A few months later, Neil was interviewed at one of New York's top cultural centers, the 92nd Street Y. He was there to promote his new children's book, but the interviewer spent most of the hour going over his career. When he got to the ten-year stretch from 1964 to '74, when Sedaka struggled to earn a living, I was surprised at how willing Neil was to talk about those hard times and to discuss some of the dives he played in order to support his family. Just 18 months before his career went south, he had been the headliner at the Copacabana.

I never gave much thought how hard those years must have been for him, yet here he was baring his soul in front of a packed audience. When he was asked about his friend Carole King's breakthrough as a performer with *Tapestry* in 1971, Neil cringed. "It marked the beginning of the singer-songwriter era," he said, "and I wanted to be a part of it badly. I wanted it with a vengeance."

At that moment, I realized that Neil Sedaka's hungry years and amazing comeback represented a truly great story. Here was a man willing to expose all of those old wounds to share the details of his inspiring turnaround. In 1982, Neil had written an autobiography, *Laughter In The Rain*, but back then those wounds were still too fresh for him to talk about in detail. Now, 30 years later, he was ready.

After the interview, Neil took to an adjoining hall to sign copies of his children's book. I had brought with me a copy of my Kirshner book to give to Neil. Inside it, I had written: "You have always been Rock & Roll Royalty to me." When I introduced myself to Neil and handed him the book, he seemed genuinely moved, so I went with my gut. "Neil," I said, "I want to write my next book about you."

"Yes," he smiled. "We'll see."

There was a line of waiting fans with books in hand for him to sign, so I thanked him and stepped away to watch.

During my research process for the Kirshner book, I'd also interviewed Sedaka's wife, Leba, on the phone, but I had never met her. I soon located her nearby, talking to some friends. I introduced myself, and I was relieved that she also was glad to meet me. I asked her if she'd had a chance to read my book.

"I had no choice," she told me. "As Neil was reading it in the next room, he would run in and read me line after line—he loved it so much."

When she said that, I knew that there was a good chance they would accept my offer to write this book. After some discussion back and forth, we organized a series of interviews to fit around Neil's busy performing schedule. (Even at 73, Neil was still performing more than 50 dates a year, including one that year at Royal Albert Hall in London with the full Royal Philharmonic Orchestra.)

It's been a long time since I first put 'The Diary' on the spindle. Fifty-four years later, I've finally been able to sit down with one of the most prolific songwriters and performers in history. What I learned was that Neil faced many more roadblocks to his successful return than I could have ever imagined. It was a struggle that just about anyone else would have abandoned, but also a struggle that, thanks to his undeniable perseverance, had resulted in some of his greatest music—a struggle that gave us 'Laughter In The Rain,' 'The Hungry Years,' 'Bad Blood,' 'Solitaire,' and many more—and, oh yes, a struggle that also produced the greatest unscripted line on a record in many a decade.

"Sedaka is back!"

INTRODUCTION

On July 28 2012, Neil Sedaka performed for an amazing 43rd time at what has become his hometown venue, The Theater at Westbury, Long Island, 30 miles from New York City. When it opened in 1956, the Westbury Music Fair, as it was then known, introduced something quite new: the theater-in-the-round, set in a relatively intimate atmosphere. On the night of Sedaka's performance, the room was packed to capacity with nearly 3,000 adoring fans. Never mind his advanced age. Even at 73, Neil didn't let them down. He looked great, and he sounded even better.

The show opened with a video projected onto a large screen that hung from the ceiling. The video featured 25 of the world's greatest recording artists covering Sedaka's greatest hits—from Frank Sinatra to Elton John, from Carole King to Elvis—one huge star after another. The audience, applauding enthusiastically, seemed to grow more impressed with each snippet. It was a stunning reminder of the enduring power of Sedaka's music.

"These are my people, my *mishpucha*," he said, using the Yiddish word for family, as the roaring applause died down. When someone called out a request, he responded, Jolson-like: "Don't worry, I've got a million of them, and I'm going to sing them all." And he did.

After performing early hits like 'The Diary,' 'Oh! Carol,' 'Happy Birthday, Sweet Sixteen,' and 'Calendar Girl,' Sedaka suddenly turned serious.

"From 1958 to 1963, I sold 25 million records," he told the audience, to warm and appreciative applause.

"Then a new group came on the scene," he added.

The crowd quieted.

"The Beatles," he whispered.

You could hear a pin drop.

"NOT GOOD!" he said, with emphasis, and then paused.

There was some nervous laughter.

"I retired."

The room was absolutely still.

"I stopped singing for ten years."

Despite having sold more records than anyone but Elvis Presley, at the age of 24 Neil Sedaka had to watch helplessly as his career collapsed.

The Beatles and the British Invasion had a lot to do with it. It wasn't just Sedaka who fell out of favor: it was just about every popular American pop singer. Paul Anka, Bobby Rydell, Frankie Avalon, Ricky Nelson, and Connie Francis all struggled. Even Elvis had his problems. From mid '63 to late '69, the King only broke into the top ten once, with 'Crying In The Chapel.

For more than a decade, Sedaka suffered one setback after another as he tried to launch a comeback. Sure, he was still making a few dollars writing hits for other singers, but supporting his family was far from easy. He was like a salesman, working for commission. The songwriting and performance royalties from his string of hits had completely stopped, and to make matters worse, Sedaka had mistakenly trusted the people managing those royalties.

Neil tried valiantly to change with the times in an attempt to win back the fans he lost to The Beatles. He took on younger, hipper songwriting partners, like Carole Bayer (latterly known as Carole Bayer Sager), with whom he wrote 'When Love Comes Knockin' At Your Door' for The Monkees, but no one wanted to hear Neil sing anything but his old hits. He had a reputation as a bubblegum singer, and the public didn't seem inclined toward associating him with anything else.

To survive, Sedaka played piano on demo recordings and took bookings in dives; with two young children, he simply needed the money. His star had fallen so far in just a few short years. During one of the interviews I conducted with him at his New York City apartment in 2012, he recalled how painful those times could be. "People would come up to me and say: didn't you used to be Neil Sedaka?"

Beginning in 1964, Neil would slowly mount a plan to get back on the charts and be accepted as a serious performer once again by the American public. Little did he know that it would take him more than a decade—a decade spent touring workingmen's clubs in Australia and the UK, changing lyricists and managers, collaborating with the British group 10cc, and battling his way back to the top.

Then, one magical night, Neil performed at the Royal Albert Hall. His set of new songs, which concluded with 'Solitaire,' was greeted with thunderous applause. Even so, he wasn't expecting much, and certainly wouldn't have predicted that Elton John—the biggest rock'n'roll star of the decade—would soon stop by to see him with an offer to release Sedaka's new songs on his own Rocket Records label.

And that was it. In October 1974, 'Laughter In The Rain' showed up on the *Billboard* charts at number 95. It was Sedaka's first appearance on the charts in over a decade. He broke down and cried when he saw it. Sixteen weeks later, the song reached number one, putting the seal on one of the most amazing comebacks in pop music history.

This is the story of how he did it.

CHAPTER 1
MY YIDDISHE MOMMA

O rphaned at the age of four and raised by her grandmother, Eleanor Sedaka grew up to be an attractive woman with a very strong personality. She had been born into a Russian-Polish family that had immigrated to Brighton Beach, Brooklyn, at the southern tip of Brooklyn, kissing the Atlantic Ocean, and she was determined to make a better life for herself.

In 1983, Neil Simon introduced Brighton Beach to the rest of the world with his charming comedy *Brighton Beach Memoirs*. Back in the 1930s, it was made up primarily of first and second-generation Russian-Jewish immigrants. Eleanor loved it there. At 17, she was a pretty, petite brunette, weighing in at just 84 pounds, and she knew how to turn on the charm. One night in 1936, out dancing at a social club on Ocean Parkway, she met her man, Mac Sedaka. He cut in on the guy she was dancing with, and the rest is history.

Mac Sedaka came from a family of Sephardic Jews who had emigrated from Turkey. He was a sweet guy with a heart of gold. Most importantly, he held down a steady job driving a cab during the Depression years. He called Eleanor 'Skinny' and was in love with her from that first dance. The attraction wasn't entirely mutual, but Eleanor married Mac for the security he offered, while secretly longing for a more glamorous life.

In 1937, Eleanor gave birth to a daughter, Ronnie, but the

pregnancy was so difficult the doctor advised her that having another child could be dangerous. Late in 1938, she fell pregnant again, and fearing for both herself and the baby she tried to induce a miscarriage by riding every whipsaw roller coaster at Coney Island. Fortunately, it didn't work, and little Neil Sedaka arrived safely on March 13 1939.

From the day he was born, Neil was babied and coddled and dominated by his mother, and protected by his sister. Worried that he was not eating enough, Eleanor hand-fed him until he was seven. He couldn't do anything without her permission, and with Mac driving 12-hour shifts there was no doubt about who ran things at the Sedaka house.

It's no wonder that by the age of seven, Neil was already considered a momma's boy and a nerd by the other kids. He wasn't interested in playing baseball or stickball in the streets; he was usually seen hanging out with his sister and her friends instead. He seemed to gravitate toward the girls, and he related to them. Ronnie even had to teach him how to carry his books to school the way the other boys did, rather than pressed against his chest like a girl.

Neil's best friend and neighbor, Freddie Gershon, would stop by each morning to pick Neil up on the way to school at PS 253. "When we were kids, Neil was very frail and I was very fat," Gershon recalled. "When I got to his apartment each morning, his mother would always give him a bowl of Del Monte peaches in heavy cream to try and fatten him up.

"When she left the room I would eat the peaches and Neil would holler 'finished!' and we'd leave for school. Neil's mother never understood why Neil wasn't gaining any weight, and my mother couldn't understand why I couldn't lose any."

Instead of sports, Neil became proficient in jacks and jump rope.

His life changed, however, when his chorus teacher, Mrs Glantz, sent home a note saying Neil had a musical gift. Eleanor was overjoyed. The note suggested he take piano lessons, if at all possible, in order to exploit that gift.

As she read the note, Eleanor's eyes started to well up. "My baby has talent!" she said lovingly, while giving him a hug. "My baby has talent."

Unfortunately, however, Mac didn't make enough money for piano lessons, let alone a piano. Things were so tight the family shared a painfully crowded two-bedroom apartment with Neil's grandparents and his three aunts. But Eleanor was determined to get Neil his lessons, so she got herself a part-time job by charming the manager at Alexander's Department Store. After six months she had saved $500 to buy a second-hand piano.

Around that same time in 1947, Freddie's mother took the two boys to see Bob Hope in his new movie, *Paleface*. While the film didn't have too many redeeming features, it did include a wonderful song-and-dance number called 'Buttons And Bows,' which later became a big hit when popularized by Dinah Shore.

"When we got home after the movie, I went over to this $25 upright we had to make us look cultural and picked out the tune to 'Buttons And Bows' by using the five black keys," Gershon recalled. "My mother was thrilled—she thought I was going to be the next Mozart."

When Freddie finished playing, Neil had a go. "It was the first time he had ever touched a piano. He not only duplicated what I had done with the song, but he quickly transposed it to the white keys as well. Right there, you knew he had a gift."

Music changed Neil's life. It gave him an outlet: a place he could be himself, and a feeling of strength. Neil's incredible talent was soon recognized, and he was invited to study at the Juilliard School at the Lincoln Center for Performing Arts—at age seven, perhaps the school's youngest scholarship student.

All of my interviews with Neil and his wife Leba were conducted at their Park Avenue apartment in Manhattan, in between Neil's concert stops during the summer of 2012. The first took place near the end of July and was scheduled for two hours. Neil greeted me at the door in a warm-up suit and couldn't have been more cordial. We walked into his den, which glowed from both the sun crashing through and from the many gold records on display. Yet there was nothing ostentatious about the room or Neil. He was friendly and down to Earth. What you saw was what you got.

Music may have given Neil an outlet, but it didn't necessarily make him many new friends. In order to become more popular, he learned to play the hits of the day, and he was soon regularly invited to attend (and play at) his schoolmates' parties.

By the time Neil turned 13 he was well on his way to becoming the next young classical piano sensation, à la Van Cliburn. But fate got in the way. While on vacation in the Catskill Mountains in upstate New York, a neighbor, Ella Greenfield—who ironically also lived in the same building as the Sedaka family in Brighton Beach—heard Neil practicing in the Kenmore Hotel lobby. She suggested that her 16-year-old son Howard, a poet of sorts, could collaborate on writing songs with him.

"I couldn't write a song," Neil told her with all certainty. "I'm afraid I don't know how."

That didn't slow Ella Greenfield down one bit. On her return to her apartment at 3260 Coney Island Avenue, she talked her son into trying to convince Neil to try songwriting with him. Eventually, Howard did convince Neil, and from that first October day in 1952 they wrote a new song every day for close to two years. Their style evolved from middle-of-the-road ballads similar to those Neil heard on his favorite radio show, *Make Believe Ballroom*, to doo-wop and rhythm & blues played by the new DJ in town, Alan Freed. Freed brought with him from Cleveland a new type of music called "rock'n'roll," and like thousands of other New York teens, Neil fell under its spell.

Rock'n'roll wasn't just a source of fun for him, though. It changed his life—literally—beginning with the Lincoln High Ballyhoo talent show, when young Neil sang a rock'n'roll song he'd written. The song was 'Mr Moon,' a bump-and-grind number that brought down the house and took Neil from nerd status to instant celebrity at his school. At the age of 16, he was on his way to becoming a rock'n'roll star.

Neil found joy and sheer excitement writing with Howie, but he had to work secretly behind his mother's back. She had loftier dreams for her son: she wanted him to excel as a classical musician. "She'd be horrified if she knew I was writing rock'n'roll instead of practicing my Beethoven and Bach," Neil recalled.

But rock'n'roll had gotten under his skin. In the next few years, Neil started a group he called The Linc-Tones with Lincoln High classmates Hank Medress, Eddie Rabkin, and Cynthia Zolotin. Jay Siegel replaced Rabkin in the group, and later along with Medress would become famous for their number one song 'The Lion Sleeps Tonight.'

Neil also began singing with another talented future rock'n'roller, Carol Klein, who went to neighboring Madison High in Brooklyn.

She had also begun writing rock'n'roll songs at an early age, and the two met through mutual friends. Sedaka, along with Siegel and Medress, would often take the bus to Klein's house after school, where they would work on their harmonies together in Carol's basement. Klein later changed her surname to King and added an "e" to "Carol." She and Neil would often get together to share their music.

In 1956, a friend of a friend suggested The Linc-Tones meet with a manager he knew called Happy Goday. The Linc-Tones had started performing at social clubs and dances in Brooklyn, and had developed a solid reputation, mainly because they played original music. Goday convinced them to change their name to The Tokens and got them a deal to record three songs for a small, local label called Melba Records. Initially, it was all very exciting, but after sparse airplay, none of the three songs made the charts.

After that, Neil and Howie decided to go their own way, determined to sell their songs to the old-line publishers of Tin Pan Alley and the up-and-coming R&B record labels such as Atlantic. They hit the pavement and started knocking on doors, clearly striking a memorable image: Greenfield, who was six feet tall, towered over Neil by nine inches, and when they stood side by side at a publisher's door they looked like Mutt and Jeff from the comic strip of the same name.

Atlantic's Jerry Wexler liked them, though, and eventually bought a few of their numbers. Two of them would become mild hits: 'I Waited Too Long' rose to number 33 for Lavern Baker, and 'Since You've Been Gone' reached number 38 for Clyde McPhatter. But it was 23-year-old publisher Don Kirshner and his partner Al Nevins at Aldon Music who made the first move. In 1958, Kirshner got Neil and Howie a top 20 hit with his pal Connie Francis singing 'Stupid Cupid,' then signed them to an exclusive five-year contract to write for Aldon Music. Because Neil was underage, Eleanor had to sign the deal for him. (She had no objections to the $50 a week Kirshner was paying the boys.)

Francis gave Greenfield the idea for their next song, 'The Diary,' when she kept consulting hers while the boys were trying to get her to listen to their songs. When she said she loved 'Stupid Cupid' and agreed to record it, Greenfield jokingly tried to get a peek at what she was writing in her diary. "No," she said brushing him away. "No one looks in my diary. That's why I have a lock and key."

Greenfield managed to incorporate Connie's line right into the song, and Kirshner thought it was perfect for Little Anthony & The Imperials, who had just had a huge hit with 'Tears On My Pillow.' The group was signed to George Goldner's End Records, located in Kirshner's building at 1650 Broadway, just down the street from the Brill Building. Goldner loved 'The Diary' as a follow-up for The Imperials and left word to have them record it when he left town, but his A&R man had the group record another song first.

Sedaka was furious at the broken promise and went to Kirshner and Nevins to ask if they could get him his own deal to record. After all, he had sung lead on several songs The Tokens had recorded. At the time, Nevins was producing recordings for RCA by his own former group, The Three Suns. He set up a meeting with Steve Shoals, the man who brought Elvis to their label, and who took a chance on the boyish and charming 19-year-old Sedaka, offering him a deal to perform his own songs. In a way, Sedaka was just what the industry needed.

As Jeff Marcus later wrote in *Goldmine* magazine, "The timing for Neil's singing debut couldn't have been better." Rock'n'roll's reputation had recently been severely tarnished by the payola scandal, when it was revealed that disc jockeys had been paid under the table to play certain recordings, and many of its biggest stars were still "missing in action—Elvis was in the Army, Little Richard found God, and Jerry Lee Lewis married his 13-year-old cousin. In an effort to clean up rock music, labels combed the landscape for the next clean teen dreamboat. They found a poster boy in Neil Sedaka."[1]

Between 1958 and 1963, Neil Sedaka was about the biggest star in the business, adored by teenyboppers from sea to shining sea. His string of hits had this in common: great repetitive melodies and catchy, memorable lyrics. His first offering, 'The Diary,' reached number 14 in 1958 and would soon be followed by 'Oh! Carol' and 'Stairway To Heaven' (both number nines) in 1959; 'Calendar Girl' (number four) and 'Little Devil' (number 11) in 1960; and 'Happy Birthday, Sweet Sixteen' (number six) in 1961. His popularity and success would be further elevated in 1962 with his first number one hit, 'Breaking Up Is Hard To Do,' and 'Next Door To An Angel,' which reached number five.

Now that his rock'n'roll songwriting had started to bring money into the house, Neil no longer had to write in secret. "After a few hits," he recalled, "my mother would open the window in Brighton Beach and holler out to the neighbors: Neil's on the radio!"

By the end of 1958, Neil had earned $42,000 in royalties, which Eleanor oversaw like a watchdog. As a reward, he was allowed one extravagant item: a white-on-white Chevy Impala Convertible. She put Neil on an allowance and hired a "friend" of hers to manage the money and give them career advice.

As it transpired, Ben Sutter was way more than just a friend to

Eleanor. He was a lover. While Mac Sedaka was working his tail off, Eleanor, now aged 40, had found someone else to pay attention to her. Mac was a sweet guy, but he was also thrifty to a fault. He wouldn't spend a dime he didn't have to, and taking Eleanor out to fancy dinners and shows was way beyond his thoughts.

With his sharkskin suits and slicked-back dark hair hidden under a fedora, Ben Sutter could have passed for one of Mafia kingpin Frank Costello's henchman. A fast-talking man in his mid forties, Sutter had the build of a Bull Von German Shepherd. He was attracted to Eleanor's looks and the way she carried herself. Although the Sedaka household income was relatively meager, she managed to dress impeccably. And Eleanor, in turn, was glad of the attention.

Sutter was a salesman, and he may have landed the best account of his life when he snagged Eleanor Sedaka. He was looking for a fish he could reel in; she was looking for romance. It didn't matter to either of them that they were married to other people. Each found what they needed in the other and harbored no shame about it.

When Neil was 19 and his sister Ronnie was 20, Eleanor called them to the side. She had a serious look on her face, and she paused before she began.

"I have something to tell you," she said, "and I want you to hear me out."

Neil and Ronnie looked at her quizzically.

"I have a lover," she said as naturally as if she were giving the time of day. "Ben Sutter," she continued. "He takes me to nice places and gives me gifts that your father can't."

Eleanor stopped to take in her children's bewilderment before continuing, half asking, half telling, "But I will only continue this affair with him if I have your permission and your father's permission."

It was almost as if she were demanding their approval. Neil and Ronnie were shocked. Eventually they acquiesced. So too, poor guy, did Mac.

"I adored my mother," Sedaka told me some 50 years later. "She was everything to me. Whatever made my mother happy made me happy. Ben would give my mother gifts and take her on trips. I was without a manager, and my mother suggested Ben, who was really just an air conditioning salesman in Queens. Later, I found out he was also married with children."

Eleanor Sedaka had done everything she could to give her children the love that she never received as a child. She worked hard to provide them with a loving home and took part-time jobs to pay for their piano lessons and vacations. She had been married to Mac for more than 20 years without any taste of the good life. Now that the kids were grown, she felt it was her time.

It was Neil's time, too. His life would take a dramatic turn during the summer of 1958. He'd formed a three-piece band in an attempt to get summer work in the thriving "Borscht Belt" of the Catskills, a hotbed for entertainers with its many hotels and nightclubs. Sedaka played piano and accordion, his friend Norman Spizz played the trumpet, and David Bass played the bass. They later added Howard Tischler on sax. They called themselves The Nordanelles, and they were booked to play all summer at the Esther Manor, just outside Monticello on Route 17B.

When the boys pulled up to report on the weekend before Memorial Day 1958, the woman who ran the venue, Esther Strassberg, looked perplexed. Although all three musicians were 19 years old, not one of them was taller than five-foot-six, and they looked more like they were about 14.

At five-foot-ten, Esther Strassberg was an imposing woman who must have seemed even taller when she looked down on Neil's group as they got out of the car. At first she thought they were inquiring about busboy jobs, which were all filled. Esther saw to it that all the waiters and busboys were either pre-med or pre-law students to ensure that there were plenty of eligible young men for the daughters of her guests.

Esther would later recount that first meeting to Myrna Katz Frommer and Harvey Frommer for their book *It Happened In The Catskills*.

"Can I help you?" she asked the group.

"Yes," Neil said. "We're the band."

"*YOU* are my band?" Strassberg replied, totally shocked. They looked like schoolboys. "Does your mother know you've left the city?"

Strassberg's next thought was to call booker Charlie Rapp in New York and give him a piece of her mind. But after a minute or so she calmed down and took into consideration the long drive the boys had just made.

"Now go to the kitchen and get some milk and cookies," she told the boys, "and tell them Esther sent you."[2]

When she called Charlie Rapp in New York he told her The Nordanelles had loads of experience, and that despite their youthful appearance they were perfect for her hotel. Strassberg had a booked a convention group into the hotel that weekend, so she needed entertainment. She decided to give the boys a chance.

Esther Manor got its start 30 years earlier as a farm that took in borders. It then became a rooming house, and by the 40s had grown into a fully fledged hotel. As the economy improved after World War II, business kept getting better, and Esther's family kept adding to the hotel. By the 50s, when Esther and her sister Irene bought out their brothers, the cows and the chickens were gone. They added a casino and hired some top talent for the big holiday weekends. It wasn't as big or as famous as the Concord Hotel or Grossinger's, but it had a great reputation. Their clever motto was "Big enough to serve you, small enough to know you."

That weekend in 1958, Esther's 16-year-old daughter, Leba, had been listening in from around the corner as the guests started checking in to the hotel. "My mother was apologizing to them ahead of time for the band," she recalled. "But when they checked out they all told her how much they liked them."

This sort of thing meant a lot to Esther. Pleasing hotel guests was tantamount to her success. "When I was very young," Leba recalled, "she told me I had to be very good to the guests or we wouldn't be able to pay the mortgage. I had no idea what a mortgage was, but I knew if we were sold out of rooms she'd sell my bed, too. The capacity of the hotel depended on how ambitious my mother was on any given weekend. Sometimes she would put three couples in a room. She'd say, don't worry, I'll put up a screen. You're never going to be in the room anyway. You have two shows Saturday night, a cocktail hour, and the midnight show. There's no time to sleep."

That weekend marked the first time Neil and Leba laid eyes on each other. Like her mother, Leba was tall and attractive, with shoulder-length brown hair and a pleasing smile.

"Neil told me that the first time he saw me, he turned to Norman and said, 'I'm going to marry that girl,'" Leba recalled, half laughing. "I'm still not sure I believe him."

When The Nordanelles realized they weren't being sent back to New York, they asked if they could get the keys to their rooms.

"You get one room with three beds," Esther told them. But after hearing so many guests gushing about them, she poured on the charm. "We'll be seeing you again next weekend, won't we?" she asked. With all the other good jobs in the Catskills already booked, the boys agreed to return.

"That summer they played dinner shows and midnight shows all weekend," Leba said. "Neil also had to play piano in the lobby before dinner, and in the cocktail lounge after dinner. And twice a week, Neil had to play the accordion for cha-cha lessons by the pool. He detested playing the accordion and refused to carry it. For all of those shows he was paid 86 dollars and 43 cents a week, plus room and board."

For Neil it was a great training ground—a great place to start. He learned how to perform before groups of all ages and in different venues. You can't buy that type of experience, as they say. He also started something else that summer—something that would last a lifetime: his courtship with Leba.

"The first thing Neil ever said to me," Leba said laughing, "was, 'Hi, I'm Neil Sedaka, and I wrote a song for Connie Francis.' I told him that was the most ridiculous thing I'd ever heard." When she heard Connie singing Neil's song, 'Stupid Cupid,' on the radio, she could hardly believe it.

That summer they started dating. They would go to the movies or to the soda shop across from Monticello Raceway to get ice cream sodas.

"Esther Manor was set back on a hill, but the casino was on the road," Leba told the Frommers. "A wonderful path with a couple of benches along the way led down to it. Neil and I would take lovely

31

walks on that road. We spent a lot of time together on the grounds."[3]

Soon, they became inseparable—except for when Neil was on the road. "When he was touring," Leba said, "I would read his fan mail while I was in study hall at Monticello High, and sign his photos for him."

In October 1958, after he recorded 'The Diary,' Neil was invited to Disney star Annette Funicello's 16th birthday party at the Plaza Hotel. Also in attendance were teenage stars Frankie Avalon, Paul Anka, and Dion DiMucci. While Neil was at the piano, Dion sat down next to him.

"I sat down next to this kid at the piano who was playing a song that blew my fucking mind," Dion told me in a phone interview. "The way he sang, I thought there was an angel inside of him. And his piano playing soared and lit up the sky. From where I was from in the Bronx, there wasn't anyone who could play piano like that."

After dating Neil for four years, Leba decided she wanted to get two things done: first, she wanted to fix her nose, which had a small bump, and second, she wanted to get engaged. Neil, on the other hand, was riding an incredibly successful streak of hit songs and was constantly on the road. At 23, he wasn't sure he was ready to get married. That didn't sit well with his girlfriend, and led to a blow-up while they were on a date at the Concord Hotel, as Neil would later recall in his autobiography:

> "'Fine, she yelled, 'don't marry me! But some day I'll walk in here with my husband—a famous doctor or lawyer—with my perfect nose, wearing my Christian Dior dress, and I'll sit in the

audience applauding ever so politely while you're sweating it out up on that stage.'"[4]

A few weeks later, while Neil was away performing in Pittsburgh, Howie convinced him that Leba was right. Neil called Leba and proposed, but she only believed he meant it when Howie got on the phone to assure her.

The wedding took place at Esther Manor on September 11 1962, a week after Labor Day. The reception was held at the Concord Hotel so that Esther could be off duty and enjoy it too. The next day, nationally syndicated Broadway columnist Earl Wilson ran a story under the headline 'Neil Sedaka Marries Catskill Mountain Heiress.'

At the reception, Eleanor approached the happy couple and announced that she was raising Neil's allowance from $200 to $225 a week. Leba was stunned. At that point she had no idea that Eleanor and Ben Sutter were making all of Neil's financial decisions. Neil's mother had another surprise, too: she had chosen and pre-planned their honeymoon. They were taking the QE1 luxury liner to Europe for a four-week whirlwind trip.

A month before the wedding, Neil and Leba had stopped by Eleanor's apartment in Brighton Beach. Nonchalantly Leba mentioned where she and Neil were hoping to live.

"Neil and I are going to look for a small apartment in Manhattan," she said. "Maybe somewhere not too far from Don Kirshner's office."

Eleanor stared at Leba for a while and then finally spoke.

"If you move into Manhattan," she replied angrily, "I'll cut you both off. The choice is yours."

At just 19 years old, Leba wasn't about to take on Eleanor. "She may have been little," Leba told me, "but she was mighty." Neil, who had grown accustomed to obeying his mother since birth, went along with his mother's wish for the two of them to live nearby in Brighton Beach.

Together, Eleanor and Neil—without Leba—picked out a beautiful apartment at Seacoast Towers, a brand new development just a few blocks away from where Neil had lived with his mother. But the construction fell behind schedule, and the apartment wasn't ready in time. Instead, Neil and his new wife would move into a much smaller apartment on Ocean Parkway, and while the kids were on their honeymoon, Eleanor supervised the decorations and the installation of their new furniture. This didn't exactly thrill Neil's new bride either, but there wasn't much she could do. Eleanor was a very strong-willed, controlling mother. But if Leba thought that was the worst of it, she was in for a big surprise.

Neil was still a hot commodity. He appeared regularly with Dick Clark on *American Bandstand* and performed three numbers as the featured performer on the number one-rated *Ed Sullivan Show*. His string of hits continued when 'Breaking Up Is Hard To Do' hit number one in the summer of 1962. It was a song, going forward, for which he would always be known.

Prior to Eleanor's intervention, Al Nevins had not only been producing Neil's recordings for RCA but also managing his performing career—not necessarily to Neil's advantage. He was more interested in plugging the songs he was publishing than plugging Neil.

"After I recorded 'The Diary,'" Sedaka recalled, "Nevins wanted to groom me for nightclubs. So they booked me at the Three Rivers Inn in Syracuse. He put together a slick production act for me of evergreen songs—they wanted to groom me like [Bobby] Darin. I played to about 12 people there, including Al and Don, and I botched up the whole show. After that they were afraid to let me appear anywhere the press might see me."

Neil was never booked to sing before his friends and family in New York, which he very much wanted. His dream was to do what his friends Bobby Darin and Connie Francis had done and play the Copacabana. The only time Neil had performed in New York, it was for free, as he lip-synched his hits live to an audience of thousands of screaming teenagers on the New York Palisades as part of a radio promotion hosted by WINS's Cousin Brucie.

The only other exception came in 1961, when Neil agreed to be one of the headliners for Clay Cole's ten-day *Rock'n'roll Christmas Show* at the Brooklyn Paramount. (Cole, a popular New York TV host, had replaced Alan Freed after the payola scandal.) The other headliners were Brenda Lee and Brian Hyland ('Itsy Bitsy Teenie Weenie Yellow Polka Dot Bikini'), and they would take turns to close the show. The rest of the featured acts formed nothing less than an all-star line-up, among them Ray Charles, Bobby Rydell, Jonny Burnett, Dion, Chubby Checker, Bo Diddley, Bobby Vee, The Drifters, The Coasters, The Shirelles, and Little Anthony & The Imperials. Bobby Vinton, believe it or not, was the bandleader.

The Paramount only held 1,200 people, but they could push close to 5,000 fans through the doors in a single day by rotating the shows. The performers were required to do four shows a day, and the backstage area soon became a little gritty. There was so much pot smoking going on that one could get high by simply breathing. Neil and Leba would avoid all of that by hanging out at Junior's Restaurant next door—or at least until the arrival of a mob of autograph-seekers led to the restaurant's management insisting Neil leave.

Diddley, who played guitar like no one had ever seen, was always the next to last act on, no matter who was nominally closing the show. He would run back and forth across the stage while singing and playing and then go into a 30-foot slide thrilling the crowd. Needless to say, he was one of the highlights of the show, especially for the many black patrons from Brooklyn.

"He got the crowd so worked up," Leba recalled. "It was impossible to go on after him. Anyone else would have been a letdown."

Neil went to see the manager of the Paramount, Eugene Pleshette (father of the actress Suzanne Pleshette), and told him that he didn't want to go on after Bo Diddley. "Let Bo close the show," Neil said. "I don't mind."

Pleshette was having none of it, however. "I pay you to close," he said sternly, "you'll close."

Left with no choice, Sedaka agreed, later lamenting the problem to a friend. "I guess all you can do is hope that in one of those slides across the stage that he breaks a leg," the friend said, half jokingly. The next day, that's exactly what happened.

Shortly before Neil and Leba were married, Eleanor went to have her fortune read by a tealeaf reader in Monticello. "I see two men in your life," the gypsy reader told her. "One is like a puppy to you and the other you're like a teenager [with]." The next time Eleanor visited, she brought Ben along with her. "That's him, that's him!" the fortune-teller exclaimed.

Eleanor used Neil's dissatisfaction with Al Nevins's management as leverage to persuade Neil to allow Ben Sutter to take over. In fact, the two of them talked Neil into buying back his own management contract. Neil duly paid Nevins–Kirshner Inc. the sum of $25,000 so that Sutter could be his new manager.

Sutter did manage to book Neil into the Copacabana—although not as a headliner but as the opening act for comedian Jan Murray. Neil was excited and disappointed at the same time. While he had always wanted to play adult supper clubs like the Copa, it was embarrassing to be the opening act for someone else in his own hometown.

When Sedaka balked at signing with Kirshner that first day they met in the spring of 1958, Kirshner tried to impress him by playing an as-yet unreleased 45 of Bobby Darin's 'Splish Splash.' Sedaka was duly impressed and agreed it was a surefire hit. Kirshner explained that he had pulled the strings to get Darin seen, and that the two of them had been a songwriting team for three years. After Sedaka wrote 'Stupid Cupid' for Darin's girlfriend, Connie Francis, it didn't take long for the two men to bond.

"He wanted to be—and would have been—the next Sinatra, if it wasn't for his [bad] heart," Sedaka told me. "He was one of the great live performers. His was incredibly versatile."

When Sedaka bumped into Darin before his first Copa engagement, he was eager to get Darin's reaction to the idea of him opening the show for Murray.

"That's not right," Darin replied. "You've got the number one record in the country … [you] should be the headliner instead of opening for a comedian." Fortunately for Neil, Murray had to cancel his appearance, so Neil became the headliner—but no thanks to Sutter.

Sedaka's opening night at the Copa was just as big a deal for Eleanor as it was for Neil. She got all dolled up and insisted that Neil

sing 'My Yiddishe Momma' during the show. The song ends with the
following lines:

How few were her pleasures, she never cared for fashion's styles
Her jewels and treasures she found them in her baby's smiles
Oh I know that I owe what I am today
To that dear little lady so old and gray
To that wonderful yiddishe momma of mine

And yet there was nothing old and gray—or out of fashion, for that
matter—about Eleanor Sedaka. By now she had bleached her hair
blond, and she sat ringside at the Copa in her new mink stole. When
Neil finished the song, Esther stood up and took a bow right along
with him.

One of the first things Ben Sutter did was to introduce Neil to his
son-in-law, Jerry Steinberg, whom he said would help Neil invest his
money. Perhaps foolishly, Neil signed papers giving Sutter carte
blanche; after that, investments were made without Neil's knowledge
or approval, with Sutter and Steinberg drawing fat fees. They bought
insurance policies along with two white-elephant buildings in
Birmingham, Alabama, of all places. The buildings soon became
worthless, costing Neil thousands.

"I was not privy to these deals," Neil said. "My mother had all the
power. The buildings in Birmingham turned out to be a fiasco."

Just when it seemed like things couldn't get worse, they did.

"My mother was wearing jewelry and furs that I thought Ben was
buying her," Neil said. "Later, I found out it was really my money, and
that I was financing all of this."

This, it turned out, was only the beginning of his problems. Sutter not only dressed like a Mafia henchman but he acted like one too, picking fights everywhere he went. In casinos in Las Vegas and Puerto Rico, Sutter called the dealers expletives to the point that Sedaka had to intercede to prevent his manager from getting a beating. Then, in October 1962, when Sedaka was recording '(I'm Living Right) Next Door To An Angel,' his mother brought Sutter to the session. Nevins and Kirshner were producing the session and warned Sutter to be quiet. When Sutter insisted on interfering, a knockdown, drag-out fight ensued, resulting in Kirshner executive Lou Adler knocking Sutter clean out.

Despite the tension, Sedaka still had momentum as a hit maker. In the spring of 1961, Ed Sullivan, host of the highest-rated TV show in America, invited Neil to be the featured performer on his show. The plan was for him to do three numbers. The first would be his current hit, 'Calendar Girl.' Next he'd show off his classical Juilliard training with a Chopin piano piece. The third number Neil wanted to do was 'My Yiddishe Momma,' as a salute to his mother and his heritage.

At first, Sullivan agreed to all three, but then told Sedaka he couldn't sing the last number. "He thought it was 'too Jewish,'" Neil recalled. But Neil had been doing the number in his nightclub act, and he knew it went over big with all audiences. He remained obstinate and threatened to walk if 'My Yiddishe Momma' was pulled. Two hours before the show, Sullivan finally relented. Sedaka sang the song, and once again the audience response was overwhelming. He wasn't surprised. "The sentiment of the song is absolutely beautiful," he told me.

In theory, at least, Sedaka should have been able to keep up his streak of creating chart-topping songs. But in 1963, just as The Beatles were revving up in England, preparing for their onslaught on the USA, Sedaka became distracted by Sutter's interference, and his songwriting and subsequent releases suffered.

Unfortunately, Don Kirshner was also distracted. He was in the process of selling his song-publishing firm to Columbia Screen Gems, and the deal consumed his energy and focus. With Kirshner preoccupied, Sutter was able to influence which songs of Sedaka's would be recorded and released, while also bullying his way in for a piece of the publishing. With all of that going on around him, it's likely that Neil may not have been putting forward his best work.

Neil had another—rather more wonderful—distraction at the same time. On June 26 1963, Leba gave birth to their daughter, Dara.

Maybe the ebbing of Neil's popularity was natural. When I interviewed him, he tossed out a theory he had regarding the shelf life of a rock'n'roll star. "Most successful performers then had no more than a five-year success cycle before the public got tired of them," he said. It happened to Bobby Darin, Connie Francis, Ricky Nelson, and The Everly Brothers. And by 1963, it seemed, it was happening to Neil, too.

That year, Neil released four songs—'Alice In Wonderland,' 'Let's Go Steady Again,' 'The Dreamer,' and 'Bad Girl'—but none rose higher than number 17 on the *Billboard* charts. His formula was no longer working. Neil was known as the king of the tra-la-las and the dooby-doos, but the public seemed hungry for another sound—a new sound emanating loudly from Britain. And it couldn't have happened at a worse time. Less than three months after 'Bad Girl' ran out of gas, The Beatles made their first appearance on *The Ed Sullivan Show*, and nothing would ever be the same again.

CHAPTER 2
IT HURTS TO BE IN LOVE

In 1950, at the age of 16, Brian Epstein started working in his family's furniture store. Soon the Epsteins added a furnishings business, and four years later, after acquiring North End Road Music Stores, they asked Brian to manage the ground floor. Until now, the store had specialized in selling pianos and wireless sets, but with all the clubs springing up in the North End, Epstein realized that they could have a thriving record business.

By 1960 he had opened another store in Liverpool near the Cavern Club, and in 1961 he began writing a record column in the *Mersey Beat*, a popular local magazine. Around the same time, he discovered that customers were requesting records by a group called The Beatles, without realizing that The Beatles were regular customers of his store. (It's possible that The Beatles themselves were the ones making the requests.)

In order to investigate this new group, Epstein arranged to see them perform at the Cavern Club, and after seeing firsthand the excitement they generated, he went backstage to meet them. Entering a dressing room the size of a broom closet, he was about to tell them how much he enjoyed their performance when George Harrison surprised him by asking, "And what brings Mr. Epstein here?"

Epstein liked their music and their sense of humor onstage, and after meeting them he was tremendously taken by their charm. It was there, then, that it really all started. Neither Don Kirshner nor Neil Sedaka or anyone else in the USA paid any notice when a small item appeared in the London papers in late January 1962, announcing that Epstein had signed a contract to manage the group. Shortly thereafter, Epstein had The Beatles record a demo at Decca Records' London studio.

Decca turned Epstein down in his attempt to get the group signed to a record deal, however, and so did just about every other record company in London. Eventually, George Martin, a producer for EMI's small Parlophone label, liked what he heard, and signed the group without ever having heard them perform live. Martin later said he was sold mostly by Epstein's enthusiasm and vision that the group could be an international success.

Within a year The Beatles had become a growing phenomenon in England, and even though Epstein had no previous experience of managing talent, he was exactly what they needed. He persuaded them to stop eating, drinking, and swearing onstage, and to stop beginning and ending songs whenever they chose. He also installed a dress code, convincing them to switch from jeans and leather jackets to suits and ties. And it was Epstein who suggested their now famous synchronized bow.

When The Beatles' first album, *Please, Please Me*, took off in 1963, Epstein began plotting to bring them to America. He was aided enormously by Ed Sullivan himself. Late in 1963, Sullivan and his wife had just landed at London's Heathrow airport when Sullivan noticed a throng of screaming teenagers waiting in the rain. When he asked what all the commotion was about, he was told they were waiting for a new group called The Beatles, who were returning from a date in Sweden. Sullivan knew a hot act when he saw it—or in this case smelled it—and set out to book the band on his show. Epstein, however, was a little more cautious, and wanted to wait until the band had a number one record in America.

The deal was finally set. The Beatles would make three separate appearances on Sullivan and receive $10,000 for their efforts, which incidentally was much more than the scale minimum Sullivan paid most of his performers. Their first US TV appearance was set for February 9 1964, just 77 days after America had mourned the assassination of President Kennedy. By then, the country was ready for a welcome distraction.

Epstein's plan was to release 'I Want To Hold Your Hand' to the US disc jockeys a few weeks ahead of The Beatles' arrival in the country. Already a number one hit in England, Epstein felt certain it could repeat the feat in the States—only someone leaked it a little too far in advance, and the record began playing on radio stations all over the country six weeks before their arrival.

Capitol Records, which owned distribution rights to the record in the USA, tried to stop the DJs from playing it, but it was too late. It seemed like everyone had it—except the buying public. Capitol acquiesced and released the single on December 26—the day after Christmas—1963.

The record sold 250,000 copies in the first three days alone. By January 10, it had sold over one million copies, and by the end of January it was number one on *Billboard*. Even before The Beatles' first performance on *The Ed Sullivan Show*, the country had started to go nuts in preparation. Radio stations played the band's music nonstop, and teenage girls were prone to bursting into tears at the mere sight of a Beatle in a fan magazine.

When The Beatles landed at Kennedy airport February 7 1964,

they were met by a mob of reporters and thousands of screaming fans. Asked how they found America, during an impromptu press conference, George Harrison introduced the press to the Beatles brand of humor by replying, "Easy—you turn left at Greenland." They hadn't even appeared on TV yet but the country had gone completely Beatles mad. An estimated 73-million people would watch the Sullivan show that Sunday night. Neil Sedaka was one of them.

After watching The Beatles on *Ed Sullivan* and measuring the reaction of the fans, Sedaka knew that this was something he had never seen before. Sure, he had seen films of girls mobbing Elvis, and he had even felt some of that kind of adulation when the kids mobbed him on the Palisades. But nobody had tried to pull the desperate tricks these girls did to try and sneak onto The Beatles' floor at the Plaza Hotel.

It was now February 1964. Unless you count 'Alice In Wonderland,' which had peaked at number 17 a year earlier, Neil Sedaka hadn't had a hit since 'Next Door To An Angel' debuted in October '62. He had tried four times since then, and four times he had failed. Now that The Beatles had arrived, he was out songs and unsure what his path should be.

Then, from out of the blue, Howie Greenfield, his writing partner all of those years, handed him a hit song. It didn't matter to Neil that someone else had written it with Howie. What mattered was that Neil knew it was a hit, and that he was being offered the first chance to record it.

While Neil was performing his string of hit songs all over the world, Greenfield had kept busy writing with other composers in

Kirshner's office. With songwriter Jack Keller he wrote a pair of number one hits for Connie Francis: 'Everybody's Somebody's Fool' and 'My Heart Has A Mind Of Its Own.' With Carole King he wrote The Everly Brothers hit 'Crying In The Rain' (number five), and with Helen Miller he had just penned the lyrics to 'Foolish Little Girl' (number four) for The Shirelles.

Helen Miller was the only songwriter aged more than 30 in Kirshner's stable at Aldon Music. She could write songs and produce nearly as well, and she could also trade barbs with any man in the office. As fellow songwriter Toni Wine put it, "She could have been the most under-appreciated songwriter in New York."

So, with Greenfield and Miller enjoying the rush as their hit 'Foolish Little Girl' climbed the charts, Howie happened to mention to Neil that he and Helen had just finished another song he liked called 'It Hurts To Be In Love.' He asked if Neil would like to do the demo. Neil listened to the song and instantly loved it. He also knew exactly how he'd arrange and sing it, and who would do the backup vocals. He might not have written it, but Sedaka wasn't too proud to turn down a hit—especially one that could resurrect his career.

Neil was still signed to RCA, which was losing its patience with him. He desperately needed this song to work, and he thought carefully about every movement, every sound. The first order of business was to record the demo.

"Instinctively, I knew exactly how I wanted to record it," Neil told me. "I flipped over the song. To make sure I got the sound I wanted, I recorded it at Dick Charles Studio on 7th Avenue."

Dick Charles's demo studio was just about every producer's favorite place to record. It had been there for decades, and the sound that could be achieved there was unmatched at any other studio—

especially RCA's new studio on East 24th Street, where the kinks had not yet been worked out.

"It was perfect," Neil said of their demo recording. "I played, sang, and clapped. Leba and [Howie's boyfriend] Tory also clapped. Toni Wine sang the backup vocals with me. I flipped over the song and flipped over the record. I took it RCA and they said: you have to record this at our studio on East 24th street. You have to record the master with us. We don't put out demos."

Sedaka didn't remember the name of the RCA executive who gave that order, but Luigi Creatore did. Creatore, born in 1921 and part of the team of Hugo & Luigi who produced The Tokens' 'The Lion Sleeps Tonight' for RCA, knew exactly who would have made such a mistake. "It had to be [A&R man Steve] Shoals," he said when I reached him by phone in Florida. "He was the only one with the authority to say that to Neil."

Backup singer Toni Wine knew a little bit about making a great record. An accomplished songwriter in her own right, having written 'Groovy Kind Of Love' with Carole Bayer, she had also sung backup on some of the biggest rock'n'roll hits of the decade.

"It was a fabulous demo and a smash as it was," she recalled. "RCA was foolish to insist it be re-recorded at their place, as if you were xeroxing a piece of paper. The reality was that magic happens once. It rarely happens twice. That's why, in those days, so many demos became masters."

Sedaka was devastated. He tried everything he could to talk RCA into allowing him to put out the Dick Charles demo. He reminded them that Goffin & King's number one song 'The Locomotion' was a demo that was used as a master. But the label wouldn't budge so, hat in hand, Neil tried to duplicate the sound at RCA's studio. No matter how many times he sang it, no matter how many times he and the others clapped in time, the magic was gone. Everyone agreed that the RCA version wasn't good enough to release.

With Sedaka out of the picture, the song's publisher, Don Kirshner, offered it to a rising young star named Gene Pitney. A successful songwriter for George Goldner, who owned two record labels at 1650 Broadway, Pitney had already written two number one songs: 'Hello Mary Lou' (Ricky Nelson) and 'He's A Rebel' (The Crystals).

As a singer, he had signed with the Musicor label in 1961 and begun a modest string of hits with 'Town Without Pity.' In 1962 he scored with '(The Man Who Shot) Liberty Valance' and 'Only Love Can Break A Heart.' But Pitney was also feeling the effect of The Beatles, and he had gone without a song in the top ten from late 1962 until April 1964 when Kirshner approached him with 'It Hurts To Be In Love.'

Sedaka chronicler Michael Turner, who first met Neil in 1975, interviewed Pitney before his death in 2005 and asked him about the song. "Don played me the Neil Sedaka demo," Pitney recalled, "and I said, that's a hit song. Why are you playing that for me? He said Neil had just changed producers at RCA and the new ones didn't want to be involved with anything old."[5]

Pitney jumped at the chance to record the song. He kept every track Sedaka had on the record—the piano, the backup musicians, the backing vocals (including Neil's own harmonies), the arrangement—everything but Neil's lead vocal, which Pitney substituted for his own.

"I even brought in the same girl [Toni Wine] who had done the background vocals on the demo," Pitney continued. "I did that song exactly as Neil did it. The record was Gene Pitney singing Neil Sedaka!"

As far as Neil was concerned, there were no hard feelings. He knew Kirshner couldn't just sit on a hit because of a foolish decision by RCA. Worst of all, though, he knew that his best hope to dig out of the slump had just passed before him.

"It was horrible," he recalled. "*That* would have been my number one song, my comeback song." Instead, of course, ten very long years would pass before Neil made his return to the upper reaches of the US charts.

For Sedaka, there was no alternative. Nevins and Kirshner had produced their last record for him. Kirshner had sold his publishing business to Columbia Screen Gems and was tied up running their music division, and Nevins was now semi-retired.

Neil's next release was a forgettable song called 'Sunny.' It barely stopped on the *Billboard* charts long enough for a cup of coffee, never rising higher than number 86. Disc jockeys were starting to whisper, "Neil who?" His name was already off the charts, and it was slowly slipping into oblivion.

CHAPTER 3
THE MONEY STOPS ROLLING IN

G rowing up in Brighton Beach in the 1940s was a joy for Sedaka. But with three families crammed into a two-bedroom apartment, things could get crowded. When Neil wanted some private time, he would find a quiet corner and listen to his favorite radio show, Martin Block's *Make Believe Ballroom*, on WNEW.

"I'd love to sit there and listen to songs by Rosemary Clooney, Patti Page, Peggy Lee, and Tony Bennett," he recalled. "I loved those songs and their voices. A few years later when I was maybe 12 or 13 I used to buy 45s and scratch out the name of the singers. Then I'd write in 'Neil Sedaka' to see how it looked."

Five years later, when he first began working in the Catskills at Esther Manor, Neil told a fib to a group of kids to see their reaction. He said he was Danny from Danny & The Juniors, who had a giant hit song at the time called 'At The Hop.'

"I did it," Neil said, "because I wanted to see how it felt to be famous. As soon as I said I was Danny of Danny & The Juniors, they all swarmed around me. I thought to myself: I want this." He paused, before adding, "I always wanted to be famous."

And for a while, Neil certainly was famous. There couldn't have been any bigger thrill than seeing his first few songs climb into the top 20 of the *Billboard* charts. 'Stupid Cupid,' written for Connie

Francis, and Neil's own recording of 'The Diary' each reached number 14. But when he saw his likeness on the 45rpm copy of 'The Diary,' Neil was beside himself with excitement. He would listen to the record while driving down Kings Highway in Brooklyn in his white Chevy Impala. All of the buttons on the radio dial were set to rock'n'roll stations, and sometimes he'd hear his song on two or three stations at the same time. It must've been thrilling. Hit after hit followed, and along with it came the adulation.

One of the major reasons Sedaka's string of hits came to an end was because RCA's record executives forced him to stay with four chords—C, A minor, D minor, and G—in order to maintain the same repetitive sound that had been selling so well. The problem was, before long the songs started sounding the same. All they wanted was a lyric sandwiched between Neil's patented tra-la-las and dooby-doos.

"I went to them and begged them to let me try something else," Neil told me. "They said, absolutely not."

By 1964, the glory days were over, and a new reality had set in. Neil's manager, his mother's 'friend,' Ben Sutter, was more of an order-taker than a manager. If a call came in asking for Neil's services, Sutter would take it and accept just about any offer put forth. But going out and drumming up business wasn't one of his best attributes.

That spring, however, Sutter announced to Neil and Leba that they were going to Las Vegas, where Neil would be playing at the world famous Fremont Hotel & Casino. The only trouble with playing the Fremont was that it was located on Freemont Street, in the downtown honky-tonk district away from the main drag. All the big stars played at hotels on the Strip, a four-mile stretch of Las Vegas Boulevard. Even a job at one of the famous lounges in those hotels—

where greats like Don Rickles became famous—would have been better than playing downtown.

"The good news was that I was the headliner at the Fremont," Sedaka said. "The bad news was that I was following a comedian, a tap dancer, and a country singer named Molly Bee." Bee was best known for her 1952 hit 'I Saw Mommy Kissing Santa Claus,' which she recorded at age 13, and for being the sidekick on the children's TV show *Pinky Lee*.

"What could I do?" Sedaka asked. "I needed the money."

In downtown Las Vegas, the barkers outside the casinos would lure patrons in to play 25-cent blackjack and penny slots. Neil knew he was a long way from his dream of headlining at the Copacabana.

Artie Kaplan, who worked alongside Sedaka at Aldon Music for years, could well understand Neil's passion—and his disappointment. "From the time he was a kid he always wanted to perform in the big rooms," Kaplan recalled. "That's all he ever wanted to do: play to an audience that loved and appreciated him."

By now, Neil was performing all over the world, but his first manager, Al Nevins, had never booked him to perform in his hometown of New York.

"I think they were afraid that a career as an artist might take away from Neil's writing and record sales," Kaplan concluded. "They were in the publishing business, not in show business. Regardless, Neil deserved better management. I don't know that Ben Sutter was the answer, but Neil deserved better than what Nevins–Kirshner Inc. was doing for him."

When Sedaka signed to record with RCA, he did so with Nevins's lawyers putting together the contract. It was the standard contract most managers and record labels subscribed to in those days—the kind where the recording artist is just about the last one to see royalties. In those days, the deck was stacked.

"We didn't have a high lifestyle," said Sedaka. "Al Nevins made a deal with RCA where he got most of the performer's royalties. I was a *pishika* [an innocent]. What did I know? And my mother—she was thrilled I was with RCA, and she signed for me [because] I was underage."

Because of Neil's ability to record his songs in other languages, Nevins sent him all over the world: South America, Europe, Japan, and the Philippines. But in 1963, with Sutter now calling the shots, Neil was sent on a trip that literally knocked him for a loop. First he traveled down to South America, both for a concert tour and also to record two albums in Spanish. Then, without a break, he flew direct to Rome to begin a tour of Italy, where he was extremely popular, having sold three million records. Sutter took the opportunity to take Eleanor to Rome to sit with him by the hotel pool while Neil battled the heat onstage.

"God bless Ben Sutter," Leba Sedaka recalled sarcastically. "When Neil got to Italy, he was sick—actually sick enough to have to postpone the tour and have me fly over."

Flying to Italy wasn't easy for Leba, since she had recently given birth to Dara, and would now have to leave her band in the hands of a nurse and her mother in Monticello. Then, when Neil began to recover, the promoter insisted he resume the tour.

"He did a few concerts," Leba recalled, "but when we got to Viareggio to a famous club called la Busola, he lost his voice after about three songs. The club owner was furious and wanted Neil to just play the piano. Neil thought the audience would be more disappointed if he did that, and we attempted to leave. The owner screamed in

Italian to get the tomatoes, which he gave to the audience. They chased us throwing tomatoes until we finally pulled away."

When the record sales stopped, Sedaka wanted to follow Bobby Darin and Connie Francis into the adult supper clubs, but that plan never came to fruition. "I didn't do the rock'n'roll bus tours—didn't want to," he told me. "Instead, I had to take a job as a demo pianist in order to provide for my family in Brighton Beach."

Sutter also booked Neil into smaller and smaller hotels in the Catskills, plus a few small clubs in Philly and Jersey and a handful of small rooms in Montreal and Quebec. Some of them were dives.

"It was humiliating," Neil recalled. "Tiny rooms that were more than half empty. And they'd talk all through the show as if it were a piano bar. But I had no choice."

One reason Neil needed the money was because his mother and Sutter had squandered most of the royalties Neil earned from his songwriting—and the 25 million records he sold between 1958 and 1963—on expensive gifts for her and gambling junkets for him.

"It came to a point that I had to sell my childhood bonds," Leba recalled. "You know, the types of [savings] bonds you'd get as birthday presents when you were kids. They left us with next to nothing."

Sutter saw Neil Sedaka as a cash cow. During his five years at the top, Neil had earned at least $400,000 from songwriting and performance royalties, but almost every penny had been frittered away on Ben and Eleanor's 'expenses' or Sutter's son-in-law Jerry Steinberg's hare-brained investment schemes. All the while, Eleanor continued to control Neil's life, doling out his allowance like he was still a child. "It got so bad, we had to get approval to buy a roll of toilet paper," Neil recalled. According to Leba, Ben and Eleanor's names were listed as beneficiaries on Neil's life insurance, not hers.

Then, one day in 1966, Leba happened to sneak a peek at the 'checkbook' Eleanor kept for Neil's work. What she found was a heap of scraps of paper—that was Eleanor's record keeping. Every check stub Leba saw related to something personal for Eleanor or Ben. Nothing seemed to pertain to Neil's business. Aware of how delicate a subject it was—she was about to tell a loving son that his mother and her lover had been cheating and stealing from him for years—Leba knew she had to tell Neil what she had discovered, and reluctantly approached him with the news.

"I don't believe it!" Neil replied, visibly upset. "This is a lie. My mother would never do such a thing. She would never cheat me," he continued, raising his voice. He was not in any mood to be rational.

Neil and Leba argued back and forth. Finally, he gave her an ultimatum: "If you don't like it, you can leave!"

With tears in her eyes and their marriage on the verge of ending, Leba begged Neil to look at the checkbook. Eventually, he calmed down, looked at the checkbook, and saw that it confirmed everything Leba had told him. There was only one thing he could do. He had to fire Sutter—and, in effect, his mother, too.

"The issue had to do with integrity and fiduciary obligations," Sedaka's boyhood friend Freddie Gershon, by now an entertainment attorney, recalled. "That and the fact that Neil, who was a very gentle soul, was wrenchingly conflicted, because of his mother. He didn't want to be hurtful. This was a devastating emotional blow to him."

So, instead of telling them that his mother and Sutter that he had caught them cooking the books, Sedaka took a much more diplomatic approach.

"I waited until I could see them together at my mother's apartment," he recalled. "I told Ben that I appreciated everything he had done for me over the years, but my career needed to go in another direction, and I was going to look for a new manager."

Sutter went crazy. He started storming around the room, screaming and hollering. "You signed a contract, you signed a contract!" Indeed, Neil had signed just about everything Sutter put in front of him during those first few years, and one of those items was a contract that tied him to Sutter for years. In order to release Neil from that contract, Sutter demanded a large payout. Not knowing what to do, Neil turned to Gershon.

I spoke with Freddie Gershon twice while researching this book. Both were phone interviews. Gershon turned out to be a powerful ally for Neil during difficult times. After studying eight years at Juilliard, he had graduated from Columbia Law School and started practicing as an entertainment lawyer. He went on to be incredibly successful, partnering with Robert Stigwood representing concert tours by acts like The Bee Gees, Chicago, and Eric Clapton, as well as producing the Broadway shows Jesus Christ Superstar, *and* Tommy. *He also arranged the financing for* La Cage Aux Folles. *Sedaka referred to him simply as "Freddie The Lawyer."*

"For a long time, Neil refused to believe that Eleanor was involved," Gershon told me. "He felt she was blinded by her feelings, that the sun rose and set on Ben, and that he could do no wrong. But she was smitten, and that was the problem."

Gershon, just three years out of Columbia law school, negotiated Neil's payout. Like everyone else, Gershon was a little scared of Sutter, whom he said reminded him of Broderick Crawford's bullying mob boss in *Born Yesterday*. "Think coarse, loud, braggadocio, with a John Gotti obsession for his appearance."

When they began negotiating, Sutter let off some steam about what he'd done for Neil. "I own him, I own his soul," Sutter yelled. "I have a piece of paper [signed by Neil], I've done everything right by him. I made him a superstar, I made him that … I made him rich!"

Gershon suggested a dollar amount for the payout; Sutter countered with a much higher figure. Not wanting to antagonize Sutter any further, Gershon kept his cool and just listened. Eventually, they agreed on an amount somewhere between $15,000 and $25,000—not much by today's standards, but it was a lot of money to Neil at the time. To top it off, Sutter wanted it all in cash—in small bills, to be exact, just like a bank robber might want.

Gershon sat down with Neil and Leba and told them what had occurred with Sutter, directing most of the business items in Leba's direction. "If you can get out, get out," he told them. "If it costs you money it's still cheap. You have your talent and you have your life and you'll make a buck and you'll recover from this."

When Sutter demanded that Gershon show up alone with a satchel full of small, unmarked bills, Gershon feared for his life. He refused, telling Sutter that they would need to consummate the deal in a public place, and that he would also need to sign a notarized release form.

Sutter called Gershon back to say that they could meet in a public place so safe that Gershon would be surprised: the Kings County Courthouse in Brooklyn. Sutter promised that the courthouse would be full, and that there would be a notary available. Of course, this being Sutter, the arrangement came with a catch. At some point during the previous two years, Jerry Steinberg—he of the life insurance schemes and investments in Alabama—had become a judge, and the Kings County Courthouse was his place of work. There were rumors that Sutter had paid someone off to make it happen.

Gershon was scared stiff, but he had a secret weapon: Morris Levy, head of Roulette Records, long rumored to have ties to the mob. "For some reason he loved me," Gershon said of Levy. When they sat down to discuss the deal, he was relieved to hear what Levy had to say.

"This guy [Sutter] is a nobody," Levy told him. "He's nothing. He can't do anything to you. Besides which, I'm putting out word that you're under my protection."

When Gershon arrived at the courtroom door he looked through the window to make sure there were plenty of people inside. He also looked at the name of the judge posted on the door, and sure enough, Judge Steinberg was presiding. A pang of distrust went through Gershon's body, but he went inside and took a seat on one of the long benches near Sutter. After a few other cases were heard, the clerk announced there would be a 15-minute recess, then escorted Sutter and Gershon into the judge's chambers.

"We all went in, including the clerk," Gershon recalled. "I handed the release to Sutter and told him we needed the notary. The clerk went out and came back with the court stenographer, who notarized the document. At that point my heart was beating fast. I wanted to get out of there, so I handed him the attaché case and walked out the building as fast as I could."

Sutter wanted one last thing from Neil: he didn't want Neil to tell anyone that he was no longer Neil's manager. Neil reluctantly agreed in order to get Sutter off his back. More than a year went by, and then one day Neil bumped into an acquaintance.

"Oh, I was just speaking to your manager, Ben Sutter," the acquaintance told him.

"Ben Sutter is not my manager," Sedaka replied, visibly upset. "I don't have a manager."

Word got back to Sutter, and once again he completely lost it.

"He made threatening phone calls night and day," Leba recalled. "We had to call the police eventually. We were afraid he might kill someone."

It turned out that cheating Neil wasn't the only thing Ben Sutter's had been up to. The New York District Attorney had since begun investigating Sutter and his son-in-law, poring over his books and deposing a multitude of characters, including Neil's wife and mother.

Eleanor couldn't take the embarrassment. After telling people she planned to take an overdose of sleeping pills, she then made good on her threat—but not before warning several relatives in advance.

"I found my mother lying on the kitchen floor," Sedaka said. "We had an ambulance rush her to Coney Island Hospital, where they pumped her stomach."

The medics had got to Eleanor in time, fortunately, but Neil had had enough of her drama. "I didn't speak to her for three months," he told me.

Eleanor made a quick recovery. Once she got Sutter out of her life, she became Neil's loving mother again, and he returned to the role of loving son. Leba might not have been quite so forgiving, but she nevertheless went along with her husband's wishes. She has also acted as Neil's manager ever since.

Eleanor lived a very long life, eventually passing away in 2006, at the age of 90, at home in the plush South Florida condo purchased for her by her son and daughter-in-law.

"We took very good care of that woman the rest of her life," Leba said. "Very good care."

CHAPTER 4
STAR-CROSSED LOVERS

With Sutter gone, Neil and Leba decided to move away from his mother's clutches. They bought a small home in Merriewold Park, an artists' community in upstate Sullivan County, New York, not far from Leba's mother's hotel in the Catskills. Marc Shcreibman, a successful artist who Leba had known in high school, was the first to suggest that the Sedakas move to Merriewold Park. But after Sutter and Steinberg squandered most of Neil's earnings, there was no way he and Leba could maintain an apartment in Brooklyn and a home upstate.

"We had to give up our Brooklyn apartment," Leba recalled. "We just couldn't afford both. It was hard to believe, with all the money Neil made all those years, there was nothing left. But I knew that if it came down to it, my mother would always take us in."

Gaining acceptance into the gated community of Merriewold Park was another thing. The community had its own board of directors, which any prospective buyers had to impress before being allowed to move in, and a rock'n'roll singer wasn't necessarily what they were looking for, but Neil and Leba did enough to persuade them. A short time later, disc jockey Bruce 'Cousin Brucie' Morrow would buy a home on the other side of the lake, giving Neil and Leba at least one friend in the community. Other neighbors included the great Broadway director George Abbott, choreographer Agnes de Mille, and Richard Rodgers's daughter Mary, who followed in her father's footsteps by finding fame as a composer of musicals.

"Merriewold Park was founded around the turn of the century," Mary Rodgers recalled when I reached her by phone. "It was the intelligentsia pocket of liberalism in that Upper New York domain. By the time we moved there, Agnes was there, and George was there, but so were a lot of very bigoted, anti-Semitic, anti-black, anti-gay folks from Nyack. When we'd go down to the lake they'd call people names like faggots and kikes. They probably didn't like Neil because they probably assumed he was peculiar and Jewish and every other bigoted thing."

Morrow, who had been friends with Neil since 1958, was an easy-going, likeable guy who helped prove to the neighbors that *some* people from his business were normal. However, Neil knew that his background meant he was likely to get a chilly reception.

"It was a bit of a scandal," he recalled of his and Leba's move to Merriewold Park. "If they didn't like you, they didn't give you electricity, so you'd have a house but you couldn't turn the lights on. Being a rock'n'roller, they were a bit concerned about me, but I was a family man."

Things soon settled down, and Neil found that—free from Sutter and his mother—his new home was a wonderful, creative place for him to write. But with the money almost gone, he now had to figure out a way to make a living.

As the 60s wore on, Sedaka's appearances had dwindled to just a few shows here and there. He wasn't making any income from recording, but the songwriting royalties from his old hits were still trickling in—

albeit not at anything like the rate they had in the old days.

The period 1963–66 was one of slim pickings. Neil was no longer headlining the Eden Roc in Miami Beach or the Copacabana in New York. In fact, the only regular work he found as a performer during those years was back in the Catskill Mountains, where the hotel patrons usually saw the shows for free, as part of their weekend package. By now, however, Sedaka was working at just about any hotel that would hire him. During those four years he appeared at least once at Grossinger's, the Concord, the Nevele Grand, the Raleigh, the Stevensville, Shady Nook, Homowack, and Lillian Lodge. Those hotel bookings were a lifesaver for the Sedakas, who were now raising two young children. Neil's son Marc Sedaka, born on October 16 1966, would join sister Dara on the road with their parents whenever possible.

Neil was also able to write a few hits for other singers. Even if Neil Sedaka the singer wasn't in demand, his songs still were. In 1966 and '67 he wrote 'When Love Comes Knockin' At Your Door' and 'The Girl I Left Behind Me' for The Monkees with Carole Bayer.

"She asked me to write with her," Neil told me, sitting back on his couch in his Manhattan apartment. "She was very pretty, very charming. I had heard and liked her song, 'Groovy Kind Of Love.' I said yes. We worked at her parents' house at 200 Central Park South. We just wrote for fun."

For Bayer, who was also writing songs for Don Kirshner at the Screen Gems offices, it was much more exciting.

Carole Bayer Sager, as she is now known, has been—and continues to be—one the most prolific and successful lyricists of the last 50 years. She has had tremendous success writing pop songs as well as music for film and Broadway shows. It has never seemed to matter who her writing partners are: the results are always something to treasure. She wrote her first number one hit 'Groovy Kind Of Love,' with Toni Wine; 'Arthur's Theme (Best That You Can Do)' with Peter Allen and Christopher Cross; 'Heartlight' with Neil Diamond; the giant Carly Simon hit 'Nobody Does It Better' and the successful Broadway musical They're Playing Our Song *with Marvin Hamlisch; 'Come In From The Rain' with Melissa Manchester; and 'That's What Friends Are For,' among others, with her second husband, Burt Bacharach. She was gracious and accommodating when I interviewed her several years ago about being discovered by and writing for Don Kirshner. Neil Sedaka was the first major songwriter she ever wrote with, and she was very happy to share those experiences with me when I reached her by phone in California.*

"I love Neil Sedaka," she told me. "I loved his voice, I loved his songs, and when I saw him [at Screen Gems] one day I introduced myself and said, do you think you'd ever want to write a song with me? He was very sweet and he said, well, yesss!"

This was a major event for Bayer, who was working as a substitute schoolteacher when Kirshner discovered her. Before that, she had approached Carole King to write with her, but King turned her down, telling Bayer she was only permitted to write with her husband, Gerry Goffin.

"Neil's wife, Leba, would send him to the city with a note telling him where he was going, and with a certain amount of money that he could use on the subway to get home," Bayer recalled. "It was almost like he had a nametag.

"Writing with Neil was fun, he was fantastic. He had a sort of childlike joy or aura around him when he wrote. He was so musical and so easy to write with. He was all melody. He'd play something very musical and I'd hear lyrics [in my head] and say them and he'd say, oh, I love that. Then he'd sing it.

"Some people you write with are much more difficult, more tedious," she continued. "Burt [Bacharach] is the master of tedious. You'd spend hours deciding between a chord. Neil was very free, very spontaneous. He loved his own melodies right away, and they were lovable. They were easy, they were melodic, they flowed. So we would write a song in rather short order. It was just always fun. Everything was easy, writing with Neil."

The reason they were writing a song for The Monkees in the first place was that Screen Gems owned The Monkees' TV show, and Don Kirshner was in charge of choosing the songs for their albums. Kirshner placed 'When Love Comes Knockin' At Your Door' on *More Of The Monkees*, which became the band's biggest-selling album. Neil and Carole also wrote 'The Girl I Left Behind Me' for the band, with Davy Jones once again singing lead.

"I begged Don to put it in the album," Sedaka recalled.

"Don't worry," Kirshner replied, "it will go in the next one."

Shortly after that, however, Kirshner was fired following a disagreement with The Monkees and a dispute with their management. The song was eventually released, but by then The Monkees' popularity had waned. Even so, both the experience and the subsequent royalty check had an enormous effect on Carole Bayer's life.

"I remember getting a check that was quite significant," she told me. "I remember thinking, oh my god, this is unbelievable. And that's when I left teaching. I got a check for $33,000. It almost didn't seem right. Here I was, working hard, teaching every day, punching the clock to make $5,200 a year, and I got a check for 33-thou for what seemed like nothing—for fun. I was very taken with the inordinate amount of money for writing a Monkees record, as opposed to teaching science and math. I remember thinking, that's quite a discrepancy. It totally freaked me out."

In 1969, the red-hot group The Fifth Dimension had a top 20 hit with Sedaka's 'Workin' On A Groovy Thing.' It was the only hit he wrote with lyricist Roger Atkins, another writer that Kirshner had signed.

"He was a good lyricist," Sedaka said. "Intellectual, very controlled, very cool and organized." Atkins may be best known for 'It's My Life,' which producer-entrepreneur Mickey Most brought to The Animals in 1965. Most was interested in Kirshner's writers' material because he had brought Barry Mann's song 'We Gotta Get Out Of This Place' for The Animals earlier in 1965. They released it right away, beating Mann's own version of the song to the punch. (Mann had been looking for four years for another hit song to follow 'Who Put The Bomp,' which remains his only success as a vocalist.)

In 1970, The Fifth Dimension scored again with Sedaka and Greenfield's song 'Puppet Man.' (Welsh crooner Tom Jones would release a successful version of the same song a year later.) Lead singer Marilyn McCoo and her husband and bandmate Billy Davis Jr have fond memories of recording the two songs.

"Our producer, Bones Howe, would bring songs to us," McCoo recalled, having taken time out from a still-busy schedule for a phone interview. "We would have listening sessions to decide. We liked 'Groovy Thing' right away. We felt it had a feeling that The Fifth Dimension could do something with."

"We thought it could be a big record for The Fifth Dimension because it fit what we were about, the things that we sung about," Davis Jr added. "It had a different feel than any Neil Sedaka song we had ever heard."

'Puppet Man' was a song they thought they could do different things with onstage. It was not only a good song to sing but a great visual song as well. "We were able to take that Neil Sedaka touch and put a Fifth Dimension flavoring to it," McCoo said.

Although his songs continued to provide hits for others, Sedaka's live appearances grew fewer and fewer. With money tight, he took whatever was offered, pretty much, even if it made no sense at all to him.

"I was booked into le Barrel [the Oyster Barrel] in Quebec," he recalled. "It was all in French. All they served were oysters, beer, and wine. I don't know why they booked me. I got five grand for the week—12 shows a week, and I played to maybe 15 or 20 people a show. I needed the money."

Playing such a tight run of shows reminded Sedaka of the schedule he had back at Esther Manor in the Catskills in the late 50s, when he was paid $86 a week. This time, he was making a lot more money—plus all the oysters he could eat. During this time he also played small clubs like Palumbo's in Philadelphia, Blinstrub's in Boston, and the Holiday House in Pittsburgh. People loved hearing the old hits, but not so much his new songs.

In the early 60s, Sedaka had toured Australia, where he was greeted by very receptive crowds—including two youngsters by the name of Barry and Maurice Gibb, who a decade later would become two of Sedaka's close friends. Now, in 1968, there was an offer on the table for him to return. But this time he had a wife and two children.

Would it be worth it to fly halfway around the world and being away from his family for so long?

The answer was yes.

"I only had a couple of gigs," Sedaka recalled. "The main gig was six weeks in Australia. Bob Rogers was the DJ there, and Richard Gray, the promoter of the Leagues' clubs, booked me. I got $50,000 for the six weeks. We lived off that most of the year."

The South Sydney Leagues Clubs were better known as workingmen's clubs. They had originally opened a century earlier to give the mill and mine workers a place to imbibe and have some private entertainment. By the 1960s, they had also become gambling clubs, and performers like Sedaka were usually well received.

Neil packed up for the six-week tour, with Leba joining him in Australia a week or so later. They were on a "budget tour," as Leba put it, so the kids remained at home in the trusted hands of their beloved nanny, Mary Moses. Leba was a combination of stage manager, business manager, and lighting director, all rolled into one.

"At the beginning, Neil did not sing his own songs," Leba recalled. "We put together a routine where he impersonated the big stars through the years. He did Elvis, he did Fats Domino, and he did Tom Jones. For each, I concocted some type of outfit for him. For Fats Domino, we had these rings; for Tom Jones, we had something very special."

Jones has become infamous over the years for having female fans throw their underwear at him while he performs—something that Neil would playfully reference onstage. "One of my aunts was quite amply endowed," Leba recalled with a laugh, "and I asked her for all of her old brassieres. In his Tom Jones outfit, Neil would toss them— along with old room keys—at the crowd."

Neil would also do a Beatles routine written for him by his old friend 'Cousin Brucie' Morrow.

"I had a pole hooked up with four mop heads," Leba continued. "Neil was the fifth Beatle. Then there was one routine where he had a makeup mirror hooked on around his neck, and he'd put blackface on and sing Eddie Cantor songs. We had a jacket made for him—it was orange and black with a bow tie. He comes out with this jacket on and he hasn't even opened his mouth and they're booing him off the stage. It turned out that orange and black were the colors of the rival team's rugby squad."

Neil and his Australian fans warmed up to each other quickly. He decided to release a record there that he and Howie Greenfield had written: a song called 'Star-Crossed Lovers' about a couple from different faiths—a very controversial topic in 1968.

"At the time, inter-faith marriages were becoming popular," Sedaka told me, "and Howie wanted to write about it, knowing it would be controversial. A smart producer asked me if I had anything new for Australia, and I thought of 'Star-Crossed Lovers.'"

Father, dear father, I come to confession
Hoping to find peace of mind.
Father, I've fallen in love with an angel
But she's not one of our kind.

If it's a sin to want her and need her,
This is what I'm guilty of.
She won't believe in the things we believe in,
But she believes in my love.

Star-crossed lovers,
Is there a place for us in this world?

Father, dear father, I can't live without her,
Is it your wish we must part?
Would you refuse to give me your blessing
If I should follow my heart?

Father, please tell me, are we so different
And is our love so unwise?
We both believe there is one God in heaven,
But we see him through different eyes.

Star-crossed lovers,
Is there a place for us in this world?

The Australian promoter listened to the beginning of the song and decided to offer it to a Christian station first. They loved it and broke the record before the rock'n'roll disc jockeys in Sydney got wind of it. With several copies of 'Star-Crossed Lovers' in hand, Sedaka set out to promote the song. Unlike the USA, Australia only had a few big radio stations, making it easier to get your record played. Sedaka decided to begin with Sydney station 2SM's Bob Rogers, who in 1964 was chosen to tour with The Beatles and bring them back to Australia. He was the biggest rock'n'roll name on the continent.

Sedaka had arranged to be on the air live with Rogers at 11:00am one morning. Rogers trailed the appearance for days; everything was set—except that Rogers thought they had agreed to 10:30. The appointed time arrived, and there was no Neil Sedaka, and nor was he there at 10:40 or 10:50. Finally, at 11:00am, Neil arrived at the station.

I was lucky to find Bob Rogers, aged 85, still spinning records in Sydney. He couldn't have been happier to share this story by phone.

"When my secretary called back to tell me Neil Sedaka was there, I was pissed off," Rogers recalled. "I had been promoting that he'd be there to talk about his new record all morning. Tell him that his time has expired, I said, and that if he'd like, he can leave his record behind."

Sedaka—never late for anything—knew it was all a misunderstanding and pleaded with Rogers to let him explain. Rogers eventually cooled off and interviewed Neil, although the first few minutes were pretty tense.

"I was pretty full of myself in those days," Rogers told me. "When I heard Neil's record, I loved it, and I decided to play it for him anyway. It was quite a controversial song for those days."

The song became so popular that Neil was asked to put out an album with Festival Records in Australia. He titled it *Workin' On A Groovy Thing* and included on it another Australian hit written with Greenfield, 'Wheeling, West Virginia,' but it was 'Star-Crossed Lovers' that rode the charts all the way up to number one.

Neil thought this could be the song to propel him back to America, but it wasn't to be. No matter how hard he tried, no record label would touch him.

"I remember I took the record to [former Kirshner employees] Charles Koppelman and Don Rubin," Sedaka recalled. "They were publishers by then and had started their own label. But they turned it down."

Back when Koppelman and Rubin first started working for Kirshner as song-pluggers at Aldon Music in the early 60s, they would hear all of Sedaka's new songs and even sit in on some of the demo sessions. There was no bigger star at the time. By 1969, however, the publishing duo was on top of the world; as far as they were concerned Neil Sedaka was a ghost from the 50s, and nothing more. And in the eyes of many, he would remain so for some time yet.

CHAPTER 5
EMERGENCE

By 1970, Neil Sedaka, like most of the great songwriters from Don Kirshner's Aldon Music office, had moved on. Carole King and Gerry Goffin had divorced and moved to Los Angeles in search of new friends and ideas; Barry Mann and Cynthia Weil remained together but also moved to LA; so too did Jack Keller and Howie Greenfield, who had written three top ten songs together for Connie Francis. Neil and Leba Sedaka were about the only ones who remained in New York.

In the late 60s, King had tried to reinvent herself by putting out her first album of songs as a singer-songwriter, *Road To Nowhere*, which Goffin produced. They had already divorced by then, and the album's lack of success probably accelerated their professional split. Settling in Laurel Canyon and surrounding herself with new friends like James Taylor, King began a move away from the depressing material found on *Road To Nowhere*. She eventually started writing again for Ode Records, run by Kirshner's West Coast A&R guy, Lou Adler. This time the results were fantastic. When Adler released King's *Tapestry* album in the spring of 1971 it was like catching lightning in a bottle. The first single from that album, 'It's Too Late,' hit the *Billboard* pop charts on May 8 and stayed on them all summer long, peaking at number one for a month. It was the fourth number one song King had written, but her first as a performer.

Sedaka had mixed feelings upon hearing King's album. He was happy for her success but sad that he was being left in the dust. Once again, music was changing. The Beatles had come and gone; the Motown sound had arrived, and now another new era was beginning.

"I heard Carole sing her *Tapestry* songs on the radio," Sedaka recalled, "and I thought, I can do that. We're from the same niche, we both started at the Brill Building, I can do that.

"The era of the singer-songwriter had begun," he added, "and I was being left behind. I needed to be a part of it. I wanted to be a part of it. I wanted it with a vengeance!"

For my previous book on Kirshner, I tried every way possible to get to Carole King without success. Once again, when I tried to reach her to discuss her early days with Sedaka, I was politely turned down, this time by her new manager, who happened to be her daughter Sherry, who told me through an assistant that Carole didn't have time in her schedule to speak. When I told Neil about this, he said he wasn't surprised.

"She's not very happy with me. My son Marc approached her on the street in New York a few years ago and she said to him, tell your father to stop talking about me." King was referring, Neil said, to his frequent mentions in interviews of her being his high-school girlfriend. "We really did go out for two months and went everywhere together," he told me. "I'm still her number one fan. I put her up on pedestal. She's still an inspiration. I'm sorry that we don't talk."

The success of *Tapestry* had to be a blow to Sedaka's ego. He had been close with Carole since they were 13, and he had always been ahead of her on the success ladder. He was the first one to sell a song to a record label, the first one to be signed, the first one to put out a record (albeit as part of The Tokens with Melba Records). Kirshner had signed Sedaka to a publishing deal two years before he signed King, and Neil's first hit record as a songwriter, 'Stupid Cupid,' came three year's before her first big success with 'Will You Love Me Tomorrow.' And although King was the first to get a number one hit, Sedaka's own songs (which he had also begun recording himself) were always in the top ten.

Yet here Neil was in 1971, trying desperately to get back on the charts for the first time in eight years, and out of nowhere King had the number one song and album in the country with 'It's Too Late' and *Tapestry*. Sure, Neil was pleased for her, but there was also a touch of jealousy. This is what drove him on even more. If Carole King could do it, he knew that could do it, too. But getting there would be the hard part.

Neil had been writing a new group of beautiful songs with Howie Greenfield that were totally different from his early 'sandwich' songs for RCA. With the likes of 'I'm A Song (Sing Me),' 'Superbird,' and 'Cardboard California,' he was convinced that he was ready to introduce a brand new Neil Sedaka to the world.

Initially, he told me, he had just wanted to work with a small group of musicians on the new material, as King had done on *Tapestry*. "But Kirshner and [arranger] Lee Holdridge had another idea. And when I heard Lee's arrangements, I was knocked over. They talked me into the big orchestrations, and I went along with it."

Like Sedaka, Holdridge had a classical background and came with a great reputation, having provided some spectacular arrangements for songs like 'Holly Holy,' 'Song Sung Blue,' and 'Play Me' for another of Kirshner's writers turned stars, Neil Diamond. When Diamond—who was also from Brighton Beach—first started, he wanted to be the next Neil Sedaka. "He had records out and you could hear them on the radio," Diamond said. "Back then, you judged yourself against Sedaka."[6] But now, in 1970, Sedaka was reaching out to Diamond's arranger.

Sedaka titled his new album, *Emergence*, hoping that was what it would bring. He wanted it to be a 'concept' album with much more elaborate songs than those he was known for. Holdridge onboard, the orchestra became an integral part of the piece, providing several exciting moments on songs like 'Superbird' and 'Cardboard California.'

"They almost verged on being 'art' songs," Holdridge told me when I reached him by phone. "They had longer bar structures and more unusual juxtaposition of phrases. Those songs were very adventurous and creative. Jimmy Webb was experimenting that way [on songs like the eight-minute 'MacArthur Park'], and I think all the major songwriters really started pushing at it. Just get rid of the eight bars, eight bars, eight bars, eight bars … they started something like, a 12-bar phrase, or two bridges—things of that sort. And Neil, because of his classical background was a natural for doing that. If you listen to that album and then his earlier songs, you'll ask yourself, is this the same guy?"

That was exactly what Neil was going for. He didn't want anyone to think this was the same Neil Sedaka who had served up all of those ready-to-order hits. His agent at William Morris, Dick Fox, had a brilliant idea: in order to show the world—and the New York press— that this was a new Neil Sedaka emerging from the 60s, he wanted to launch Neil on a four-date tour beginning at the hippest club in the city, the Bitter End. The only problem would be convincing Paul Colby, the manager and booking agent of the club, to go for it.

The Bitter End became popular in the 60s when Colby started booking folk acts such as Peter Paul & Mary. Avant-garde comedians like Woody Allen, Bill Cosby, and Joan Rivers had played there, too, and slowly Colby was bringing rock music to the club. In the mid 70s, the Bitter End would gain nationwide recognition when Bob Dylan kicked off his Rolling Thunder Revue there.

"I went down to the club one day around lunch time," Fox recalled. "When I pitched the idea to Colby and his group, they laughed in my face. 'You mean *Breaking-Up-is-Hard-To-Do* Neil Sedaka? *That* Neil Sedaka?' They asked laughing hysterically."

After explaining what Sedaka's new music was about and assuring him it would fit right in with the new singer-songwriter trend, Fox made Colby an offer he couldn't refuse.

"I said, how about you don't have to pay him at all? He'll do a week without pay, other than what he brings in the door. If he brings in six people, you pay him for six. If he brings in a thousand, you pay him for a thousand."

I was able to track down Colby, aged 94, at his home in Montclair, New Jersey. Despite his advanced age, he remembered the deal vividly.

Colby had little to lose, and realizing he had a weeklong slot available without a headliner, he agreed to the plan. "[Fox] didn't want much money," Colby told me, "and that was a good starting point. And after all, Neil Sedaka was still going to draw a crowd. I really didn't have much too lose."

Once the shows were announced, Neil began to get nervous—not about performing, but about having the right outfit to wear for such a hip club. "Carole Bayer had been writing some songs with me and volunteered to help," he recalled. "She brought me down to the Village and helped me pick out the right jeans and shirt to wear."

Ironically, when Neil appeared at the Bitter End he only had a small group of musicians behind him—just the way he had originally imagined *Emergence* might sound, without the orchestral arrangements Holdridge brought to it.

"It was a tremendous success," Fox said. "They loved it, and the reviews were amazing. We thought that would be it"—that Sedaka would be back on his way up the charts—"but the records didn't sell. The DJs wouldn't play them. The public wasn't ready to meet the new Neil Sedaka."

Opening night at the Bitter End might have been a tremendous success, but once Neil hit the road the reception was much more chilly. He played to small, intimate clubs like the Quiet Nights in Chicago and Marvelous Marv's in Denver. A writer for the *Chicago Tribune* ripped him to shreds. "It was very mean-spirited," Sedaka recalled. "He wrote, what is this guy trying to do? He'll never come back."

It may have been that disc jockeys in 1970 had the same reaction Paul Colby had when they first heard Neil's name. Maybe they just wanted to remember 'Calendar Girl' and 'Breaking Up Is Hard To Do.' Maybe they just weren't ready for the 'new' Neil Sedaka. Or maybe the full, orchestral sound of *Emergence* didn't slide comfortably into the top 40 sound of the day; maybe the songs, beautiful as they were, missed the mark. Whatever it was, this was not to be the golden ticket to bring Sedaka back.

For the first time in his career, Neil felt that he had failed. The album's lack of success put him in a funk, but not for long. "When they said, he'll never come back, it made me all the more determined," he told me. "It gave me more fight, more drive. Nothing was going to stop me."

Thirty years earlier, another young composer had followed a similar path. Like Neil, Jule Styne had studied classical piano as a child but yearned for a way to be more popular. He solved the problem by buying the sheet music for and memorizing 20 of Irving Berlin's most famous tunes. This in turn led him to Broadway, where he composed two of the all-time great musicals, *Gypsy* and *Funny Girl*.

Sedaka too had wondered about writing for Broadway, and decided that now was the time to explore a road he hadn't tried before. In Merriewold Park, he sought the council of a new friend, Mary Rodgers Guettel, daughter of the legendary Richard Rodgers and an accomplished composer in her own right.

"He was trying to reestablish himself," she told me. "He never complained. They had this wonderful little house with a circular bed. The minute he went to the piano, I thought this is a guy with a classical ear. I could tell when he was playing all of his absolutely charming pop songs. I could hear really good training going into that. I found out later that he had studied at Juilliard."

Sedaka was already a huge fan of her father's music. At Lincoln High, he had directed and performed songs from Rodgers & Hammerstein's *Carousel*. He loved the big Broadway musicals but never pictured himself composing one. Mary, however, had seen and heard Neil's brilliant classical piano talent and enjoyed many of his popular songs, and thought it was time to set up a meeting with her father.

Richard Rodgers is probably responsible for more standards than any other composer. With Lorenz Hart in the 1920s and 30s, he wrote such classics as '(I'll Take) Manhattan,' 'Where Or When,' 'My Funny Valentine,' 'Isn't It Romantic,' and 'The Lady Is A Tramp.' With Oscar Hammerstein in the 40s and 50s, Rodgers wrote some of the most beloved musicals of all time, including *Oklahoma*, *Carousel*, *South Pacific*, *The King And I*, and *The Sound Of Music*.

Although he had been slowed by a heart attack in 1969, Rodgers was still writing music well into his seventies when Sedaka met with him in 1971. Mary Rodgers arranged the meeting, which took place at her father's office on Madison Avenue.

"I remember I put on a new suit," said Sedaka. "When I got there he told me he had already heard the *Emergence* album and liked it very much. I sat down at the piano and played 'Superbird' and a few other songs for him."

Rodgers listened to Neil play both classical and pop material before offering a suggestion.

"This is much too easy for you," he told Neil. "You must write something for the theater. Come back to me with an idea—a concept—for a show and I'll help you develop it."

Sedaka was thrilled to get such a response from one of the greatest composers of all time, but he was also unsure as to whether he was up to the task.

"I was intimidated by the idea of writing for the theater," he said. "I didn't know if I could write for other voices beside my own."

Maybe some day, he thought, maybe some day. But he still had an itch to prove that he could write and sing popular music.

"My father was right," Mary recalled. "He could have written for the theater. We'd all go over and listen to Neil play, and [his daughter] Dara could instinctively harmonize with him. He was so gutsy then. He didn't complain about what had happened to him, or having been so famous before. You know he just started right over again. He just worked his ass off to get back up."

Meanwhile, Dick Fox came up with an alternative suggestion: "Why don't you go to England? Move there. The English still love your music. They still respect you. They're much more loyal. They still love the early rock'n'rollers."

The more Neil thought about it, the more he thought this might be a way to engineer a way back onto the charts in America—through England's back door. If he could be successful and have a few hits in the UK, maybe, just maybe, he could come back to the States on his own terms.

"This country [America] had a preconceived notion of me," Sedaka said in 1976.[7] He talked it over with Leba and decided to make the move. "I was either going to kill it, or it was going to kill me!"

Of course, moving would mean uprooting the kids. In 1972, Dara was nine years old and Marc was six. They had been living in Merriewold Park, near Monticello, and Dara had been attending Monticello Middle School. Now they would be going to the American Community School along with Indian princesses and the sons and daughters of some of wealthy industrialists.

"I never knew they were going through challenging times," Dara told me when I reached her by phone. "I had no idea whatsoever. They should be saluted for how they kept it separated from us. I'm sure there was tension and issues, but we never saw the problems.

"No matter where we lived, we were always happy together. Whether it was Brooklyn or Merriewold, London or Park Avenue, we were always happy together. And no matter how challenging the times were for Dad, it was never an issue," she continued. "They always indulged me—probably too much. And from the time I was two years old, Dad and I always sang together."

Eventually, Neil and Leba rented a nine-room flat in Mayfair behind the Dorchester Hotel, completely furnished, for the ridiculously low price of $1,000 a month. This would be their home, off and on, for the next two years. To keep things as normal as possible, they brought along Mary Moses, the beloved family nanny. When Neil went on the road, however, Leba would pack up the kids and bring them along whenever possible. For the kids, it was the adventure of a lifetime. Neil, however, was about to find out just how tough the road could be.

CHAPTER 6
HEY NEIL, SING 'EMBRACEABLE YOU'

W hen the Sedakas accepted his proposal, Dick Fox, too, packed up and headed for the UK to survey the lay of the land. He booked Neil into large and small clubs from London to Liverpool and from Manchester to Stockport.

Fox wound up booking Neil in a series of halls known as the workingmen's clubs (or WMCs) over the next two years. Neil knew these would not necessarily be the UK's version of the Copacabana, but he still wasn't quite ready for the reception he'd get.

Working men's clubs first sprang up in the early 19th century in the North of England and the Midlands, as well as in the South Wales Valleys and on the other side of the world in Australia. In those days, they offered the working man a place to socialize and partake in liquid refreshment in a controlled environment. There would be a bar that offered alcohol and food, and usually a snooker or billiard table.

"Your average workingmen's club in the late 60s and 70s would attract a regular crowd from its local streets," Gary Kitchen, a former regular, told me. "The bar was reserved exclusively for men; the 'lounge' would be for those unfortunate men who had been coerced into bringing their wives—and even under these circumstances it would only be a matter of a few minutes before the menfolk snuck out of the lounge for the comfort of the men-only bar."

Eventually, many of these clubs began providing entertainment to go with the alcohol. One of the first of these clubs that Sedaka appeared at was the Wooky Hollow, on the outskirts of Liverpool in the Northwest of England, its name derived from that of the caves in the Southwest where tourists go looking for evidences of the legendary witches of the same name. The club itself was a landmark in the area during the late 60s and early 70s.

"There weren't many night clubs nearby at that time," former local resident Paul McDermott told me in an email. "And here was the real drawing card—it was open later than the pubs. The place was considered posh because they served steak and chips or chicken in the basket. People would come from all over for their big night out."

The Wooky Hollow could be either a great place to perform or a nightmare, depending on the mood of the crowd. The stage was lit up, like the one in *Saturday Night Fever*, and there were tiers of tables banked high around it so that everyone could see the acts. If they liked you, you were the toast of the town. If not, those tables provided the perfect vantage point from which to toss beer or just about anything else.

"The Northern audiences smell bullshit very quickly," Graham Gouldman of 10cc, who would later play a key role in the Neil Sedaka story, told me when I reached him by phone. "They don't take any showbiz-y stuff very well. It can be a very tough environment."

The acts themselves would vary from established names like Sedaka to such bizarre fare as a boxing kangaroo, depending on the night. Regardless of their stature (or not), many of these performers would leave the stage with a renewed empathy for the lions at the Roman Coliseum.

"There was a bridge that you walked over from backstage to front, like a little drawbridge," Neil told me. "I only had a drummer traveling with me—I had to pick up and rehearse a band at each spot. Usually, I only had a few hours before the show to work with them, and often I had to sing over them just trying to be heard."

The first offer came in from promoter Henry Sellers for a cabaret act in Northern England. Sedaka decided to take the gig but wished he hadn't. He drove from town to town in a VW Beetle with his drummer.

"The clubs turned out to be real holes," Neil later wrote. "The first was a depressing beer joint in Liverpool catering to a rowdy clientele. I sang mostly old material, while the audience drank and talked through the act. After the show I was seized with depression. What was I trying to do? Perhaps I would never achieve stardom again."[8]

The self-doubt rose in Manchester, when only 20 people turned up for the show and Neil had to follow a stripper. The acoustics were terrible, and the audience started talking, loudly, every time he tried to sing something new. But he wasn't about to give up.

Leba traveled with Neil as much as possible. She was his manager now, and for these shows she was his stage manager as well. She worked the spotlight and often would introduce him. Sometimes they'd have four or five-hour drives from club to club. Yes, Neil was a long way from the limo that brought him to the Copacabana for his opening night in 1962, which felt like a million light years away.

"On one particular night at the Wooky Hollow the crowd was really worked up," Neil recalled fondly. "They'd holler out, half drunk, hey Neil, sing 'Embraceable You.' And if they didn't like your song, they'd throw beer or lit cigarettes at the stage."

One of the problems for the performers was that the Wooky Hollow was only a short distance from Anfield Football Stadium, home of Liverpool FC, at the time one of the most successful teams in the country. "If there were a comedy act, the club would fill up with lads from the pubs on Breck Road," McDermott told me. "Often, the funniest lines would come from the floor. If the artists were rubbish, they could expect things thrown in their general direction. People would turn up half-drunk after football matches. After all, the club was within house brick-heaving distance of Anfield."

Another club that Sedaka appeared at regularly was the Golden Garter in Wythenshawe, Greater Manchester, about 35 miles inland from Liverpool. A former bowling alley, the Garter, as its patrons affectionately called it, had opened its doors for the first time on October 7 1968 and was intended to be a step up from most other workingmen's clubs. It could cater for up to 1,400 diners, while the thick, plush carpet and gold-and-crimson décor made clear that this wasn't just any old club.

According to the Wythenshaw History & Heritage website, the club's 50 barmen wore green-and-gold-striped waistcoats, while the food menu included Golden Fried Scampi and gammon ham (replaced after a few years with something much simpler: chicken in a basket.)[9] In the 70s, Maurice Gibb from The Bee Gees would come by to watch his wife, Lulu, perform. Unbeknownst to the crowd, he would stand in the back every night and have a drink while Lulu performed. Maurice became good friends with Sedaka during those years, and would play a key role in his comeback, while other stars who made regular stops at the Garter included Mary Wilson & The Supremes, The Drifters, The Hollies, and Gene Pitney.

"It was a huge club in its day," Pitney later told Sedaka chronicler Michael Turner. "It was fantastic. It was a smoke-filled drinking atmosphere and a late-night place. Sometimes it was like looking through a haze [of smoke] to see your audience. And it got pretty rowdy at times, but it was fun. There were ladies who'd rush the stage and grab whatever they could from you."[10]

For the most part, Sedaka enjoyed the atmosphere—at least when the crowd wasn't too rowdy—but felt he had been reduced to a mere "nostalgia act."

"They only knew 'Oh! Carol,' 'I Go Ape' [a UK hit in 1958, despite bombing in the USA], 'Happy Birthday, Sweet Sixteen,' and 'Calendar Girl,'" he told me. "I also sang songs by Cat Stevens, Joanie Mitchell and Gordon Lightfoot—the singer-songwriter songs of the 70s. I desperately wanted to throw in some of my own new songs, but they weren't open to it. They just wanted their beer, and to hear the hits. I had to swallow a lot of pride."

The Batley Variety Club near Leeds in West Yorkshire offered a further step up from the average workingmen's club, referring to itself instead as a theater club. The Batley had a capacity of 1,600, offering dinner for six shillings and sixpence (about $30 today), and was fitted with plush velvet benches installed in horseshoe-like pods that could seat five couples, with an open end facing the stage.

"Two remarkable things distinguished the Variety Club from the run-of-the-mill workingmen's club," former regular Gary Kitchen told me in an email. "They fed you during the night, and they attracted the world's top performing acts. They fed you with a dish that had been specially invented for the club-land audience—the ubiquitous chicken-in-a-basket. And when I say they attracted the world's top performing acts, I mean the world's top performing acts that were going through a bit of a drought year. They would follow the chicken-in-a-basket and take to the stage to the smell of cooking oil and the sound of smacking lips to entertain the masses of coalminers and millworkers and then get offstage and into a taxi before the fights started."

Annette Burnely used to drive the acts back and forth to the club with her husband, Jimmy. "There were fights all the time," she told me, "in the good Yorkshire tradition: a few pints and bit of a feed and a good biff and smack."

The Sedakas became favorites of James and Betty Corrigan, the owners of the Batley Variety Club. These gracious people had at one time worked the carnival circuit for a living and lived in the back of a wagon. After Neil had appeared at the Batley several times, the Corrigans invited the Sedakas to stay with them. James Corrigan had sold off one of the bingo halls the couple also owned and decided to hide his cash under the floorboards of his home. Unfortunately, he had chosen to hide it right in a spot where his cats tended to urinate. One day, Neil walked in and to his surprise found Corrigan ironing £5 and £10 notes. Shocked by the sight, he asked what was going on. "Trying to get the smell out," Corrigan replied, as if it was all perfectly natural.

"In the spring, Betty and James were invited by the Queen to have tea in the Royal Garden," Leba recalled. "There might have been 1,500 people invited, but it was still an honor. There were certain prerequisites for Betty, though—the gloves, the hat, the dress. So she said, please come shopping with me. The first place we go to is Christian Dior, right off Bond Street. We walk in and she's trying on things, and she picks the hat. Then she opened her pocketbook and took out a bag of this [foul-smelling] money and handed it to the clerk. The lady at Dior was thrown back, startled, but she took the money anyway."

Sedaka would make regular stops at these clubs for several years, from late 1971 through to early '74. In between, there was quality time back in London with his family, and the occasional flight back to

New York. After a while, however, performing at the Wooky Hollow, the Garter, and the Batley Variety Club began to grind him down. The smoke and the haze and the rowdy crowds would have worn anyone down. At some point, you have to wonder whether Neil ever thought about throwing in the towel and giving up his comeback attempt.

"Never! Never!" he told me. "I had this driving ambition, even as a kid. I always wanted to be famous. Once you get a taste, you never lose that—that high of being number one. I was determined to make it all the way back."

CHAPTER 7
PHIL CODY, PHIL CODY

Prior to leaving for the UK, Sedaka's setbacks were adding up. After his failure to find a label to release his Australian hit 'Star-Crossed Lovers,' and the ultimate failure of *Emergence* in 1970, you had to wonder what kept him going. By 1971, he hadn't had a top ten hit as a performer for nearly a decade.

After *Emergence*, but before he decided to pack his bags for England, Sedaka decided to try yet another lyricist. He had found some success writing with Carole Bayer, but at that time she was busy writing the Broadway musical *Georgy Girl*.

Sedaka had also written a little with lyricist Roger Atkins, with whom he collaborated on 'Workin' On A Groovy Thing' for The Fifth Dimension, and he was still writing occasionally with Howie Greenfield, but he wanted a new sound for his songs, and that required a new kind of lyricist. That lyricist turned out to be Philip Feliciotto, a hippie by nature, and therefore the very opposite of what Neil Sedaka represented. Few would have seen it coming.

Philip Feliciotto (pronounced Fell-ah-chotto) was the son of a musician named Anthony Feliciotto, who had longed to be an opera star when he came over from Sicily in 1930 at the age of 17. Anthony settled on becoming a carpenter instead and raised a family near Bridgeport, Connecticut. His son, Philip, became proficient in music and formed a band with some friends from college.

In 1966 they tried out at the Night Owl Café in Greenwich Village, where The Lovin' Spoonful had been discovered, but were told they needed original material. Feliciotto was elected by the group to be the lyric writer, since he was studying English at Bridgeport University. When the group eventually disbanded, Philip decided to quit school and stay in Greenwich Village.

"I was a pot-smoking hippie," he said during an interview over lunch in Santa Monica in July 2012. "I was knocking around, and I got married, and then all of a sudden I wasn't married and I moved back home with my parents. I had found some work writing for commercials, and then in 1970 somebody suggested I go see Donnie Kirshner."

By now, Kirshner had parted ways with Columbia Screen Gems, following the dispute about The Monkees, and had opened a gorgeous suite of offices on the 28th floor at the corner of 56th Street and 6th Avenue in New York. Kirshner liked Feliciotto immediately, and after an audition offered him a publishing deal and a recording contract. Philip jumped at the chance.

Kirshner always had a great ear for talent. He had started his songwriting career in 1955, at the age of 20, in partnership with a guy named Walden Robert Cassotto, but they struggled to get the established Brill Building publishers to listen to their songs. When Cassotto changed his name to Bobby Darin and had a hit with 'Splish Splash,' Kirshner decided to open his own publishing firm to accommodate all the great teenage songwriters that were being turned away at the Brill Building: Goffin & King, Mann & Weil, Sedaka & Greenfield. In many cases, Kirshner had to guide and groom his writers for years before they began turning out hits (Goffin & King, for example, published 45 flops before they made the charts).

Sedaka and Greenfield didn't need help that way, however. They were writing hits from the moment they walked in the door—which made it all the more difficult for Kirshner to know what advice to give to Sedaka once he fell out of favor.

Around the time Sedaka released *Emergence*, Kirshner got Feliciotto a recording deal with RCA, the first fruits of which was an album of original songs called *Laughing Sandwich*. Just before the album came out, Feliciotto received a phone call from the RCA accounting department.

"Jose Feliciano was one of RCA's mainstays," he told me, "and their accounting department [asked] if I wouldn't mind changing my name because they were getting confused. That night I was watching an old movie about Buffalo Bill Cody, and I said, there it is—Cody—and I became Phil Cody!"

Regardless of whether it was credited to Feliciotto or Cody, however, *Laughing Sandwich* would not find an audience. It was not, all told, a great experience.

"I blotted so much of it out," he said. "I didn't really enjoy the recording experience, and I didn't enjoy the results, because the album seemed to come out and disappear. I still get letters and fan mail from people who actually loved that album and I don't know why. I thought it was a total failure, and I was depressed about the whole thing. But I remember Donnie Kirshner coming up to me and saying, don't worry kid, you're gonna be all right."

Cody would hang out at Kirshner's office with Jay Siegel, Mitch Margo, and Phil Margo, three members of The Tokens, who at that time were writing and producing for Kirshner. One of the few people who had heard and liked *Laughing Sandwich* was Neil Sedaka. He took a copy home and played it from cover to cover one night. A few days later, he came tapping at Cody's door, calling out "Phil Co-dee, Phil Co-dee" in a singsong fashion, accenting every syllable.

"He mentioned that he heard my album and that he liked my lyric writing and that we should write together," Cody recalled. "I wasn't sure it would work. The kind of music I liked was folk-rock and the blues. Neil Sedaka was nowhere on my radar. I was not an idol-worshipper of Neil Sedaka, not a member of the cult of Neil."

But Neil was sure that Phil was exactly the kind of lyric writer he was looking for. "I was fascinated by his lyrics," Neil told me. "Fascinated because they were poetic, they painted pictures, they were elusive, evasive, whereas Howie Greenfield's lyrics were tie-it-with-a-ribbon and perfectly polished. Phil's were artistic. And I needed a change. I needed to get into the 70s. I was fascinated—and he was shocked. I could practically read his mind: write with Neil Sedaka? He's a ghost!"

Neil wasn't far off. Cody certainly had his doubts.

"I was a hippie who lived in a little studio in Greenwich Village," Cody recalled. "I was two steps out of a commune, and here was this guy who looked like he had just come in off the tennis court, asking me if I wanted to write songs with him. I do remember expressing some doubts to Wally Gold [who ran Kirshner's publishing company] as to whether or not this was a good idea."

Gold looked at Cody as if he was considering turning down a chance to write with Gershwin.

"Are you fucking kidding?" he asked.

Jay Siegel, who had played with Sedaka in The Linc-Tones before they became The Tokens, remembered discussing Cody's dilemma.

"Cody thought Neil was too *pop* for his style of music," he told me. "He was afraid Neil would try to make him write another 'Calendar

Girl.' But that's exactly what Sedaka was trying to get away from, and that convinced Cody to give it a try. And that was the beauty of the environment Kirshner encouraged: that a Neil Sedaka and a Phil Cody could find each other."

Phil and Neil began by writing together late one afternoon at Kirshner's baby grand piano. The huge office, 28 floors above ground, had floor-to-ceiling windows that faced west, overlooking 6th Avenue, and when Neil sat behind the piano he faced north and looked out over Central Park. They wrote three songs together that first day: 'Trying To Say Goodbye,' 'Don't Let It Mess Your Mind,' and 'Solitaire.'

Cody found the transition to writing with Sedaka much easier once he realized that there was a personal connection.

"It was really fun," he said. "I couldn't believe how much fun songwriting was. And I mean I never experienced anything like that. The guy just pumped pure optimism into the room. I didn't want it to stop, and neither did he. We had nothing in common other than the joy to make music.

"It was much easier than I thought. In retrospect, my dad was passionate about music and I learned about being passionate from my dad. He had a great tenor voice—his hero was [Enrico] Caruso. If you were on a job where my dad was pounding nails on a roof, he was singing at the top of his lungs all day long. He was Tony the singing carpenter. He had that kind of passion—and Neil had that kind of passion. And I think I recognized that."

Cody had never written a song like 'Solitaire' before. There are certain things in the song that he recognized as having a Mediterranean feel to them, which didn't feel alien to him.

"Here I was this bluesy, folksy hippie kind of person, and I just fell into it," he recalled. "I felt at home, musically, with him. It was very strange, and at the same time it just felt natural. Basically, I sat at Neil's elbow and I got a free songwriting education from him. He was very patient with me and had the capacity to repeat melodic lines over and over again while I tried to fit words into the melodic phrases he was playing."

"We were unlike," Neil told me. "He was a hippie and more introverted. I was very outgoing and impulsive, compulsive. But it flowed. Our songs flowed."

Sedaka's melody for 'Solitaire' was inspired by listening to Roberta Flack sing 'The First Time Ever I Saw Your Face.' Right before they got together, one of Neil's friends—somebody he respected greatly—had told him, "You know, you still haven't written that one great one." When Neil played the melody he had written while thinking about Flack's voice he asked Cody to make him cry, and sure enough Sedaka—always an emotional performer—would cry repeatedly during the completion of the number. The melody came from his classical roots. He called it "Chopanesque."

"There wasn't any contrivance," Cody recalled. "It was all there in the moment he was playing and I was feeling, and I had no idea where those feelings came from inside me. It felt very natural."

According to Sedaka, sometimes when you get a spiritual feeling you just have to go with it, no matter what you originally had in mind. "Sometimes you're chosen by something spiritual at that moment in time," he said, "and it passes through my voice and my fingers and the piano and it actually comes from somewhere else. It's a very marvelous feeling."

When we spoke over lunch, Cody explained that his recent divorce might have been part of the inspiration, adding that the inspiration for the song title and lyrics came from the tedious train trips he had been taking into the city each morning from his parents' home in Connecticut. During the ride each day he would take out a deck of cards and play Solitaire.

As happy as Sedaka and Cody were with these first three songs, nothing would happen with them immediately. After playing them again at home that night, Sedaka was sure 'Solitaire' was going to be a hit, but he couldn't get anyone else to believe him. Even Don Kirshner's golden ear let him down on this occasion when Phil and Neil presented 'Solitaire' to Kirshner, Wally Gold, and Kirshner's moneyman, Herb Moelis.

"They had no interest in it whatsoever," Cody recalled. "There seemed to be a general lack of faith in the song's potential earning power—the feeling at the company being that we had written a 'nice' song, and that we would be better served devoting our efforts to writing hits. Yet, here I am, four decades and at least 47 cover recordings later, talking about what is, essentially, the most covered song that Neil and I have ever written."

It wasn't the first time Kirshner had dropped the ball on a potential hit. When Barry Mann and Cynthia Weil first played him 'Uptown' (which Phil Spector would shortly turn into a hit for The Crystals), Kirshner advised them to try to write something like The Diamonds' 'Little Darlin'' instead.

"I don't think they [Kirshner and Gold] had any idea that "Solitaire" was as good as it was," Cody continued. "And I think it really pissed Neil off. And that's where I think the break with Donnie started, or got exacerbated. The next thing I heard, Neil was working in dives in Northern England, and I didn't really understand what any of that was about."

It took four more years for 'Solitaire' to become a hit, first for Andy Williams in the UK and then for the Carpenters in the USA. Cody had to change the lyrics slightly for both acts. For one thing, they were afraid the line "a little hope goes up in smoke" would be interpreted as being about smoking pot, and with their middle-of-the road audiences, they didn't want to chance it.

"I remember that producer Richard Perry called and wanted Andy Williams to record 'Solitaire,' but there were lyrics Andy was uncomfortable singing. So Perry had me rewrite the lyric over the phone. It was word for word over the telephone. I didn't mind because Neil really believed in the song, and I wanted to help him get it out there."

Andy Williams, born in 1927, was the youngest of four brothers who enjoyed singing together. By the 50s his singing career was in full bloom, with constant appearances on *The Tonight Show*. It didn't take long for him to get his own TV show and become one of the most popular male singers in the world. By the time he recorded 'Solitaire' in 1973, Williams was 46 and in the prime of his career. He had a long line of hits and 18 gold albums. Although he had never recorded Henry Mancini and Johnny Mercer's 'Moon River,' it became his theme song after he sang it during the 34th Academy Awards telecast in 1962.

Richard Perry had first heard 'Solitaire' on the UK only album of the same name Sedaka recorded for RCA in 1972, but he wanted the song to be softer, more personal, when Williams sung it.

"For Richard, getting me to change the lyrics for Andy may have been one of 400 things he had to do that day," Cody continued, "but for me it was a seminal experience, a career changing—no, a life changing experience."

Here are the lines that Williams sang, after Cody agreed to the changes:

There was a man, a lonely man
Who lost his love through his indifference
A heart that cared, that went unshared
And so it dies within his silence
Now Solitaire's the only game in town
And every road that takes me, takes me down
And by myself, it's easy to pretend
I'll never love again

And keeping to myself he plays the game
Without your love it always ends the same
While life goes on around me everywhere
I'm playing Solitaire

Another day, a lonely day
So much to say that goes unspoken
And through the night, each sleepless night
The eyes are closed, the heart is broken

And Solitaire's the only game in town ...

When I reached Perry in Los Angeles to ask him why he chose the song, he didn't have much time to talk and he didn't recall asking Cody to change the lyrics, but he did say that record mogul Clive Davis had "turned me on to it." At that point I reached out to Davis for an answer, and I caught up with him at his New York office early in 2013.

"You know, it's been 40 years since Andy Williams made that recording," he began. "All I know is that I heard Neil sing 'Solitaire' and I knew it was a great song. I thought it would be a great combination to have Andy sing it. That's why I recommended it to Richard.

"Years later, after Clay Aiken sang it on *American Idol*, I insisted he record it, and of course it became a big, big hit. Knowing Neil and Leba, and working with Clay, it was great fun watching that happen."

The fact that Andy Williams—one of the most popular singers in the world—could have a big hit covering a new Neil Sedaka song was a signal to many that Sedaka was on his way back. Williams's version went all the way to number two in the UK, while the Carpenters' version peaked at number 18 in the USA. Aiken, who had not even been born when the song was written, hit number one with his version of the song after his groundbreaking performance of it on *Idol*.

'Solitaire' is now a standard only because Sedaka believed so strongly in the haunting melody he had written and in the magnificent lyric he extracted from the hippie lyricist who had never written a hit song before. By the end of the '70s, they would become one of the hottest songwriting teams in the country.

Shortly after Sedaka moved to London, he got a call from out of the blue from Maurice Gibb of The Bee Gees, who happened to be staying right around the corner from Neil's London flat. Gibb suggested they get together for a drink. Sedaka found him to be a bright, witty, and charming man and a great musician. The Bee Gees were going through a little bit of a slump in their own at that point, and the two of them would console each other over afternoon drinks at the Saddle Room next door to the Inn On The Park. Gibb was on his way to a divorce with Lulu, and introduced Neil to the drink that John Lennon had earlier introduced to him: scotch and coke.

"We were all friends," Maurice's brother and fellow Bee Gee, Barry Gibb, told me when I contacted him in Florida early in 2013. "Maurice and Neil were very close. Neil had been an influence on our songwriting from the beginning. The whole concept of Neil making a comeback is just not reality to me. He never went away. Around that time, we played at Sheffield and the Batley Variety Club, where Maurice met his [next] wife Yvonne."

Maurice and Neil consoled each other through this rough period, and at times took turns being over-served and helping each other get home. They quickly became close friends. If Neil had to take a four-hour drive to play the Wooky Hollow or Golden Garter, Maurice would often tag along for support.

Soon after that, The Bee Gees were performing in London, and Neil and Leba were invited. Maurice introduced them to Elton John at the after-party, and the two composers and pianists soon hit it off.

"I think it was at our London concert with the London Philharmonic," Barry Gibb recalled. "I had the 'flu, and Elton and Neil were sitting in the first row, and in that point in time they were just starting to get together. You could tell that they were both so alike."

Not long after that, Elton played back-to-back concerts at Carnegie Hall in New York, just before Thanksgiving in 1972. Neil was pleasantly surprised to receive a call from Elton's office inviting the Sedakas to attend the concert. Instead of taking Leba, however, Neil brought along nine-year-old Dara, already a huge Elton John fan.

When Sedaka mentioned meeting Elton to his boyhood pal Freddie Gershon, aka Freddie The Lawyer, Gershon encouraged him to make the most of the friendship.

"These people can help you accomplish what you've always wanted," he told Neil. "Don't be afraid to ask them."

Gershon had no idea at the time just how right he was.

CHAPTER 8
SOLITAIRE

Whenever Sedaka returned to Merriewold Park, he put himself under enormous pressure to write new material. It wasn't easy. There were times in the 60s when Howie Greenfield had had to lock Neil in a room in order to get him to write.

"That blank piece of paper," Sedaka recalled with a sigh. "It was very stressful. You had to keep reinventing yourself, raise the bar, top yourself, get out of that comfortable sphere, take a chance. You couldn't do the same 'Calendar Girl' over and over and over."

Neil's aim now was to be recognized among the elite singer-songwriters of the 70s. The pressure must have been overwhelming.

"Was I uncomfortable, trying to reinvent myself?" he asked. "No, I knew there were hits inside of me. I had a lot of confidence. I was a studied musician. I wasn't a four-chord rock'n'roller. I listened to the radio constantly, bought records constantly. I was inspired by other creative people. Early in my career I wrote for Dinah Washington's voice. If I heard something on the radio, I would say, gee, I could do that, but better. I could do it Sedaka-esque."

During these difficult years Sedaka experimented with marijuana, which helped relax him, and there were also times when he tried to drink his problems away when he was with Maurice Gibb. But for the most part, Neil kept those demons away and continued his efforts to reinvent his music.

One night in Merriewold Park, the Sedakas were expected at a friend's party. He told Leba to go without him and stayed behind to face the blank page and the "menacing-looking piano." Carole Bayer had urged him to try writing his own lyrics sometime, and he decided that this would be the night—but he needed a little more courage to do it.

"In those days, everybody tried smoking pot," he told me. "Of course I was curious."

There was a stash of marijuana in the house. Neil rolled a joint, took a couple of hits, and started to relax. He began to think about all the roadblocks he'd encountered in the last ten years, wondering if he'd ever have a comeback. Roadblocks like his mother and her lover bungling his career and squandering his funds; RCA refusing to release his demo of 'It Hurts To Be In Love'; no US record label being willing to release 'Star-Crossed Lovers,' his number one hit in Australia; the failure of his comeback album, *Emergence*; and Kirshner failing to get behind 'Solitaire'—a song Sedaka felt could be the cornerstone of any future success.

Neil stewed over all of these things and got angry, then took a few more hits and began to think about how he feels when he writes his music, and the kind of high he gets from it. Two hours later, he had an almost-finished song, 'That's When The Music Takes Me,' including lyrics. He played it and let himself relax and enjoy it. Then he sang the lyrics—*his lyrics*:

That's when the music takes me
Takes me to a brighter day
That's when the music takes me
Helpin' me to find my way

When the bluebird sings her sad, sad song
And the wind brings a cold to tag along
Oh, yeah,
I can feel the spirit move me
I can almost touch the sky
Reachin' for a new tomorrow
I know it's hard
But music makes me waaaaanna try
Wanna try

He loved it all, but he had to wait until the morning to make sure the pot hadn't clouded his judgment.

"I always thought everything I wrote when I was smoking pot was great until I played it the next day," he told me.

Not this time, however. He was sure 'That's When The Music Takes Me' could be a hit. It was a joyous, up-tempo song, perfect for use on a future album.

Now that he was rebuilding his reputation in Britain, Sedaka kept hoping for some better offers to come in. And then it happened, the one that would set everything in motion: an offer to play at Royal Albert Hall in London on September 29 1972. This wasn't Liverpool or Stockport or Manchester, with the crowds from the hinterlands demanding more beer and more oldies. It was London, with its media center and sophisticated audiences who could appreciate what he was trying to do.

The Royal Albert Hall first opened in 1871 as a tribute to Prince Albert. It's a huge hall with seating for around 4,000 people for concerts. The building has a beautiful architectural design with a slight resemblance to a domed wedding cake. It has held many historic events, including the famous Salute To The British Empire in 1936, while Alfred Hitchcock shot the spine-tingling climax to *The Man Who Knew Too Much* at the venue.

Sedaka had reason for concern, however. He described the Royal Albert Hall as a "menacing edifice." He had only brought three other musicians with him as instrumental backup: a drummer, a bassist, and a cellist. The soundcheck he took that afternoon gave him even more reason for concern. "The acoustics were terrible," he told me. He went out and downed three gin martinis, back to back to back.

When he walked out on the stage that night the hall looked only half full, but he had to consider that the crowd was still much bigger than any he had performed for in a long time. He decided to start out with his old, familiar hits and then slowly introduce his new songs. The crowd greeted the golden oldies with warm applause that grew stronger as he made his way from the 50s into the early 60s.

Then it was time for the new songs. Neil had decided to sing the trio of songs he and Phil Cody had written on their first attempt, the first of which was 'Trying To Say Goodbye.' The end of the song was met with silence, so he went right into the next one, 'Don't Let It Mess Your Mind,' hoping to temper the awkwardness. When he finished it, however, the room was so quiet you could hear a woman snap her purse shut. The bright lights prevented Neil from seeing many of the audience members, and he wondered if there was anyone left out there.

Now he had arrived at the final song of the night, 'Solitaire,' just Neil and the piano, alone on the stage. Not knowing what the crowd was thinking, he lumbered on. The long, slow melody seemed endless to him as he sang it. He wanted to get it over with, but he was careful not to rush the tempo. Finally he got to the last eight lines of the song:

And keeping to himself begins to deal
And still the king of hearts is well concealed
Another losing game comes to an end
And he deals them out again

And solitaire's the only game in town
And every road that takes him, takes him down
While life goes on around him everywhere
He's playing solitaire

Neil finished the song and stopped cold. The silence continued for a moment—and then it was broken by thunderous applause.

"They were stamping their feet and cheering wildly," Neil told me with a look of satisfaction on his face as he recalled the moment. "I stood up and was in shock. They were yelling bravo, bravo."

Neil took bow after bow while the audience stood and screamed for him. He hadn't had a reception like that for a long, long time. The press poured backstage—suddenly journalists were all over him. The reviews in the papers the next day were sensational, with the highest praise reserved for 'Solitaire.' Sedaka thought he was dreaming. This was the turning point. He knew it. He could feel it in his bones.

"I was in tears by the time I reached Leba," he recalled. "The reception they gave me was overwhelming. After everything I had been through, to come to London, to the Royal Albert Hall, and hear them stamping and cheering for 'Solitaire' like that ..."

Neil's voice trailed off, and there were tears in his eyes. There was no doubt that he was back in that moment again. Like Babe Ruth reliving one of his famous home runs, Neil Sedaka was back in 1972, contemplating the exact moment his life and career changed. He had turned the corner. Everything was going to be all right, he felt, for the first time in a decade. Yes, everything was going to be just fine.

CHAPTER 9
THE HUNGRY YEARS

After his confidence-building performance at the Royal Albert Hall, Neil's creative juices started to flow again. He had written some new songs that audiences were responding to, and he felt that in Phil Cody he had finally found the lyricist to carry him into the 70s.

But ending his working relationship with Howie Greenfield—one that he had begun 20 years earlier, in 1952—would not be easy. Fortunately, Greenfield made it easy for both of them. With Neil spending at least 50 percent of his time in England, Greenfield had bought a home in Beverly Hills with his partner Tory Damon, and decided to make Southern California his base. They were now half a world apart, which was no way to be a songwriting team.

Around the turn of the year, 1973—no one is quite sure of the exact date—Sedaka came back to New York for a few days. Neil had been working on a few new tunes and he invited Cody to come over and listen to one of them. When Cody arrived, Neil began playing a haunting melody that Cody just couldn't get his head around. Neil asked him if had a lyric that might work with it.

"That's not for me," Cody told him. "Give it to Howie. He'll do it justice."

When Neil sat down to write the song he was inspired by The Stylistics, an R&B group from Philadelphia, whose lead singer, Russell

Thompkins Jr, had a voice so high that he made Sedaka sound like a baritone. Neil had been listening to the group's hits 'You Are Everything,' 'Betcha By Golly Wow,' and 'Break-Up To Make Up' before settling down to write the melody for 'The Hungry Years.'

"I thought they were marvelous," Neil said of The Stylistics. "I'm inspired by listening to voices. I listened to theirs and I said to myself, I can write for that voice. I could write a song that they could do in their repertoire."

In fact, as Sedaka would make clear during our conversations, when he writes he's mostly inspired by two things: an artist's voice and the dance beat.

"I came from Dick Clark's *American Bandstand*, where the beat was very important to dance to. So in essence, 'Oh! Carol' was inspired by the dance beat of The Diamonds' 'Little Darlin',' 'Calendar Girl' by the dance beat of 'Personality' by Lloyd Price, 'The Diary' by Little Anthony & The Imperials' 'Tears On My Pillow,' 'Breaking Up Is Hard To Do' by the beat of The Everly Brothers' 'Cathy's Clown,' 'Happy Birthday, Sweet Sixteen,' by the dance beat of Bobby Vee's 'Take Good Care Of My Baby' (written by his old friend Carole King), and 'Bad Blood' was inspired by Gordon Lightfoot's 'Sundown.'"

Sedaka took pride in listening to hit songs and picking out the one thing that made them tick. He'd take a song apart, looking for the hook, then see if it was something he could improve upon with a different melody. It was a method known as writing a song sideways.

In this case, Cody was right about 'The Hungry Years' being perfect for Greenfield. The more Sedaka tinkered with it, the more he liked it. He was going out to California with Leba, and while out there they stopped at Greenfield's house in Beverly Hills, where Neil played Howie the tune Cody turned down.

Howie told him that the sadness he heard in the song reminded him of Sonny & Cher, who by now had fallen into a pattern of constantly bickering in public and on their TV show. Greenfield knew how much happier they had been back when they had nothing.

Sonny Bono and Cherilyn Sarkesian first met in 1962 at a coffee shop in Hollywood when he was 27 she was just 16. He had been bouncing between jobs and at the time was working as a combination gofer/producer for Phil Spector. Cher was hoping to become a backup singer, and Bono helped make that happen. Before long she was backing up The Ronettes and The Righteous Brothers, among others, on some of the biggest hits of the decade.

Sonny kept writing and working on songs the two of them could do together. In 1964, they had a local success in LA with 'Baby Don't Go,' and then the following year they released an album, *Look At Us*, that contained the song for which they will forever be known. 'I Got You Babe' broke out as a single in July 1965 and quickly went to the top of the *Billboard* charts. It also made them stars.

After 'I Got You Babe,' Sonny & Cher began appearing on just about every major primetime television show there was, and the public got to know their kooky personalities a little bit. By 1968, however, their success was beginning to dry up, and by 1970 they were in the same boat as Sedaka—looking for that comeback number to get them back on top. In the meantime, Sonny put together a nightclub act for the two of them. The venues weren't always glamorous, but it gave them time to work out the kinks and learn to play off each other onstage.

In 1971, CBS programmer Fred Silverman offered them a one-hour slot as a summer replacement show. Their brand of music and comedy was a hit from the start and soon *The Sonny & Cher Show* was one of CBS's top shows. It always seemed like Sonny was the butt of their jokes, but after a while they weren't really jokes anymore.

Greenfield knew it wasn't an act. He remembered how happy Sonny and Cher had been back when they were nobodies. He started writing down the words to a song that he called 'The Hungry Years':

Girl, we made it to the top
We went so high we couldn't stop
We climbed the ladder leading us nowhere
Two of us together, building castles in the air

We spun so fast we couldn't tell
The gold ring from the carousel
How could we know the ride would turn out bad
Everything we wanted, was everything we had

I miss the hungry years, the once upon a time
The lovely long ago, we didn't have a dime
Those days of me and you, we lost along the way

How could I be so blind, not to see the door
Closing on the world, I now hunger for
Looking through my tears, I miss the hungry years ...

Sonny & Cher would remain on the air in various forms until 1977—two years after the couple were officially divorced. "I don't think Howie ever told them that they inspired the lyrics to 'The Hungry Years,'" Sedaka told me.

Greenfield apparently had another couple in mind, too, according to Connie Francis, perhaps his closest friend—somebody he would confide in about almost everything he wrote.

I caught up with Connie Francis again in September 2012, when she came to New York to be honored at the annual Feast of San Gennaro in Little Italy. A few years earlier, I had asked her about her relationship with Don Kirshner and her love affair with Bobby Darin for my previous book, and this time she was happy to share with me her thoughts about her friends Sedaka and Greenfield.

"When he was writing 'The Hungry Years,' Howie would call me every five minutes to read me the lines," she told me. "He was very excited about the song. I asked him, are you writing it about me? He said, this one's for you and Bobby [Darin]. I think it was the best song [he and Neil] ever wrote together."

When Neil and Howie finished the song they called Leba and Tory into the room to the room to play the song for them. "We all had a good cry," Neil told me. Today, when he sings the song, he thinks back to his own early days in Brighton Beach.

"You have to have hungry years. You have to starve to top yourself," Sedaka told critic and broadcaster Paul Gambaccini in 2006. "Yes, I miss the hungry years. My father drove a taxi and we never had much but we were always a close-knit family and happy. Even when I was hungry, I was happy because I had my family."[11]

Many others share Connie Francis's view that 'The Hungry Years' is the best lyric Greenfield ever wrote. It's also possible that Greenfield—knowing his partnership with Sedaka had reached its end—set out to write a song that reflected how he missed what they once had together. Both men were happy with the result, but it wasn't going to change anything. Neil was going to continue to pursue his comeback in the UK, and Howie was in the midst of pursuing new ventures in Los Angeles.

As far as 'The Hungry Years' was concerned, Sedaka kept it on the back burner, as he had 'Solitaire,' waiting for the right time and the right place. A few years later, when he had an album on which to place it, Neil brought in his old friend Artie Butler to arrange the song.

"Neil played me this song that he had written with Howie Greenfield and I wept," Butler recalled. "I wept right in front of him. And I remember saying to him right there at my house, leave me alone with this song—I knew exactly what to do with it. I wept for its beauty as a song, for its depth of emotion. Having been in and out of love affairs, and having hurt someone not wanting to—we've all been there. It was Howie Greenfield at his best."

Before Sedaka moved his family to England, he was pretty much resigned to the fact that his songwriting partnership with Greenfield had run its course. For years, Greenfield had found success with other melody writers while Neil was on the road. Now Neil felt that he needed a different kind of lyricist—and he felt he had found him in Phil Cody. He and Greenfield would be a million miles apart anyway. But when Neil broke the news, Howie took it hard.

"He was shattered," Leba recalled. "He was in tears. But later that night he called Neil and said he had a surprise."

"What kind of surprise?" Neil asked.

"You'll see," Howie replied.

Howie told Neil he would bring the surprise to his apartment in Brooklyn. When he arrived he pulled out a piece of paper with a song title at the top. It read 'Our Last Song Together.' Neil loved the idea and thought he had the perfect tune to go with it. Greenfield's nostalgic lyrics cleverly combined titles and lines from many of their hits through the years. And Howie didn't hold back how difficult this all was for him. The words he wrote are filled with sadness:

Yesterday is yesterday
The past is dead and gone
Nostalgia just gets in the way
Let's stop hanging on …

Now we go our separate ways
And leave the world we used to know
Scratchy worn out 45s
An echo on the radio
Tra la days are over now
Those days of me and you
Now we know that breaking up is
Really hard to do

This will be our last song together
Words will only make us cry
This will be our last song together
There's no other way we can say goodbye

Neil told Howie that he and Leba were going to fly to London the next day. Howie went home and wrote a lyric for yet another new song—one for which they will forever be known. When Greenfield returned the next morning with the lyric, Sedaka was trying out a new tune on the piano. This one really would be their last song together. Taken by nostalgia, they decided to call it 'Love Will Keep Us Together.' Sedaka treasured these two songs, tucking them away, along with several others, for the right moment.

In 1973, while Neil was performing at the Golden Garter in Manchester, he ran into Harvey Listberg, a well-known artist manager. They had first met a year earlier when Listberg happened to stop by Kirshner's office looking for a song for British pop singer Tony Christie.

"Harvey said that Tony was a Tom Jones type," Neil recalled, "so I played 'Is This The Way To Amarillo' for him, and he loved it." The song was a top 20 UK hit for Christie in 1971, and then, 34 years later, the same recording hit number one when it was reissued—complete with a star-studded promo video—to raise money for the Comic Relief charity.

At their chance meeting at the Golden Garter, Listberg began singing the praises of this new group he represented called Hot Legs who not only played and sang rock'n'roll but also co-owned Strawberry Studios in Stockport, a few miles from the club. When conversation turned to Neil's new songs, Listberg suggested he record some of them at Strawberry Studios.

Hot Legs consisted of bassist Graham Gouldman, guitarists Eric Stewart and Lol Creme, and drummer Kevin Godley. They were all basically studio musicians, but within a year they would change their name to 10cc and receive worldwide acclaim for songs like 'I'm Not In Love' and 'The Things We Do For Love.'

Neil went over to the studio one day and found the group in the midst of recording. "I was extremely impressed," he recalled. "They had an extraordinary sound." Later, he met with Gouldman at the Queens Hotel in Leeds, where Neil was staying. They went into a small room with a piano and Neil played Graham the songs that would make up his album *Solitaire*.

"The idea was that we'd record two or three songs to see how it went," Gouldman recalled when I reached him by phone in 2012. "Neil came to the studio and it went like a dream. I think we finished the album in two weeks. We finished it so quickly because Neil would sing the lead vocal as we were recording. The feel of it was great. We were playing together instead of recording everything [separately]. Neil was a great keyboard player, he was funny and he was emotional. We really got on with him and grew very fond of him. Like anybody of our age, Neil Sedaka was part of our DNA."

The songs they recorded were all new, most of them written with Phil Cody. In fact, the last three songs on side two were the three songs they wrote together that very first day at Kirshner's baby grand: 'Trying To Say Goodbye,' 'Solitaire,' and 'Don't Let It Mess Your Mind.' 'That's When The Music Takes Me' was the first song on side one and would also become a hit single in the UK.

Sedaka was very pleased with the album and couldn't believe that he was able to record all the songs and master them for the paltry sum of $5,000. The experience was an important one for Graham Gouldman and his group, too.

"I have a tremendous affection for both the album and for working with Neil," Gouldman recalled. "In a way he was part of the glue that kept us together before we became 10cc." Shortly after that, Gouldman took a call from Jonathan King, who had recently started a label called UK. "He had heard us sing 'Donna,' which became our first single, and he loved it. He called and said he wanted to come up and see us, and he asked what our name was. Well, we really didn't have one. That's when he said, I had a dream last night that I was standing in front of the Hammersmith Odeon [a London theater], and on the [marquee] it said, *10cc—The Best Band In The World*."

With the *Solitaire* sessions complete, Sedaka mixed the album with Eric Stewart and then went to Apple Records to cut the master. Then, in a taxi on the way to the airport, Sedaka decided the album lacked clarity, so instructed the driver to take him back to Apple, where he remixed the album himself.

When he finally got on the plane back to New York, Neil had a smile on his face and all the master recordings in his briefcase.

"Just wait until Donnie Kirshner hears these," he thought to himself. "He'll certainly want to get my album released in America."

Kirshner, however, wasn't so sure.

CHAPTER 10
THE TRA-LA DAYS ARE OVER

W hen Sedaka got back to New York, despite being jet-lagged, he tracked down Don Kirshner the next day and arranged to meet him at his office to play him the master. Kirshner had not been crazy about 'Solitaire' the first time Neil played it for him, right after he wrote it with Phil Cody, and he still wasn't crazy about it now—or the rest of the album, for that matter. It was as if Kirshner had been taking too many beatings from record labels and DJs asking him, "Neil who?"

"His attitude quickly changed when I offered to buy it from him and put it out myself," Sedaka recalled. "Then all of a sudden he loved it."

Kirshner had no problem getting RCA to distribute the *Solitaire* album in England via the Polydor label. He also released the album on his own label in the USA, but he didn't put much marketing and promotion behind it. The result was that the public at large never got a chance to hear the album, and Sedaka was bitterly disappointed. But it turned out to be very successful in the UK, at least—so successful that RCA decided to break out the bluesy 'Beautiful You' as a single. Then, just as 'Beautiful You' began to climb the charts, something strange happened.

There was a trend at the time for reissuing hits from the 50s in the UK, and Sedaka's song 'Oh! Carol,' from 1959, was one of them. It took off and started climbing the charts. It was good news and bad news for Neil. Just as he had finally started to shake his 50s image, people were playing 'Oh! Carol' again.

With all the buzz surrounding his music, Neil was invited to sing 'Oh! Carol'—which by now had made its way back into the top 20 all over again—on *Top Of The Pops*. The primetime show had been a key fixture of Thursday night programming on the BBC for the best part of a decade, and would remain on the air for 42 years. The very first show, which aired on January 1 1964, was a classic. Counting down to that week's number one (The Beatles' 'I Want To Hold Your Hand'), the show had all the stars of the day present and correct to lip-synch their latest hits: The Rolling Stones with 'I Wanna Be Your Man,' Dusty Springfield with 'I Only Want To Be With You,' The Dave Clark Five with 'Glad All Over,' The Hollies with 'Stay,' and The Swinging Blue Jeans with 'Hippy Hippy Shake.'

Leba knew that appearing on the show would be great for Neil, but he was upset not to be asked to sing his new song, 'Beautiful You,' instead. "I'll never be able to shake this 50s image," he told her, visibly frustrated. He had faced a mountain of opposition just to get to this point in his comeback. He had been shot down in 1964, when RCA refused to put out his version of 'It Hurts to Be In Love'; he had been humiliated working dives and following strippers; he had been ignored in the USA in 1969 when no one wanted to release his Australian number one hit, 'Star-Crossed Lovers'; his 1970 comeback attempt with his *Emergence* album had been stopped cold when the DJs refused to play it. Since then, he had moved to England, and worked his way back up from workingmen's clubs to the Royal Albert Hall and now, just when it seemed like he was making tremendous strides with his new songs, they wanted him to go on TV and sing something from the 50s!

"I won't do it," he told Leba. "They can't put me back into that 50s box again."

Wisely, Leba got him to calm down, explaining that a BBC TV appearance in primetime could do nothing but help his image and record sales.

"There are thousands of 13-year-old kids here that weren't even born when 'Oh! Carol' was a hit [in 1959]," she told him. "To them, it's a new song and they love it. Why don't you go on the show and sing it as if it was a brand new song." Somehow, Leba convinced him—and, of course, she was right.

(One silver lining was that it turned out that 'Oh! Carol' was a special song for somebody else, too. Elton John told Neil that it was the inspiration for his 'Crocodile Rock.' Neil loved the compliment but never expected he'd have a hit with the song again.)

By now the Sedaka family was firmly entrenched in their nine-room rented flat in Mayfair, just behind the Dorchester Hotel. With Neil's resurgent success in the UK now just about assured, the Sedakas fell into a pattern of living six months in London then six months back in upstate New York. Their Merriewold Park home was in a quiet and beautiful artist community. Neil loved writing there, with his piano stationed in front of a huge picture window overlooking the woods.

With Neil picking up steam in England, Leba agreed to a deal with Polydor Records for Neil to release another album of all new songs in Europe. With this new assignment to focus on, Neil traveled back to New York and summoned Phil Cody to Merriewold Park to work on the new collection.

Neil was so happy about the prospect of a new album that he knew what he was going to call it even before he had written any of the songs. This was going to be the record that announced to the world that he was no longer a ghost from the 50s. This would be his true emergence: *The Tra-la Days Are Over*.

Once he decided on the songs, Sedaka rushed back to England and drove to Stockport to record them all with 10cc at their Strawberry Studios. By now, 10cc had become a hit band in their own right, but they were only too happy to do it. It was a labor of love for all of them.

The album would combine new songs Sedaka had written with both Howie Greenfield and Phil Cody. Cody's other songs included 'Little Brother,' 'Suspicions,' and 'Rock'n'roll Wedding Day,' while Greenfield's contributions were the two final numbers he and Neil wrote together: 'Our Last Song Together' and 'Love Will Keep Us Together.' The album also included another song, 'Standing On The Inside,' for which Sedaka wrote his own lyrics, which reflect how he felt at the time:

Standin' on the outside
Lookin' in
You know it's been a long time,
Don't know where to begin …
I've been through the hard times
Of searchin' souls,
You know it's been a hard climb
From rock'n'roll
Now I feel a need in me, so hard to explain,
Now I've seen the joy and light,
And I want to remain …

119

Listening to Neil's lyrics, you couldn't help but empathize with how he felt about his tortured comeback attempt. 'Standing On The Outside' was well received, but the big song in the album turned out to be 'Love Will Keep Us Together'—not that anybody knew it at the time.

Sedaka had loved working with 10cc on the album, and he couldn't have been happier about the success they were achieving in their own right. He would later credit them as being a large part of the reason why the albums he recorded at Strawberry Studios were so successful.

"They certainly inspired me," he told interviewers Simon Barber and Brian O'Connor in 2012. "The musicianship, the production, the playing—they blues-ed it up, they pushed me in another direction. I didn't have to look at a clock like I did at the RCA Victor sessions [where they gave me] three hours to do three songs."[12]

On his return to New York, Neil had an idea for another song he wanted to work on, so Phil Cody duly made the drive once more up to Merriewold Park. Arriving after a hot summer's-day drive from the city, Cody was not in the mood to write anything when Neil sat down at the piano and began playing the tune to 'Laughter In The Rain.'

"Neil was sitting at the piano and he played me this song," he recalled. "And I had nothing. I had absolutely nothing. I kept shooting blanks, I kept looking at him like, I don't know what this song is, Neil. I had to excuse myself.

"I went out and I took a walk. There was a little deserted golf course along the road to Neil's home. There were deer out on the fairway. I was sitting there for a while and smoked some pot, nodded out for a while, and then went back to the house. And in about five minutes, the song just happened."

That was the day when Cody felt like he had graduated as a fully fledged songwriter.

"There was a section of the song, where Neil sings, I feel the warmth of her hand in mine," he continued. "And that line originally was doubled up. I said to Neil, why don't you make it just one? He looked at it, he tried it, and he said, I like it better. It made me feel really good, because he listened to a suggestion of mine. That was a great elevation in status for me."

Even on a hot day with bright sunshine, Cody conjured up an image of a rainy day. "One reason I drew blanks at first was because I just wanted to get back to my new girlfriend in the city," he told me. "It made me think of some happy moments we had together on a rainy day."

What Sedaka loved about Cody was how he could paint a picture with his lyrics, and nothing painted a picture better than the lyrics for 'Laughter In The Rain.'

Strolling along country roads with my baby
It starts to rain, it begins to pour
Without an umbrella we're soaked to the skin
I feel a shiver run up my spine
I feel the warmth of her hand in mine

Ooo, I hear laughter in the rain
Walking hand in hand with the one I love
Ooo, how I love the rainy days
And the happy way I feel inside …

They actually began writing the song from the middle. When Cody came back from his walk he sat down next to Sedaka at the piano with a yellow pad in hand. Sedaka explained the process during his interview with Barber and O'Connor:

"I started 'Laughter In The Rain' with the 'ooo, da-da-da,' and I told [Cody] that I wanted to get to this chord. In the key of F, it's a B-flat minor chord. At the end, I went to 'strolling along country roads with my baby,' which is pentatonic. I call it the American Indian sound—the Grand Canyon sound. All the black keys on the piano fascinate me. It's very ethnic, very Americana. I try to write something that's simple, yet has a surprise chord, and I think 'Laughter In The Rain' is the great masterpiece of that."[13]

Sedaka enjoyed retelling a story Billy Joel told him about this song.

"He was having a dream, and he woke up and wrote something in the middle of the night. Then he asked his band to come over and he played them the tune. They said, it's nice, but it's Neil Sedaka's 'Laughter In The Rain.' A melody can stay in your subconscious mind, so of course he had to change it. It became 'Moving Out.'"

Sedaka knew right away that 'Laughter' was a special song.

"I remember he called me when I got back to New York later that night," Cody recalled. "He said he had been working on it since I left, and that it was going to be our first big hit together. Even though we hadn't had a hit together yet, he was positive."

With the *Tra-la Days Are Over* selling well, and both 'Oh! Carol' and 'Beautiful You' in the charts, the Sedakas were happy to receive the additional good news that Kirshner had made a deal with Mike Curb at MGM Records to release the new album in America. Curb told

Kirshner he planned to issue the album on an MGM subsidiary owned by Curb and his sister Carol, with 'Standing On The Inside' selected as the single.

The Sedakas were thrilled and took off for a few restful days at La Costa, near San Diego, where Neil planned to work on losing a few pounds. A combination of stress, drinking, and a poor diet had caused his weight to get away from him. Since they were out on the West Coast anyway, they thought they would visit Curb in Los Angeles.

"We rented a car in San Diego," Leba recalled, "and we drove to MGM in LA to see the Curbs, to find out how the record was doing."

When they stopped by the MGM offices, however, they were treated like unknowns and had to cool their heels for nearly a half-hour before Carol Curb finally came out. Not only did she know nothing about 'Standing On The Inside' being released, she acted like she had never heard of Neil Sedaka.

"What album?" she asked.

Neil was steaming mad—so furious he stormed right out of the building. He and Leba got back in the car and drove to a nearby Hamburger Hamlet where he could let off some more steam.

"That's it," he told Leba. He was determined to take a more aggressive stance with whatever happened from then on. He thought about it some more on the drive back and eventually broke the silence about halfway to La Costa.

"I've decided, all the great musicians have moved out to California," he said. "I'm going to record my next album in Los Angeles."

Neil knew that music had changed over the last ten years, and he felt he had changed with it. The success Carole King and Neil Diamond had achieved in recent years made him confident that he, too, could be accepted again by American audiences.

"I wanted that very badly," he recalled. "All of those record executives who said my day was done—[they] didn't have the foresight to anticipate a changing market, one which would welcome artists like myself. I wanted to be back—in the worst way."

Now, he realized, trusting his future to record executives like Mike Curb was very much *the* worst possible way.

CHAPTER 11
ELTON TO THE RESCUE

One day, at 1:30pm in the afternoon, there was a knock at the door of Sedakas' flat in Mayfair. "Marc," Neil yelled to his seven-year-old son, "why don't you see who's there."

Obeying his dad, Marc skipped to the front door and opened it. The boy couldn't believe his eyes. Standing there in the flesh—with his tri-colored hair and his green platform shoes—was Elton John, the biggest rock star in the world. Marc nearly fainted. Neil rushed over and welcomed him in.

"I was a big Elton fan and had his posters on all the walls," Marc recalled nearly 40 years later. "In retrospect, it was a very charmed, privileged, amazing upbringing I had. But at the time, he [Elton] was just a guy my dad worked with."

When they first moved to London, Marc had the perspective of a seven-year-old. Perhaps his greatest disappointment was that there were only three channels on the TV.

"We traveled a lot," he told me, "and I took for granted that that was what families do. You pack and move to different countries for six months and then move back. But it was dad's profession, and that's where the work was, and that's what we did."

The Elton John visit wasn't quite such a surprise for Neil as it was for Marc because Elton had already surprised him the day before when he called out of the blue. In his autobiography, Neil recalled

125

how Elton began by telling Neil he had heard about his new album, *The Tra-La Days Are Over*, and wanted to wish Neil "all the success in England."

Sedaka graciously thanked him.

"You know what they're saying about you," Elton continued. "That you're better than Carole King, that you're the next American superstar."[14]

Neil had to pinch himself to make sure he wasn't dreaming. Then Elton asked if he could stop by for a visit.

From day one, I knew Elton John was the hero of this book, and that I'd have to try every way possible to get an interview. Neil and Leba suggested Fran Curtis, who represented Elton for Rogers & Cowan Public Relations. She tried several times but ultimately said it didn't look possible. He was out of the country, then under the weather, then touring. I pleaded that all I'd need would be a few minutes on the phone but no luck.

Six months went by, and I began to lose hope. Then a friend who was an executive with EMI put me in touch with John Barbis, Elton's manager and the president of Rocket Music Entertainment Group for North America. Mr Barbis was sympathetic to my plight and my deadline but could not offer much more hope. Every two or three weeks I called or emailed him but my deadline was fast approaching.

Then, suddenly, he called from Los Angeles and asked if I could be available for a call two days after the Grammy Awards. On February 12 2013, I answered the phone and the caller said, "Richard, this is Elton. Do you mind that I'm calling a little early?" I am extremely grateful to Sir Elton for his time and for Mr Barbis for making the interview possible.

It turned out that Elton John had always been a huge Neil Sedaka fan.

They sat side by side at Neil's piano and played several Sedaka oldies together. Then Neil played 'Solitaire' and a few of his other new ones, at which point Elton played a new song of his own.

"He played me 'Candle In The Wind,'" Neil recalled. "I cried. I'm a crier. It was beautiful. He was the biggest rock star in the world."

Shortly after that, Elton invited Leba and Neil to a concert by Paul McCartney. At the party that followed, Neil was introduced to McCartney for the first time. "As soon as Paul saw me, he began singing, 'That's When The Music Takes Me,'" Neil recalled. "He was marvelous."

Sedaka also spent time that night with another hot superstar of the day Rod Stewart. Here he was, hobnobbing with British rock'n'roll royalty and feeling like he absolutely belonged with these people. Back in America, however, people were still asking, "Neil who?"

On February 1 1974, Neil had been asked to perform at London's prestigious Royal Festival Hall, an intimate 2,500-seat theater. He asked the famous Tommy Nutter on Saville Row to make him an all-white tuxedo with satin braiding. It cost a small fortune, but he felt it was worth it.

For some reason, however, Neil started to get nervous ahead of the performance, even to the extent of feeling like he was losing his voice just a few days before the show. He gargled with warm salt water, he sprayed, he drank hot toddies, he called his voice doctors in New York and Los Angeles—and he drove Leba nuts. Then, on the morning of the engagement, he woke up and his voice was had returned.

That night, Neil and Leba arrived in a limo and were excited to see people selling Neil Sedaka programs and T-shirts outside. Inside, everyone was dressed to the nines. Neil had decided to perform a program of mostly new songs. He opened with 'Sing Me' and continued with 'Cardboard California' and 'Superbird,' three songs from *Emergence* that had been rejected in the USA, but the crowd at Royal Festival Hall loved them. He also played 'Love Will Keep Us Together,' 'Solitaire,' and 'Standing On The Inside,' finishing with a rousing rendition of 'That's When The Music Takes Me.'

By the time he reached the end of the show, Neil had sweat pouring down his face. The audience jumped to their feet. Neil couldn't have been happier. Leba was waiting for him with open arms as he danced off the stage. Waiting in his dressing room was Freddie Gershon, making a surprise visit with the actor Rex Harrison by his side. Harrison went on and on about how much he enjoyed the show.

A few weeks later, Sedaka played an incredible weeklong sold-out run at the London Palladium. "Just me and the piano onstage," Sedaka recalled with joy. "It was one of the happiest weeks of my life."

In the spring of 1974, a couple of *Washington Post* reporters named Woodward and Bernstein kept digging up dirt about Richard Nixon on Watergate, which would lead a few months later to Nixon's resignation. Sedaka hardly noticed. At that point, he was feeling so good about his career in the UK that he decided to throw a big party at their flat in Mayfair—a star-studded affair attended by Elton John and his manager and business partner John Reid, Paul McCartney, Rod Stewart, the Carpenters, 10cc, and record executive Seymour Stein, among others.

The assembled guests got through five cases of champagne. It was a joyous occasion, with all the stars taking turns at the piano, playing

Neil at his bar mitzvah with mother Eleanor, father Mac, and sister Ronnie.

NEIL SEDAKA   3260 Coney Is. Ave.
Supply Squad, Pres. Choral, Music Dir. Class
Night, Dance Band, Pianist for Assembly.

ABOVE: Eddie Rabkin (top), Hank Medress (in glasses), Cynthia Zolotin and Neil as The Linc-Tones, before they became The Tokens.

LEFT: Neil's Lincoln High graduation photo.

OH' CAROL OH' NEIL

CLOCKWISE FROM TOP: David Bass (drums),
Howard Tischler (sax), Norman Spizz (trumpet), and
Neil as The Nordannells; Al Nevins, RCA Victor A&R
executive Steve Sholes, and Don Kirshner surround
Neil; Carole King poses for a publicity shot with Neil
after recording 'Oh Neil' in answer to his 'Oh! Carol.'

THIS PAGE: Neil with his first car, a 1959 white-on-white Chevy Impala Convertible.

OPPOSITE PAGE: Neil with his parents, Eleanor and Mac; Eleanor leans back on her car in a seductive pose.

NEIL SEDAKA
Exclusive RCA Recording Artist
Personal Management
BEN SUTTER

NEIL SEDAKA

NEIL SEDAKA
Exclusive RCA Recording Artist
Personal Management
BEN SUTTER

OPPOSITE PAGE: Howie
Greenfield, Neil, and Connie
Francis.

THIS PAGE: Three different
postcards Neil sent to fans; Neil
on the cover of a vintage 1960
edition of *Records* magazine.

records
MAGAZINE
No. 3 VOL. 3 MARCH   1960 SIXPENCE

NEIL SEDAKA   Hear him on his LP *Neil Sedaka*
RCA RD 07160

The FLOWER DRUM SONG
Songs From The American Hit Musical
Recorded on 'Ace of Clubs'
(See Story Inside)

ABOVE AND LEFT: Two shots of Neil mobbed by fans at autograph appearances during the peak of his popularity as a teen idol.

RIGHT: Neil with Ed Sullivan.

THIS PAGE: Two shots of Neil and Leba Sedaka on their wedding day, September 11, 1962.

OPPOSITE PAGE: Neil and Howie Greenfield at work on a song; a 1963 RCA ad for *Neil Sedaka Sings His Greatest Hits*.

HEAR
NEIL SEDAKA'S
great new album

"NEIL SEDAKA SINGS HIS GREATEST HITS"

exclusive on RCA VICTOR

Jules Podell's **COPACABANA**

CLOCKWISE FROM RIGHT:
Neil with Dick Clark; Neil with
Phil Cody; clowning around
with Elton John.

OPPOSITE PAGE: Neil and
Elton in the studio.

THIS PAGE: Neil and best friend Maurice Gibb of The Bee Gees; Neil onstage with Andy Gibb, Dara Sedaka, Neil, Toni Tennille, and Daryl Dragon.

OPPOSITE PAGE: Neil and Leba with Elton John; Neil performs with The Captain & Tennille, aka Daryl Dragon and Toni Tennille.

RIGHT: Neil and his daughter, Dara.

BELOW: Toni Tennille sings with Neil at the Lincoln Center celebration of his 50 years in show business.

Neil's songs and their own. Then, at around 2am, Neil pulled Elton and Reid aside and told them he had a proposition for them.

"My friend and attorney Freddie Gershon has told me about your new venture that you're starting in America, Rocket Records," he told them. "Would you be interested in signing me to your company and releasing my new songs there?" (Looking back, Neil recalled his embarrassment when he came to ask the question, but he needn't have worried. From 1971 through '73, he had put out four top 20 albums in the UK and had five hit singles in a row, including the reissue of 'Oh! Carol.')

Thanks to Sire Records boss Seymour Stein, I was able to contact John Reid in London. Despite the disagreements and legal conflicts that followed, there's no doubt that Elton John's career was elevated by his business and personal partnerships with Reid.

"Elton and I just looked at each other in amazement," Reid told me. "At the same time we turned back to Neil and said in unison, yes! We'll release them!"

Reid, who may have been a touch over-served by that point in the evening, then revealed what a great deal it was for Rocket when he said, "These songs are like gold bricks you're handing us."

And in a way, they were gold bricks. Many of the songs for Neil's first album with Rocket were songs that, for the most part, were already hits in England.

"These records are hits," Elton told him. "I can make you a record star again. You're as good as Carole King."

"I couldn't believe what I was hearing," Sedaka recalled. "I couldn't have been happier."

They broke from their impromptu meeting and rejoined the party, but not before Neil flashed a telling look toward Leba.

"He couldn't really say anything with everyone still there," she recalled, "but I knew what was going down. And all I had to do was look at Neil's face or listen to his voice to know."

Before long, Neil found a quiet corner and whispered the good news to Gershon. When just about everyone had left, Leba and Neil finally embraced. A huge roadblock had been removed from his path. All he had to do now was sprint to the finish line.

The original aim for Rocket Records was not to distribute established stars, because it didn't have the financial firepower to compete with the majors, but to introduce new talent. When Elton learned that Neil was available, however, it was a no-brainer. Likewise, US-born broadcaster and critic Paul Gambaccini, who had moved to the UK in the early 70s to take up a post at *Rolling Stone* magazine's London bureau and had written a cover story on Elton John a year prior to this, felt it was too good a situation for Elton and John Reid to pass on.

"Elton could not believe that Neil was not being released in America, because it was happening in England," Gambaccini told me by phone. "As a matter of fact, before 'Laughter In The Rain,' Neil had five top 40 singles in Britain: 'That's When The Music Takes Me,' 'Standing On The Inside,' 'Our Last Song Together,' 'A Little Lovin',' and 'Oh! Carol.' To Elton, Neil wasn't an oldies artist, he was a current artist."

To work out all the details, Elton and John invited Neil and Leba to join them at Caribou Ranch in Colorado, where Elton was recording *Lucy In The Sky* with producer Gus Dudgeon.

After the session, Elton told Neil they were going to give him carte blanche on his choice of songs for his Rocket Records album—and why not, since Elton considered Neil's offer to be a stroke of luck for the company. It was decided that all the songs would be drawn from Neil's recent British albums, plus the batch of new material he was about to record in Los Angeles.

"I had always been a Neil Sedaka fan, anyway," Elton told the BBC radio documentary series *The Story Of Pop*. "It was like Elvis coming up and giving us a chance to release his records. We couldn't believe our good luck."

Now Neil was ready to record the rest of his new songs in California, and Rocket Records was picking up the tab. And there was one song he was especially looking forward to recording: 'Laughter In The Rain.'

CHAPTER 12
LAUGHTER IN THE RAIN

" That day we wrote 'Laughter In The Rain,' Phil asked me, how did you come up with that melody? I told him it takes years of building up, growing. It just doesn't happen in one day."

Neil told me that the melody for 'Laughter In The Rain' came from the same line of thinking as the one he wrote for 'Workin' On A Groovy Thing.' But the lyric Phil Cody came up with in response left even Neil in awe.

"It was his painting of two people soaked without an umbrella, married to that magnificent melody. It gave you goose bumps. It was a piece of art. It was a masterpiece. That doesn't come very readily. It's spiritual."

When Neil was ready to record in Los Angeles, he put in a call to a man named Robert Appere, who had a reputation as a great engineer but hadn't produced many albums at that point.

"A fellow I worked with named Kenny Young recommended me to Neil," Appere told me when I caught up with him by phone. "He wanted to come out in a few weeks and make an album with me. At that point I hadn't been the producer for a whole lot of things. I had been engineering a whole lot of things and produced just as many that I never got credit for."

Appere began his career at Herb Alpert's A&M Records, where he worked with the Carpenters, Joe Cocker, Leon Russell, James Taylor, The Average White Band, and Earth Wind & Fire. But he had never met Neil, and at first he shared America's disc jockey's misguided view of Sedaka's music.

"At first I wasn't that excited or that serious about it," Appere continued. "Neil had represented another type of music to me, and I didn't realize what a talent he was until we actually got together.

"I remember the first time I spoke to Neil, his voice sounded high. It didn't sound strong and powerful. I had an image in mind—and I couldn't have been more incorrect of who he actually was."

Things changed immediately when Neil played Robert his new song.

"The first time he played 'Laughter In The Rain' for me, I had very strong feelings about it. I thought it was a great pop record."

Appere chose Clover Studios on Santa Monica Boulevard for the sessions, but as Sedaka recalled, the musicians Appere initially called upon weren't quite up to the task, and the songs didn't sound great. He quickly realized he needed the best, and the next day brought in James Taylor's backup band, The Section: Leland Sklar on bass, Craig Doerge on keyboards, Russ Kunkel on drums, and Danny Kortchmar on guitar. Regarded as the best backing crew in the business, The Section had also worked with Carly Simon, Jackson Browne, and Crosby Stills & Nash. Appere also brought in the best backup singers in town: Abigail Haness, Brian and Brenda Russell, William Smith, and Donny Gerard. When it came to recording the basic tracks, Neil sang live with the band—something that was extremely unusual, then and now.

"That's the unique thing about Neil," Appere told me, beaming. "On all five albums we've done, there's never been a vocal overdub.

Neil sang live—every song, every take, every album. They were all first and second takes. When you have a talent like that, you have to have support people that don't screw up. And it's pretty hard to screw up with Neil Sedaka and a band like that."

That's where Artie Butler, the arranger, came in. If melody and lyrics are the real estate of a song, the arranger is the song's architect, deciding which instruments to choose and how they'll be used to enhance the overall effect. At that time, in 1974, Butler had quite a reputation himself, having arranged songs by Neil Diamond ('Solitary Man,' 'Cherry, Cherry'), Gladys Knight ('Neither One Of Us Wants To Be The First To Say Goodbye'), Joe Cocker ('Feelin' All Right'), and Vicki Lawrence ('The Night The Lights Went Out In Georgia'), among others. He also arranged the Louis Armstrong classic 'It's A Wonderful World.'

At the Brill Building, a decade earlier, he cut his teeth playing on dozens of demos by Sedaka & Greenfield and Goffin & King. He also played keyboards for songwriter/producer Jeff Barry and for the deans of rock'n'roll, Jerry Leiber and Mike Stoller.

Like Sedaka, Artie Butler was born and raised in Brooklyn and began playing several different instruments at the age of four. By the time he was 16, he was playing piano, vibes, drums, and clarinet—all he cared about was music, to the absolute neglect of his schoolwork. In other words, he was flunking out.

"The Dean of Boys at Erasmus High School called my father in," he recalled. "He talked him into letting me quit school to pursue a career in music. My father took me straight from there to the musician's union on 52nd Street and had me join the union. That's a day you don't forget."

While waiting to hear of jobs from the musicians' union, Butler

150

took a job in the record department of Korvettes department store. "This guy used to come in and ask me about some obsolete Miles Davis tracks," he continued. "And I knew where to find them. He said, you really know your stuff—would you like to work at a recording studio?"

The job was at Bell Sound Studios, as a button pusher—a second engineer. Butler's role entailed setting up the studio and then pressing a button to start the tape machines when the producer was ready to record. His tongue was hanging out. He was 16 and working with some of the greatest musicians in the world.

"I was button-pushing a Leiber & Stoller session one day in 1958 or '59," he recalled. "They were recording a world-famous piano duo, and one of the duo couldn't play a section of the music. Take after take after take after take he failed to get it. Leiber and Stoller were getting frustrated. I whispered to Mike and Gerry, I can play that part. Get rid of the orchestra and I'll play it."

They sent everyone home—the orchestra, the engineer, the world-famous duo, everyone—until only Butler- at this point just a stocky teenager with long sideburns—Leiber, Stoller, and the tape machines were left. First, he did a dry run of how long it would take him to start the tape machines and run out of the control room to the piano.

"I backed up the tape a little further than the section the guy couldn't play," Butler recalled. "I put it in record and ran outside to the piano. When the passage came I played it perfectly, ran back inside, and turned off the machine."

After that, Butler's days as a button-pusher were over, and he started playing keyboards for "every date Leiber & Stoller had."

Working in the Brill Building and at the demo studios on Broadway, Butler received quite an education. The two main demo studios in those days were Dick Charles and Associated, located nearly side-by-side on Broadway, with only the Metropole Theater in between.

"That's where all of us got impregnated with the music business," Butler told me. "All we were doing was just going by the seat of our pants. It was pure passion, instinct and a desire to be a part of this thing that was in our blood. Chasing our dreams, that's all we were doing."

One of those dreams Butler had back in the beginning was of working with an artist like Neil Sedaka, and he distinctly remembered getting the call for 'Laughter In The Rain.'

"I remember the conversation so well," he said. "[Neil] called me up and said, Artie, I'm going to make an album for Elton John's label and I'm going to record it Los Angeles. Would you like to write the arrangements?"

Butler, of course, said yes. Neil recorded the rhythm tracks for the song and brought them to Butler's house in Los Angeles.

"Do what you do," Neil told him. "Add the strings, whatever is right. Do your magic."

What Butler did took in violins, violas, cello, harp, and percussion. He recorded the parts on a separate track and laid it on top of what Appere had recorded.

"I just sensed that it was a very good record and a different sound for him," he recalled. "It didn't have that 50s sound anymore. What I wrote were counter melodies to Neil's melodies."

What Artie Butler did was create an entire sound and mood around Sedaka. The arranger, if he does his job right, has an awful lot to do with the way the record sounds.

"I wrapped him in an atmosphere that presented both his vocal and the song, in the commercial and theatrical sense," he said.

Sedaka felt the same connection. "Artie Butler's arrangement was like a magnificent song in itself," he said. Thinking back to that time, Sedaka got lost and began singing the string lines. "He feels me," he continued. "I have to surround myself with people I emotionally connect with."

Another person Neil connected with during these recording sessions was David Foster, an award-winning composer, singer, and producer who was born in 1949 and grew up in Victoria, British Columbia, Canada.

Knowing that Foster had produced some of the greats, like Whitney Houston ('I Will Always Love You'), Celine Dion ('The Power Of Love'), Natalie Cole ('Unforgettable'), and Toni Braxton ('Unbreak My Heart'), I was naturally excited to talk to him about his early days, growing up in Canada, and working with Neil on 'Laughter In The Rain.' Aside from winning 16 Grammy Awards—as well as Emmys, Golden Globes, and three Oscar nominations—one of his greatest achievements is the David Foster Foundation, which helps provide financial support to Canadian families with children who need to undergo life-saving organ transplants. I was fortunate to reach him by phone during his very busy schedule.

"I grew up on Vancouver Island," he told me, "and when I ordered a record back then it took about three months to arrive. When I first heard 'Breaking Up Is Hard To Do' in 1962 it was a pivotal moment in my life. I always come back to that song because it was an epic, epic moment in my career—although meeting him in '75 was pretty epic, too."

Foster was called in once Appere had decided to assemble the best musicians in the city. At that point, Foster was perhaps best known for his creative and groundbreaking work on the electric keyboard.

"I played auxiliary keyboards for that record ['Laughter']," he continued. "Neil was the main piano player, of course, but I played some electric piano on it. Meeting Neil was a great thrill. Having him welcome me in as a secondary keyboardist on that album brought things semi-full-circle for me. It was a time in my career when I was pretty hot as a studio musician but wanting more. I wanted to arrange and wanted to write, and Neil nurtured me and gave me confidence that I was more than just a piano player, and that I could do it.

"Appere was a very supportive producer," he added. "He had a great love of music and they made magic together, him and Neil. I don't think it would have been as successful with anyone else producing."

Foster was blown away by Sedaka's ability to do the vocals live. "It was at a time when producers liked to keep each track separate," he recalled. "In the end, it didn't matter—it was a great record."

Foster also had a theory about Sedaka's decade off the charts. "He was a victim of his own success. I mean who doesn't remember 'down dooby-doo, down, down, come-a, come-a'? But thank God he had more in him, and thank God he was able to expose it to the world and get it out there. You couldn't keep a guy like Neil down. He was destined to write beyond the four chords."

During that week, going to the studio each day was absolute joy for Neil. Like Sinatra, he appreciated and loved playing with great musicians, and the feeling was mutual.

"Neil has always been one of those people who always surrounded himself with great musicians and was never threatened by great musicians because he was a great musician himself," Foster said. "And when I say he's a great musician himself, let's not underplay that.

There are certain stars that you meet that have a great affinity for musicians, and other star singers just don't care. It's not that they're bad people. They can be making a record and be in a room with the greatest musicians in the world and they just don't notice.

"And then there are other people like Paul McCartney and Neil Sedaka and Elton John—they love musicians and they'd just as soon have dinner with the guy who played drums on their record than the Queen of England."

During one of the sessions that week, a surprise guest decided to drop by.

"Gus Dudgeon, who was Elton John's great producer, came and sat in the booth," Sedaka recalled. "And I politely asked him to leave."

"You're asking me to leave?" Dudgeon replied, seemingly incredulous. "I'm part-owner of this company [Rocket Records]."

"Yes," Neil replied. "I'm sorry, but I don't like visitors while I'm recording. I start to perform, and stop focusing on the recording."

Dudgeon grudgingly departed.

When Sedaka danced out of Clover Studios at the end of the week, he thought he had just recorded the perfect song. He loved his melody and Phil Cody's beautiful, spiritual lyrics. He loved the group backing him up and Artie Butler's arrangements. And he loved the overall sound. 'Laughter In The Rain' represented to him everything that the new Neil Sedaka was all about.

Several months had passed since Neil sat down at the piano with Phil to write the song, so he felt it was time to send over a copy of the finished product. Back when he was writing with Howie Greenfield, they would both be in the studio together, and they often argued. Neil didn't want that to happen this time, and Phil was happy to stay at home.

"I was in my little studio apartment in Greenwich Village," he recalled, "and a messenger came with an acetate of the song. It was the complete record from beginning to end. The last time I heard it was a few months earlier, when we had written it. And there it was, all decked out, and I just beamed. I thought to myself, oh, that's what a hit song sounds like!"

Neil brought 'Laughter In The Rain' back to the UK and released it as a single. It quickly began to rise up the charts before stalling at number 14. Neil was disappointed, but he hoped that, with the right promotion, the song would do a lot better in the USA. What he could never have expected, however, was that somebody else would release it there first.

CHAPTER 13
SEDAKA'S BACK

On his return to the UK, Neil was thoroughly satisfied with the Clover Studios recordings and certain that 'Laughter In The Rain' should be the title track and first single from his next British album. But he was also looking ahead to his big US comeback, and would get together often with Elton John to discuss his Rocket Records debut, which they had decided should bring together tracks from *Solitaire*, *The Tra-La Days Are Over*, and *Laughter In The Rain*.

It wasn't all work, however. Sometimes Elton would stop by Neil's flat late at night. His daughter Dara, who was 11 at the time, distinctly remembers one of those occasions.

"One night he came over our apartment in London very late and I was already asleep," she recalled. "He was one of my idols, and Dad brought him to my room at three in the morning and turned on the light. I was groggy, in my pajamas, and opened my eyes and saw Elton standing there in his platform shoes and thought I was dreaming. My dad said, Dara, he loves 'Benny & The Jets.' Sing it for him. I tried, and [it] sounded horrible."

They all had a good laugh, however, and it was probably the last time Dara Sedaka sounded anything less than great.

As the summer of 1974 drew to a close, plans were finalized for the October release of Neil's Rocket Records album, which now had the title *Sedaka's Back*. It was now set to include 'Standing On The Inside,' 'Love Will Keep Us Together,' 'Little Brother,' 'The Other Side Of Me,' and 'Our Last Song Together' from *The Tra-La Days Are Over*; 'That's When The Music Takes Me' and, of course, the title track from *Solitaire*; and 'Laughter In The Rain,' 'The Immigrant,' 'Sad Eyes,' 'The Way I Am,' and 'A Little Lovin'' from his newest LP.

Freddie Gershon drew up a deal and along with Neil waited in a private room at the prestigious Sign Of The Dove restaurant, on the corner of 65th Street and 3rd Avenue in Manhattan, for Elton to arrive and sign the papers. The restaurant had the look of a French museum, with a grand piano at the top of the steps leading to the private room. It was the kind of place you would go to impress a date or an important client. Elton John was certainly that, but there was also the more practical reason that the restaurant was a few blocks from the East 63rd pied-a-terre Neil had taken as his main base of operations in the city.

"When Elton arrived it was around two in the afternoon and the place was wall-to-wall with gentlemen in suits and elegantly dressed ladies," Gershon recalled. "And in walked Elton in one of his crazy outfits, acting as if he fit right in."

No one could recall what they ordered or even how long they were there, just that they all agreed that 'Laughter In The Rain' was the song with the best chance to break out in America. Both Neil and Elton felt the key to its success in the USA would lie in convincing DJs to play it. Elton felt the best way to do that was to promote it himself. He went all out for Neil, traveling across the country, visiting all the top disc jockeys.

"He was E.J. the DJ," Sedaka said. "He was unbelievable. He'd go in and he'd tell everyone how great my new songs were, and then they'd play 'Laughter In The Rain' and talk about it."

As Elton's then-manager, John Reid, put it, "Elton has quite a bit of clout when he gets behind a cause." He also wrote the liner notes for *Sedaka's Back*, which every DJ and music fan in the country would take note of:

Neil is proud of his past, but he's even prouder of what he's doing now. And so he should be! This album contains some of his best work ever. Listen to songs like 'Solitaire' and 'Laughter In The Rain,' then you'll see what I mean. We at Rocket Records have been given the privilege of releasing these tracks, which are a compilation of Neil's hit albums in Great Britain. If you watch the charts in the next few months, you'll see that even though he's never been away, SEDAKA'S BACK.

Everything seemed to be going smoothly for Neil as the release date approached. All of those horrible years were almost behind him. All of those aborted comeback attempts were about to be over.

On October 12 1974, *Billboard* ran a full page ad proclaiming: *"Rocket Records is proud to announce a new single by Neil Sedaka, 'Laughter In The Rain.'"* Everything seemed perfect. And then the unthinkable happened.

"I had a release date all set with MCA," Neil recalled. "MCA was releasing Rocket records in America. I was driving in New York and I had an R&B station on in my car, and they said, and now, Lea Roberts, singing a new song— 'Laughter In The Rain.'"

Lea Roberts sang with a style that was a little bit of funk, soul, and R&B all rolled into one. She sounded like a combination of Aretha Franklin and Della Reese. Unbeknown to Neil, she had heard a demo of the song and recorded a great R&B version of it.

In a panic, Sedaka telephoned Elton. "It's phenomenal," he said. "We've got to do something. We've got to move up the release date of my record."

All Neil could think of was how Barry Mann had *his* comeback cut short the same way with 'We Gotta Get Out Of This Place.' Mann was all set to release it in the USA, only to find out two days earlier that The Animals had beaten him to the punch in the UK. It was an instant hit, and there was nothing Mann could do.

Elton and John Reid were not about to let that happen to Sedaka. They went to Mike Maitland at MCA and asked him to rush Sedaka's version out. Five days later, it was released—and just in time, because Roberts's version had reached number 20 on the *Billboard* R&B charts.

"In the process, unfortunately, it destroyed that marvelous effort of Lea Roberts," Neil recalled. "I don't think she had a career [after that]. But I still play that marvelous record. Thank God they did it. I would have never had a comeback."

On October 19, Sedaka's version hit the *Billboard* pop charts for the first time at number 95. The Sedakas were all back in Merriewold, New York, when it happened; Neil was out shopping and unaware of the news until he returned home later that day.

"Leba and the kids made up a sign that they taped on the front door for me to see when I came home," said Sedaka, who became very emotional while retelling this part of the story. "It said, 'Laughter In The Rain' is number 95 on *Billboard*. I broke down and cried when I saw it."

Slowly but surely, the record moved up the charts. When Neil heard it on the radio in New York, it once again struck and emotional chord.

"It was the thrill of a lifetime, because it showed a survivor—someone who had longevity. It showed someone who wanted it with a vengeance. It showed someone that sang well, and it was a beautiful, smooth romantic piece." Then, pounding his heart with his fist for emphasis, he said, "I sang it from my kishkas. After 12 years off the charts, I was finally back."

Every week the single moved up five, six, seven notches. For the Sedakas, the song was climbing the charts at a torturous pace. It finally got into the 20s, and then the teens, and then the top ten after 12 long weeks. One of the reasons it kept moving up was that the Sedakas had their own family style of promotion.

"I remember that one of our family activities was writing letters to radio stations," Marc Sedaka, who was eight at the time, recalled. "We had stacks of paper and envelopes and stamps and we'd write 'please play Neil Sedaka'—whatever song at the time—and we'd make up different names to sign with. We wrote dozens and dozens of letters to radio station DJs. There were certain stations where there was no other way to tell them than by sending an actual, physical, snail-mail letter."

Meanwhile, on a trip to Los Angeles, Neil and Leba ran into Don and Sheila Kirshner by the pool at the Beverly Hills Hotel. Kirshner's TV show *Don Kirshner's Rock Concert*, was only a few months old at this time but had already met with some success, so Neil saw a golden opportunity to sing 'Laughter' on screen.

"Donnie," Neil began, "since you are the publisher of 'Laughter,' why don't you put me on your show?"

"Neil, I have bigger plans for you. The timing is not right now," Kirshner told him. "However, if you can get Elton to do a few songs, I'll put you both on."[15]

Sedaka began a slow burn. He turned and jumped into the pool.

"Neil just swam away from me," a surprised Kirshner said to Leba.

"Forever, Donnie," Leba replied. "Forever."

As 'Laughter In The Rain' rose up the charts, Neil was invited to perform at the famous Troubadour club in Los Angeles—one of the greatest rock'n'roll clubs in the country. Elton John had made his first splash on the American scene at the very same club a few years earlier. This time it was Neil who received a raucous reception.

For his three nights at the club, Neil was backed by the same top players from the *Laughter In The Rain* sessions: David Foster on keyboards, Leland Sklar on bass, Russ Kunkel on drums, Dean Parks and Danny Kooch on guitars, and backing vocalists Abigail Haness plus Brian and Brenda Russell. Even Robert Appere was there to make sure the sound was just right.

With so many stars in attendance on opening night, it was nearly impossible for a regular fan to get in. James Taylor, Carly Simon, Neil Diamond, and of course Elton John were all there; so too was Andy Williams, whose version of 'Solitaire' reached number two in the UK. This time, Neil didn't feel the need to perform any of his early songs. Almost the entire Troubadour program was from *Sedaka's Back*. It was a great feeling to get standing ovation after standing ovation from his peers. The tears flowed as he took his final bows.

Even greater was hearing his new songs on the radio. By now, Sedaka's comeback was big news. The press clamored for interviews, and Neil popped up on TV with Johnny Carson, Merv Griffin, Mike Douglas, and Dinah Shore, who even sang 'Solitaire' with him on her show.

That week, Neil and Leba took a suite at the Beverly Hills Hotel. 'Laughter"'s slow rise to the top continued. A few weeks earlier, it had reached number three, where it remained for three weeks, and by the time they had arrived in LA it had climbed to number two. They both well remember the moment that Sunday when they tuned it to Casey

Kasem's *American Top 40* countdown show on the radio. "This is the number one song in the country," Kasem announced, and then he played 'Laughter In The Rain.'

"Leba and I danced to it and we cried," Sedaka told me, misty-eyed just recalling it all. Sixteen weeks it took to hit number one. Sixteen weeks!"

Sixteen weeks and 12 long years Neil had waited since his last visit to the top ten. And it felt all the sweeter for it.

"Neil Sedaka might have been off the charts for 12 years [from 1963 to 1975], but he never really left," disc jockey Bruce 'Cousin Brucie' Morrow told me. "The music was there and the talent was there. The public had decided it wanted a little change of where music was going. Neil wasn't part of that, but he didn't disappear. He kept writing. He wasn't going to let anything stop him. It took a lot of courage to change partners and move into another genre. When he returned with 'Laughter' and 'Bad Blood,' and 'Love Will Keep Us Together,' they all said it was a great comeback. But I don't think he ever left."

CHAPTER 14
LOVE WILL KEEP US TOGETHER

Neil Sedaka's life became a wonderful whirlwind when 'Laughter In The Rain' hit number one. He got the word in advance while taping NBC's *The Midnight Special* just before his shows at the Troubadour. While preparing to go on, someone grabbed his arm from behind: John Reid, who was standing there with a big smile and a gift in his hand.

"Go ahead and open it," Reid said. Inside the little box was a charm in the shape of a disc. "Congratulations," it read, "you are number one in *Cashbox*, *Billboard*, and *Record World*."

"Ya-hoo!" Neil exclaimed. He later returned the favor by giving blue Tiffany & Co gift boxes to Elton and Reid. Inside, Reid told me, was a silver whistle inscribed with the words, "Anything you want, just whistle."

At first, sales of *Sedaka's Back* were slower than hoped for, partly because the record's distributors were waiting to see how the single did first. A similar thing happened on the radio in New York. At first, only WNEW—the MOR station with Frank Sinatra on heavy rotation—was playing 'Laughter In The Rain,' but eventually the rock'n'roll station WABC picked it up too. After that, both single and album took off.

The first major review came from *Rolling Stone* critic Ken Barnes, and was an unquestionable rave:

This is the year for the return of veteran popsters, and while I wish we had been spared Paul Anka and Bobby Vinton, Neil Sedaka is welcome back any old time … He again proves himself a highly skilled, sophisticated songwriter, both lyrically and melodically … The good songs are a fascinatingly varied lot, from the affecting, straight 'Solitaire' to the 50s-styled raver, 'A Little Lovin'.' 'Standing On The Inside' has a terrific chorus, 'Little Brother' is quite infectious, and 'Our Last Song Together' is a lovely closer. 'Laughter In The Rain' isn't a personal favorite but I'm glad it's a hit, because it assures Sedaka the wide audience that his imaginative pop creations deserve.[16]

At the very end of March, 'The Immigrant' was chosen for release as Neil's next single. "It was the first controversial song I had written with Phil Cody," Neil said. "It was not a love song. The record was magnificent."

As well as 'Laughter In The Rain,' Neil also recorded a half-dozen other songs during his week at Clover Studios with Robert Appere, including one that was very personal to him: 'The Immigrant.' At the time, John Lennon was battling the US Immigration and Naturalization Services over his right to remain living in New York, and Neil planned to dedicate the song to him—even though it had been The Beatles, ironically, who had helped put Neil's career into obscurity a decade earlier.

One day, even though they had never met, Sedaka decided to give Lennon a call. "He [had been] on the radio in New York and said whenever anyone called, they always wanted something," Neil recalled. "He couldn't imagine why I was calling [now], and was taken aback when I told him I was dedicating my record to him."

Lennon would eventually win his Green Card in 1976, after a four-year battle, begun by then-President Richard Nixon, to deport him for leading peace rallies against the Vietnam War. When Phil Cody sat down to write the words to 'The Immigrant,' he started to think about how America got started.

"I don't know what was going on [politically] in the country at the time," he told me, "but I felt an early wave of people not being friendly to people from other countries. And I was well aware that politically, this country was what it was because it *did* welcome people from other countries."

Once he got going, Cody started to think about his father's experiences as an Italian immigrant, as well as his own childhood.

"It's a strange song," Cody recalled. "It was inspired by my dad, but a tribute to my upbringing. I spent a lifetime being teased about being a little dark Italian kid in a white Protestant neighborhood. I tried to deny my cultural heritage. I'm sure my dad, when he heard I changed my name from Feliciotto to Cody, went apoplectic."

The song also touched on the differences between Cody and his co-songwriter. "Here were Neil and I—two signs of the old world," he continued. "Understanding that we were so different together in our musical tastes, I spent a lot of time thinking about our commonalities—that seemed important to me."

Three weeks after 'The Immigrant' made its debut, A&M Records released a song by a totally unknown duo, Daryl Dragon and Toni Tennille, better known as The Captain & Tennille. Their song: Sedaka & Greenfield's 'Love Will Keep Us Together.'

"I didn't even think about releasing 'Love Will Keep Us Together' [as a single]," Sedaka admitted. "I wanted 'The Immigrant' [to be a hit] so badly. I wanted to get to another plateau. I remember my brother-in-law saying, you're not putting out 'Love Will Keep Us Together?' And my mother-in-law said, this is 1975—it's love that keeps us together. And I said I could put it out at a later date. When I was writing it, I knew it was great, but I got away from it.

"It was on the *Sedaka's Back* album, and was released nearly two years earlier in England on *The Tra-la Days Are Over*. But unbeknown to me, Kip Cohen of A&M played my record for Toni and Daryl, and Toni fell off her chair. They recorded it while I was living in England, and I got it in the mail. I put it on the turntable and I fell off *my* chair. It was a great record!"

Not knowing who The Captain & Tennille were, Neil was in for a big surprise.

"I was living in London at the time and a lot of cover records of my songs were being mailed to my apartment," he said. "My daughter, who was about 11 at the time, brought it to me and said, Daddy, wait until you hear this one. When I first listened to the record, I was positive [Toni] was a black R&B singer. She has a great voice. She sounds like Ella Fitzgerald. I was shocked to find out otherwise. I didn't even know how to pronounce her name. What a voice she has!

"The first time Howie Greenfield heard the record on the radio he pulled his car over and called the radio station and asked who was singing," he continued. "My version was good, but theirs was great."

Cathryn Antoinette Tennille was born to a musical family in Montgomery, Alabama. Her father, Frank, sang with Bob Cosby & The Bobcats, and her mother was a TV talk-show host. Like Neil, Toni had studied classical piano, in her case at Auburn University.

In 1971, she had co-written a show and was looking to hire a keyboard player when she met Daryl Dragon, who was on a break from performing with The Beach Boys on tour. When she hired him she got a lot more than a keyboard player—he would become her professional life partner, and eventually her husband.

The pair became quite popular locally in Southern California performing at venues like the Smokehouse in Burbank. Although they weren't singer-songwriter types or rock'n'rollers, A&M Records' Kip Cohen was keen to sign them.

"They had a local single," Cohen recalled when I reached him by phone in California. "Their song, 'The Way I Want To Touch You,' had been making some noise in the Los Angeles market for some little independent label, which was a nice foot in the door. Then I saw them perform live, and I knew she had the ability and that he had the musicianship."

When it came to choosing songs for their first A&M album, the duo realized they needed another upbeat number. Cohen came up with the answer.

"I knew Neil had come out with an album," said Cohen. "I remember the morning I bought a cassette of [*Sedaka's Back*] I was driving around listening to it, and there were a number of wonderful pop songs. Then I heard this track that was a very spare production— basically just him and the piano, and not too much else. It had a multiplicity of hooks, plus the construction was strong. There were so many hooks—it was perfect for them. I played it about two more times and I picked up the phone and called them and said, you've got to come here and listen to this song."

Toni and Dragon had a similar reaction when Cohen played 'Love Will Keep Us Together' for them.

"We both knew immediately that it was the perfect song for us!"

Tennille told me. "Actually, Kip played the entire album for us, and all the songs were great, but we really needed an up-tempo song to round out our first album."

Daryl worked up an arrangement, keeping it simple but punching it up a little and overdubbing Tennille's voice. The final touch involved adding Tennille's famous line—"Sedaka is back"—to the fadeout. It came about almost by accident.

"When my sisters, Louisa, Meilla, and I were recording the backgrounds for 'Love Will Keep Us Together,' we did a run through for levels," Tennille told me. "We were having such a good time we just threw in 'Sedaka is back' for fun. We decided to keep it in the final recording as a tribute to Neil.

"Thanks to Daryl's arrangement, we took Neil's great song and made it our own. The bassline Daryl created for the intro was irresistible."

Although they were unknowns, the record still got to the top quickly. It remained at number one for a month, and in all spent an astounding 23 weeks on the charts. "We were in the right place at the right time with the right song," Tennille said.

The duo's album of the same name also did well, while the single won a Grammy Award for Record of the Year. By then, the newly married double-act had recorded a Spanish-language version of the song, 'Por Amor Viviremos,' which rose to number 49 on the pop charts, marking the first time a song had charted in two different languages simultaneously.

Six months later, they went back to the Sedaka well again, recording their own arrangement of 'Lonely Night (Angel Face),' for which Neil had also written the catchy lyrics. The Captain & Tennille's version made it to number three and stayed on the charts for 19 weeks. And they would reach into the Sedaka song-bag one last time in 1978 for their top ten version of 'You Never Done It Like That.'

Sedaka & Cody were far from finished after 'Laughter In The Rain' and 'The Immigrant.' Before the year was out, they would co-write Neil's third number one hit of the year, 'Bad Blood.'

"I felt like I again had to reinvent myself," Neil told me. "I wrote it at my little apartment on 63rd Street in Manhattan. I played him the whole tune, and Phil said, oh, my mother used to say in Italian— don't talk to that woman, she has bad blood. And it was edgy—just edgy enough—both the tune and the lyric."

The lyric brought Cody back to his roots, making him both comfortable and uncomfortable at the same time.

"The title came from my grandmother," he recalled, adding that the lady down the street from her was known as a *strega*—Italian for witch. "Be careful," his grandmother would say, "she'll give you the *malocchio*"—the evil eye.

"There was something in the music that sounded primitive to me," Cody told me. "[It] made me think of my grandmother and primitive superstition, old-world superstition."

Cody was unhappy with his first attempt at the lyric, but Neil was unsympathetic.

"I wanted to take that lyric back," Cody continued. "I wanted to redo it. But with Neil, once the session is over and the song is out the door, there's no getting it back. I was never able to talk him into giving me another hour to redo some of the stuff on that. It seemed to me that the song had a somewhat misogynistic slant to it that I wasn't really very proud to have, because I wasn't that way. But I got myself involved in playing a role. Neil was having fun with the song, and I thought, what the hell."

In Neil's mind, the song was finished, and he liked it right away. Around that time, Elton called and said he'd like to sing a duet with Neil because "you're on my record label."

"He came to a closed studio on Santa Monica Boulevard, with Robert Appere there, and I played him a few songs," Sedaka recalled. "He said, that one, 'Bad Blood,' I want to sing background on that one."

Many of the musicians from the *Laughter In The Rain* sessions were called back, including David Foster on keyboards. Neil had a finished track, so when Elton arrived, all he had to do was sing his part over it. After an hour passed, however, they started to wonder whether Elton would be coming at all.

"I was really getting worried," Neil told me. "I knew what it meant to do a duet with Elton John. There were very few duets in those days, and I thought it would almost guarantee it to be number one. We waited two hours for Elton, and I was worried that he wasn't going to get there. But then he did, and it was marvelous."

As 'Bad Blood' made its way up to number one, Neil received a call out of the blue from James Brown, the Godfather of Soul.

"I want to congratulate you, Neil," he said. "But I also want to warn you," he added, with a devilish laugh. "You're in my territory now."

CHAPTER 15
BREAKING UP IS HARD TO DO (AGAIN)

W hen 'Breaking Up Is Hard To Do' first hit the airwaves in 1962, it hit the ground running. Teenagers all over North America and Europe were moved and incredibly intrigued by the beat, the chords, and the very unique opening to the song. It was, as critic Joe Viglione later put it, "Two minutes and sixteen seconds of pure pop magic."[17] As far as Elton John was concerned, it was "one of the greatest songs of all time—a classic, a standard that will always be sung."

Among those backing up Sedaka on the original were Charlie Macey on guitar and Artie Kaplan on sax. The Cookies, who doubled as Ray Charles's backing group The Raelettes, sang the backing vocals. Sedaka picked them up in a car and taught them their parts on the way to the studio.

Three of the kids who would be forever influenced by the song were Barry Gibb, Paul Shaffer, and David Foster.

"We were in Australia around 1960 or '62 when we first heard 'Breaking Up Is Hard To Do,'" Gibb told me when I reached him by phone. "That was the light—it was the beacon for us, songwriting-wise. Neil has influenced us from when we first started writing songs. What got us about the song were the multi-harmonies and the dual vocal leads. That's what probably influenced us the most as a group. We loved that. No one in Australia was doing that—having two tracks doing the lead vocal in unison. I'm talking about how someone like that can influence you without you ever having met them. It's what really leads you into the whole concept of making records, and that's what did it for us."

Foster had a similar experience when he first heard the record.

"When I first heard 'Breaking Up Is Hard To Do,' it was a pivotal moment in my life," he told me. "Who doesn't know 'down, dooby-doo, down, down, com-a, com-a?'"

With this song, Sedaka lured Foster pied piper-like into a career in music. Then, 13 years later, Foster was invited to play auxiliary keyboards on *Sedaka's Back*.

"The first time I met and got to work with Neil was when he was recording 'Breaking Up' the second time," he continued. "It was extraordinary that it could be a hit twice. It speaks to the power of that song."

Foster has since become a very successful songwriter and producer in his own right. "I believe that I write songs that the whole world knows," he said. "Neil writes songs the whole world sings."

Shaffer, who grew up in Ontario, Canada, and went on to become the leader of the house band on *The Late Show With David Letterman*, would also describe hearing the song for the first time as a major event in his musical life.

"We all remember when we first heard 'dom, dooby-doo, dom, dom,'" he said. "It was revolutionary. It was irresistible for so many different reasons. One was that it was right in tune with the time—it sounded right at home on the radio. On that record, he did things most people had never heard before, most notably tracking and re-tracking the vocal."

Shaffer was referring to the fact that Sedaka sang two parts—the lead and the harmony—himself. Neil was a Juilliard graduate and understood every mechanism that went into the making of a record. At that time, Les Paul and Mary Ford were among the few using Paul's invention of over-dubbing, but Sedaka made great use of every track recording 'Breaking Up Is Hard To Do.'

"His delivery on each of the tracks was so remarkable," Shaffer continued. "It was a different inflection, a different language. It was like our own language, spoken our own way, the way he inflicted the syllables and the notes together. It was R&B influenced, certainly, [but] he brought it mainstream."

Shaffer also remembered seeing Sedaka's appearance as the featured performer on *The Ed Sullivan Show* a year earlier. "To see him on *Ed Sullivan* with Ed so proud of him … he'd talk about Neil just like he did The Beatles: 'These are nice upstanding young men. We've worked with them all week.' And Ed was that way with Neil.

"He made a big deal about Neil being asked to compete in the Tchaikovsky Festival in Moscow, which Van Cliburn had won. And he had him play some classical before breaking into some rock'n'roll. For me, being a little bit of a classical prodigy as a kid in Northern Canada, I related to Neil. I grew up loving rock'n'roll and all of his records."

Sedaka recorded 'Breaking Up Is Hard To Do' in Spanish and Italian, and it also became a hit in French and German. It's hard to tell how many languages it's been translated into, but what's clear is that it's a song known all over the world.

In 1963, 25-year-old ballad singer Lenny Welch put out a compelling cover of the Big Band-era song 'Since I Fell For You.' It climbed the pop charts all the way up to number four, and Welch became an overnight success. Seven years later, however, he was still looking to capture that magic again when he approached Neil with a request.

"Lenny was a friend and he came to me and asked for a song," Neil recalled. "I was just doodling at the piano and I discovered that 'Breaking Up Is Hard To Do' would work as a gin-mill song, a ballad. It was a perfect slow ballad, because Howie Greenfield's lyric was very apropos for a slow ballad."

Welch's slow version of the song did get some airplay and made it into the *Billboard* top 40, but it just didn't have the same buzz as Neil's rock'n'roll original.

"The inspiration [for the slow version] was Dinah Washington," Neil told me. "She had recorded a song of mine way back called 'Never Again.' I loved Ella Fitzgerald, Kay Starr, Rosemary Clooney, Patti Page. I was inspired to slow down 'Breaking Up' by hearing those voices in my head, but Dinah Washington was the one that I thought of the most."

Several years later, Sedaka started including the song in his club act as an encore. "People were shocked," he said, "because they knew it as a rock'n'roll tempo."

At the tail end of 1975, after 'Laughter In The Rain' and 'The Immigrant' had run their course, Neil got together with producer Robert Appere to do another album for Rocket Records. This time he was going to use the beautiful song he and Howie had written a few years earlier and title the album *The Hungry Years*.

"When we were selecting the songs for the album, Robert Appere—I must commend him—said, let's put your slow version of 'Breaking Up Is Hard To Do' on an album," Neil told me. "I think it's the only song in history to be a hit twice with a different tempo."

Indeed, it was a hit all over again, rising to number eight on the *Billboard* pop charts and to number one on the Adult Contemporary charts in early 1976. It is also one of Sedaka's most covered songs, having been recorded by a wide range of artists including David Cassidy & The Partridge Family, the Carpenters, Carole King, The Four Seasons, Tom Jones, Little Eva, The Happenings, Gloria Estefan, Dee Dee Sharp, Andy Williams, and Shelley Fabares.

Like its predecessor, *The Hungry Years* received a very favorable write-up in *Rolling Stone*, this time from Stephen Holden, now one of the lead critics at the *New York Times*:

> Sedaka's comeback has helped reassert the idea of the pop album as a collection of thematically unrelated material. Like Elton John, who informally promoted his re-emergence, Sedaka is far more concerned that a pop album work as entertainment than as "art." *The Hungry Years* features 11 songs, most of them collaborations by Sedaka with Phil Cody and Howard Greenfield, whose simple tunes, skillfully co-produced by Sedaka and Robert Appere, add up to an enjoyable collection of possible singles for other artists as well as Sedaka … Sedaka's singing is perfectly consistent with his material— dry, energetic and detached, allowing just the right amount of pathos. It is a mark of Sedaka's all-around craftsmanship that the resetting of one of his biggest hits, 'Breaking Up Is Hard To Do,' as a cabaret torch song should work almost as well as the original.[18]

Turning 'Breaking Up Is Hard To Do' into a ballad was a brilliant move. But Neil didn't do it to be brilliant, or even to sell another hit song. He did it because he loved the song and wanted to enjoy it himself, in another way. And now the rest of the world loves the slow version, too. Drop into a karaoke bar and see which version of the song they have. It's almost always the slow version. It's as beautiful a song as Sedaka has ever written. Back in 1975, meanwhile, discovering both 'The Hungry Years' and 'Breaking Up' on the same album was almost too much for a Sedaka fan to endure.

"'Breaking Up Is Hard To Do' is without doubt his greatest song," music journalist Paul Gambaccini told me. "It has proven that it transcends genre. It's been an up-tempo hit and a hit as a ballad. Its title has become part of the language. It's a case where he probably didn't realize he was summarizing the feelings of millions of people who had had a rough time. And in a popular format, he nonetheless still found truth."

CHAPTER 16
YESTERDAY ONCE MORE

W ith Neil's popularity in England rising with each passing month, and his comeback in the USA all but assured, he and Leba found themselves under pursuit by a number of different management companies. Ever since Freddie The Lawyer rid Neil of Ben Sutter and his crude, mafia-like tendencies, Leba had been managing Neil's career. Now, they felt, it was time to get some professional assistance to help enhance and extend Neil's career.

After meeting with several prospective candidates, they settled on BNB, one of the top management companies in the USA. BNB had been managing Jim Croce up until his death in a plane crash in September 1973, and also handled Richard and Karen Carpenter. The company seemed a good fit with Neil, and what he liked best was the agents' easygoing, unassuming manner.

With 'Laughter In The Rain' becoming such a huge hit, BNB booked Sedaka as the opening act for the Carpenters' summer 1975 tour. The move made total sense as the two acts shared a similar audience.

Richard and Karen Carpenter grew up in New Haven, Connecticut, before moving to Southern California in the 60s. Richard was born in 1946 and Karen in 1950, and both took up instruments at a young age. Richard began playing piano at the age of nine while Karen, who was much shyer, felt happier hiding behind her drumkit. After several failed attempts to start a band, Richard and Karen started performing as a duo, and in 1969 were signed by Herb Alpert to A&M Records. Within a year they had struck gold with 'Close To You,' written by Burt Bacharach and Hal David, and by 1975 they were established superstars.

Sedaka's comeback was on solid ground. This wasn't like 1962, when Ben Sutter booked Neil to open for comedian Jan Murray at the Copacabana. The Carpenters were as hot as any group in the country. Everyone knew their songs, from recent chart-toppers 'Top Of The World' and 'Please Mr Postman' to early hits like 'We've Only Just Begun,' 'Superstar,' and 'Yesterday Once More.'

Neil and the Carpenters knew each other already, too. The siblings had attended the party Neil threw to celebrate singing his deal with Elton John, while Richard had decided to issue Karen's version of 'Solitaire' as a single. Everything looked hunky dory.

"The Carpenters were marvelous," Neil told me, "but they sounded exactly like the record—they were not performers. I went on for 40 minutes and I jumped and I sweated and screamed and danced and the audience would get up on their feet [and beg for more]."

When the Carpenters went on, however, nearly all of their songs were ballads, and their set felt in stark contrast to the excitement Sedaka's generated.

"Richard had put together those clever duets we did together," Neil continued. "Me with Richard and me with Karen at the very end of the show."

As the tour wound its way toward Las Vegas, however, the resentment appeared to be building—not least when a *New York Daily News* headline blared out, 'Sedaka Steals Show From Carpenters.' Now the two acts were due to open at the Riviera Hotel on the Las Vegas Strip—a big deal for Neil, since ten years earlier he had been forced to appear downtown, sharing the stage with a comedian, a tap dancer, and the co-star of a kids TV show.

To give you an idea how big the Riviera was in those days, it was one of the five hotels Frank Sinatra's crew robbed in the original version of *Ocean's Eleven*. By the third night, word had gotten out among the celebs in town that Sedaka was truly back. The room was packed.

Writer Tom Nolan was there that night to capture the scene for *Rolling Stone*. Here's how he described Sedaka's performance:

> The first show [with the Carpenters at the Riviera] is, for Sedaka, a rewarding debut. It is the traditional dinner-show family crowd, never a group to whistle and stomp their approval. But Sedaka gives them the full treatment, eager to wring from them whatever is there to be wrung. Seated at the piano, dressed in a three-piece white ensemble, flanked by his two singers in midnight blue, he pumps his foot, beams, and exudes contagious enthusiasm for the occasion. Neil walks to the lip of the stage and does a modified Mashed Potato; he has a repertoire of other moves, none too overt, but giving the impression that the heart of a rock'n'roller still pumps somewhere beneath his dazzling white breast. Through sheer force of showmanship—a good sense of pacing and ability to sell his songs—he is pulling the diners up to his level of zest. "Let me assure you," he assures them, "Sedaka is very glad to be back with you."

> The reaction to Sedaka at the second show was remarkable. The audience whistled and stomped, and when Sedaka's 42-minute turn was up they cheered for more, like rock fans at the Roxy.[19]

Glen Campbell was there in the audience, while both Dick Clark and Tom Jones called Neil to say they were coming by. Sedaka introduced his celebrity friends to the crowd from the stage, while out back Richard Carpenter began to seethe.

Carpenter lived by the credo that only the headliners made introductions. When Neil left the stage, he heard Richard scream, "Get that son of a bitch out!" The next day, Neil's name was off the marquee. He'd been fired.

"I had no idea that there was a protocol that the starring act was supposed to introduce celebrities in the audience," Neil recalled. "I never heard of it. It was the Riviera Hotel in Las Vegas. I had already been on tour with the Carpenters for several weeks. I'd known Dick Clark since I was a teenager."

Carpenter, it seemed, just couldn't handle Sedaka's sudden success. Neil was getting tremendous reviews, he had two recent number ones, and he was definitely stealing the show. When Neil introduced Clark and Jones from the stage, it drove Richard over the edge, as he confirmed when he finally broke his silence on the matter two months later.

"I mean, that's a no-no," he told Tom Nolan. "It's just not good manners. Anybody in the business knows, the introduction of guests is left to the people who close the show—it's like an unwritten law. ... He [Sedaka] really had a great opportunity; there had to be over a million people who saw [our] summer tour. It was a helluva showcase for him. ... The introductions and other things I don't want to discuss were really like a direct slap in the face."

Still, Neil was stunned by what happened. The next morning, somebody from the management company called to tell him he was off the tour. "While Neil was on the call," Leba told me, "I looked out the window and could see the maintenance crew removing Neil's name from the marquee by the hotel entrance."

I first met Richard and Karen Carpenter in Philadelphia in 1970 and was looking forward to talking with Richard Carpenter again but was unable to locate him. It wasn't for a lack of trying. Calls and emails to the Carpenters' website and the Carpenter Center in California went unanswered. For months I tried to find him to get his side of the story, which Neil Sedaka urged me to do. I've spoken with dozens of producers, musicians, and singers who knew or worked with Richard Carpenter at one time, and no one had been in contact with him of late. Composer and arranger Artie Butler tried to contact former members of Carpenter's band and came back with this comment: "The man just doesn't want to be found."

One moment Neil was on top of the world; the next he'd been left fired and embarrassed. And for what reason—because he was too good? He started making some calls to New York, including to Dick Fox and Freddie 'The Lawyer' Gershon. Gershon, who by now was involved with Robert Stigwood and numerous Broadway producers, put Neil in touch with showbiz mogul Alan Carr, who knew exactly how to handle things.

His first piece of advice was, "Don't leave Vegas without securing a contract with you as the headliner." The second was, "As soon as you get back to LA, have [PR agency] Rogers & Cowan call a press conference for you."

The press conference drew writers from all the top trade papers, including *Variety* and the *Hollywood Reporter*, as well as journalists from the Associated Press and United Press International. The headlines the next day said it all: 'Sedaka Fired For Being Too Strong.' And it seemed the Riviera agreed, offering Neil a deal to return as headliner. For the Carpenters, the fallout was awful. A few days later, Karen entered the hospital with fatigue—possibly the first public indication of her battle with anorexia, to which she would eventually succumb. Many Carpenters fans were also Sedaka fans, and the incident forced Richard Carpenter to make this public statement in the 45th edition of the Carpenters Fan Club Newsletter, dated October 1975:

> When the Carpenters play concerts, they invite someone to be their opening act. In the case of our last summer tour and Las Vegas engagements, we asked Neil Sedaka to open the show. It often happens in our business, not only with the Carpenters but also with other headliners, that the choice of the opening act proves to be unsuitable for personal, or other reasons. Under those circumstances, the headliner has no option but to terminate the engagement of the opener. This was the situation with Neil.
>
> Please be assured that we DID NOT fire Neil Sedaka for doing too well. In fact we were delighted that he was receiving a nice response from the audience. It was a result of other circumstances of which he is totally aware that made it necessary for us to terminate his engagement. Since he has full knowledge of all the background acts, it is a disappointment to us that he had found it necessary to make statements concerning same to the press. Personally, the Las Vegas/Sedaka issue is an old matter, and right now I am much more concerned with Karen's health, and writing new songs.

A few months after the Carpenters debacle, Sedaka opened at the Riviera as headliner, with Artie Butler called in to arrange the sold-out shows.

"When the Carpenters fired him, Neil called me up and asked me to be his musical director and arranger and travel with him," Butler told me. "He brought me all the old arrangements he had used, and we spread them out on my floor, and I said, oh my god, Neil we've got to fix this—you're headlining in Vegas now. We rewrote all his arrangements, plus wrote new ones. I added horns and strings. We had three weeks to do it."

Once Butler had finished the arrangements he hired an orchestra and found a place to rehearse. Neil was scheduled to open a two-week stint at the Riviera on November 6, but they couldn't rehearse at the hotel until the day before. Thinking fast, Butler rented out a huge space for the day from Modern Van & Storage in Los Angeles, and Neil and his band had their first full rehearsal there on November 3. Three days later, they opened to a star-studded crowd at the Riviera.

Butler traveled all over the world with Sedaka from 1975 to 1980 and was struck by how much of himself Neil gave his audiences night after night.

"He's not a slick singer," Butler told me. "He doesn't come out in a $3,000 tuxedo with flashy cufflinks. He's not a cufflink adjuster. He's this little guy that comes out, and when he opens up to sing, this ten-foot tall heart comes out of his mouth, followed by a 20-foot soul. I'm telling you, night after night after night after night he would take his heart out, he would put it on the stage, and he would just tear the audiences' guts out. Then he'd close, and he'd put his heart back inside."

CHAPTER 17
SHOULD'VE NEVER LET YOU GO

B y the end of 1975, Gerald Ford was firmly entrenched in the White House and facing a heavy backlash from pardoning Richard Nixon for his Watergate crimes. If he wasn't getting lambasted by the *Washington Post* or the *New York Times*, he was being mocked at every opportunity by Chevy Chase on *Saturday Night Live*.

The country needed a little relief from the Vietnam War, which may be one reason 'Love Will Keep Us Together' was so successful. It was upbeat and fun, and along with 'Laughter In The Rain' and 'Bad Blood,' it helped catapult Sedaka back to the top. Wherever they booked him, the show sold out.

After struggling to make ends meet for more than a decade, Neil now found that everyone wanted to see and hear him. No one, except maybe Elton John, was hotter. So, with opportunity at his doorstep, he decided it was the time to make as much money as he could to ensure his family's security for years to come.

"I did it for the money," he said frankly when I asked him about the insane schedule he embarked upon during the late 70s. It was hard to turn down shows that paid such exorbitant sums each night.

After the near disaster with the Carpenters, the Sedakas decided they couldn't be with BNB any longer. One of the agents left the firm and started a new management company along with Neil and Leba. Offers poured in and they booked Neil for 40 weeks nonstop. They

185

were mostly one-nighters—there wasn't a county fair or a theater-in-the-round that Neil didn't play.

It was during this period that Neil missed what might have been one of the greatest evenings of his life. While he was onstage at the Riviera in Las Vegas, Leba and the children attended the annual BMI (Broadcast Music Inc) Awards in New York. Every year, BMI presents awards to the songwriters and publishers of the 100 songs that received the most airplay during the previous year. That night, Sedaka received an incredible five BMI Awards for 'Laughter In The Rain,' 'Love Will Keep Us Together,' 'Bad Blood,' 'Solitaire,' and 'Lonely Night.' And his popularity was re-emphasized shortly after that when he placed second (behind Elton John) in *Billboard*'s poll of the most popular male vocalists of the year.

Before going out on the road, Neil spent a quiet week in Merriewold Park with Leba, Marc, and Dara. He talked at length with his father, Mac, who was enjoying his new life in Fort Lauderdale, Florida, where Neil and Leba had bought his parents a condo. (Eleanor, of course, picked it out without ever consulting her husband.)

Neil loved his Dad no end. Mac had always tried to be there for his son, teaching him to play tennis or taking him to see the Dodgers play at Ebbets Field. When a nervous Neil flew to South America to perform for the first time, Mac was there by his side. As the plane approached the airfield in Rio de Janeiro, Neil looked out the window and saw thousands of people waiting.

"Someone important must be in this plane," the naive 20-year-old told his father. "I wonder who they're waiting for."

"They're waiting for you, Neil," Mac replied. "They're all here for you."

The only way Neil could make this crazy 40-week schedule work was to rent a hotel suite in Chicago and use it as his hub.

"I had my own plane that I bought with Maurice Gibb," he recalled. "It was a [Dassault Aviation] Falcon 20 jet, French made. It was two-and-a-half mill. We spilt it. I was working nine, ten months of the year—all those one-nighters. My main base was Chicago. We flew to a gig at night and came back to Chicago and slept. On the plane was a stewardess offering Bloody Marys, starting at 12 noon. It was a very exhausting time being on the road all those months and I found myself drinking more than I should. Too much food and whiskey."

Neil was consuming a couple of Bloody Marys on the plane, two vodka martinis on arrival, plus a half-bottle of wine after the show at midnight dinner. His weight was ballooning, too: at just five-foot-six tall, he now weighed around 175–180lbs. "The brutal pace was driving me to drink," he said. "And I would eat greasy food every night." The press was starting to take notice, too:

"I was horrified to see how much weight I was putting on with the return to the good life. When I toured the UK, I was looking like a fat pig. The press called me 'the Disco Doughboy,' and 'a bowling pin with a smile button for a face,' and another said I was 'the most unlikely looking rock'n'roll star.'"[20]

In order to address the problem, Neil went to Los Angeles to see Dr Charles Kivowitz, who advised him to lose 30–35lbs and to cut down to 'just' two drinks a day. Sedaka faced another type of pressure as well—the pressure to top himself.

"My blood pressure was going up," he recalled. "The pressure was on. The bigger the records were, you had to top it with the next. And then, when it starts to slip, it's a terrible ego-deflator."

Eventually, he knew, it was going to slip. Rocket Records tried to get more mileage out of *Sedaka's Back* by releasing 'That's When The Music Takes Me' as the third single from the album. It was well received but only went as high as number 22.

After 'Bad Blood,' Neil was on the road so much it was difficult to find time to write or to get into the studio to record. Writing every day was what he kept him sharp, but now he had slipped into a pattern of only trying to write when he had a new album to make.

"The piano became a symbol of fear," he told me. "It seemed to scream to me, Neil, let's see how good you really are. Are you afraid? Have you run out of melodies?"

'Love In The Shadows' made it to number 16 on *Billboard* in late 1976, but the follow-up, 'Steppin' Out,' the title track for Neil's third and final Rocket Records album, only reached number 36—despite featuring Elton John once again on backing vocals. Asked by the British press whether he was singing with Sedaka to help him sell records, Elton bullishly replied, "I only appear on the records of people I really know or like."[21]

In the mid 70s, the Sedakas felt comfortable enough to take an apartment in Manhattan—something they had wanted to do back when they first got married, only to be prevented from doing so by Neil's mother. They moved to the Upper East Side and sent the children to the equally prestigious Dalton School. At Dalton, Dara found that life wasn't as simple as it had been in London.

"Dalton was a very difficult adjustment," she said, "coming from the American School in London. The workload was much greater, and the student body much more sophisticated. It was never important before what I wore to school, but at Dalton I was teased and picked on for my outfits. They opened my locker and laughed at my raincoat when they saw it came from a discount department store. My mother had to take me shopping at Charivari just so I'd have the right clothes."

In the late 70s, the Sedakas settled into their home life in New York as Neil's hot streak came to an end. Perhaps the public had been oversaturated with Sedaka songs for a while. No one was quite sure what was happening and Neil began to worry.

"I had a strange obsession to suffer, to set up obstacles, to make things harder for myself," Neil wrote. "I actually looked for new things to worry about. Still quaking over the trauma of my professional life falling apart after The Beatles, I lived in constant fear that my career would bottom out again."[22]

It didn't bottom out, of course—it simply reached a comfortable plateau. He was still very much in demand and slid into a very comfortable life as a performer in the 80s and 90s. Before that, however, the pop music gods planted one more surprise hit on him— one that he could share.

In 1978, Sedaka recorded another song co-written with Phil Cody called 'Should've Never Let Her Go,' which he placed on his first album for his new label, Elektra Records, *All You Need Is The Music*. People told him it was "a very nice song."

Then, one night in 1980, shortly after Margaret Thatcher became Britain's first female Prime Minister, the Sedakas were having a dinner party at their new apartment at 72nd Street and 5th Avenue in Manhattan.

"Dad and I always sang something together at these parties," Dara Sedaka, who was 17 at the time, recalled. "The day before the party I sat next to him [at the piano], and he said, you always liked this song, let's sing this. It was 'Should've Never Let You Go.' He said, I'll sing this line then you sing that one ... we always harmonized in sync. It was a special blend. I knew when he was going to breathe and he knew when I was. We were like one voice. It was very serendipitous."

Neil remembered the moment slightly differently.

"We were all at a party at Freddie Gershon's in the Hamptons," he told me. "He was developing *Saturday Night Fever* with Robert Stigwood, and they were all there at this party including [John] Travolta and Olivia Newton John. Freddie said, Dara has such a beautiful voice, get her up to sing with you. And for some reason I thought of 'Should've Never Let You Go.' Freddie said, you should record that again with your daughter—she has a beautiful voice. And we did."

In this case, Dara's version of events seems more accurate. While I don't doubt that Neil and Dara sang at parties at Freddie Gershon's place in the Hamptons, it's unlikely that the stars of *Saturday Night Fever* would have been there with him in 1980, three years after the film's release. But whatever the exact circumstances, the beauty of Neil and Dara's voices together took everyone by surprise. It was an amazingly sweet duet—impossible not to like.

"People have always told me it's their favorite song," Dara told me. "I think it's the combination of the father-daughter thing and the blending of our voices that makes it so special. People are really moved by it. I can't imagine how great it is for him when he sings it."

Sedaka pointed out that there is a "family blend" in their voices. Their breathing is the same, and their harmonies are very tight. He also noted that it was one of only a handful of other successful father-daughter duets, the others being Frank and Nancy Sinatra's 'Somethin' Stupid' and Natalie Cole's posthumous duet with her dad, Nat 'King' Cole, on 'Unforgettable.'

"During 'Should've Never Let You Go and other duets we sang, there are literally moments when you don't know whether it's dad singing or me," Dara recalled. "It's one voice."

'Should've Never Let You Go' was another successful collaboration by Sedaka and Phil Cody, who said the lyrics were deeply personal to him. (He had originally called the song 'Should've Never Let Her Go.') The father-daughter version was an instant hit, peaking at number 19 on the *Billboard* pop charts and number one on the Adult Contemporary charts.

"It's particularly thrilling to have a hit record with my daughter," Sedaka told the audience of *The Mike Douglas Show* in 1980. "She is very talented and very beautiful, and it's thrilling to have this with your own offspring. She is a natural singer and I suppose she got some of that musical ability from her dad."

Like her father at the start of his career, however, Dara had stage fright and decided to curtail thoughts of a singing career of her own. "When the song became a hit we went on the road together to promote it," she recalled. "We did just about every talk show: Mike, Dinah, Merv, and *The Tonight Show* with David Letterman pinch-hooting. I tried to overcome it [the stage fright]. I would take beta-blockers for the performance anxiety. But they calmed me down so much I wasn't breathing, so I had to give it up."

Instead, Dara became a jingle-writer and behind-the-scenes singer. Today she just sings them, and you've probably heard her voice on many a record. She doesn't mind, she told me, because she received the greatest possible compliment many years ago.

"The great Luther Vandross had seen a video of me singing an R&B version of 'Laughter In The Rain,'" she said. "He told my dad I sounded just like Aretha Franklin. That was the greatest compliment I ever received."

And as for growing up the daughter of a celebrity with people like Elton John visiting all the time, Dara had a compliment of her own to dish out. "My parents did a superlative job keeping things normal for us. It was not a celebrity upbringing. My father is a wonderful man as a person and that supersedes his genius as a singer, writer and performer."

In the years since, Neil has continued to perform 'Should've Never Let You Go' as a duet during his shows, with Dara singing her lines on video. "It's so special to so many people," she said of the song. "You can only imagine how special it is for my dad."

The song's success came as a surprise and meant Sedaka had secured hits during four decades and under seven different US presidents, from Eisenhower to Reagan. Not bad for a classical pianist.

CHAPTER 18
SAYING GOODBYE TO HOWIE

Whenever I think of the famous double negative that Madison Avenue created for the Sara Lee Corporation, "Nobody doesn't like Sara Lee," Howie Greenfield immediately comes to mind. He always had a big smile and a good word for everyone. He was never catty or mean-spirited. While researching this book, and my previous one, I must've spoken to 50 people who knew and worked with Howie, and not a single person had a bad word to say.

Howie Greenfield was not just a great songwriter. He was also an important trendsetter, as one of the first openly gay songwriters in the rock'n'roll era. As Don Charles Hampton put it on the *Pop Culture Cantina* website, "He was a genius of a musical collaborator who dared to be openly homosexual long before it was safe to do so. He was warm, sweet, impulsive, bossy, funny, sexy, ambitious, energetic, emotional, and a great friend. Everybody who knew him seemed to love him, and pop singers went absolutely crazy for his songs."[23]

Among those pop singers who had hits with Greenfield records were Connie Francis, The Everly Brothers, The Captain & Tennille, Cher, Tom Jones, Tony Orlando, Brenda Lee, Jimmy Clanton, Gene Pitney, Dionne Warwick, Tony Christie—and of course Neil Sedaka. "His idol was [Broadway lyricist] Lorenz Hart," Neil told me, "and he always kept that in mind when writing for rock'n'roll."

Hart, who was also gay, partnered with Richard Rodgers to pen all-time standards such as 'Blue Moon,' 'Where Or When,' 'The Lady Is A Tramp,' and 'My Funny Valentine.' Decades from now, it's entirely possible that Sedaka & Greenfield's work will be considered as important as Rodgers & Hart's, and that songs like 'Breaking Up Is Hard To Do,' 'The Hungry Years,' and 'Love Will Keep Us Together' will also be counted as standards.

Greenfield and Sedaka first began working together in 1952; by the time they auditioned for Don Kirshner in 1958, they had written more than 500 songs. By then they were writing rhythm & blues and doo-wop and meeting with some success. From 1958 through '63, they wrote one hit after another, many of them recorded by Sedaka. 'Oh! Carol,' 'Stupid Cupid,' 'Stairway To Heaven,' 'Calendar Girl,' 'Where The Boys Are,' 'Little Devil,' 'Happy Birthday, Sweet Sixteen,' 'Next Door To An Angel,' and 'Breaking Up Is Hard To Do' were all big hits, and it seemed like their string of successes would never end. But when The Beatles forged a cultural change in America in 1964, their songs fell out of favor.

To music journalist and broadcaster Paul Gambaccini, Sedaka & Greenfield formed the perfect team. "There are very few partnerships which establish the single authorial voice," he said. "When you listen to Elton John sing 'Someone Saved My Life Tonight,' knowing it's about what he called his Woody Allen suicide attempt—putting his head in the gas oven while keeping the windows open—it never occurs to you that somebody else wrote the words, because it sounds so first person. That was the magic of the Elton and Bernie partnership. Well, Neil could sing one of Howie's songs and you'd vow—you'd bet money—that he wrote the words. Because somehow, it wasn't just a words-and-music partnership, it was an identity fusion."

For ten more years they continued to write together, although by 1970 Sedaka had sought out other lyricists in an attempt to be identified more with the new music. Greenfield, however, had been writing with other partners ever since Sedaka first went on the road to promote 'The Diary' and 'Oh! Carol.' With Jack Keller, Greenfield wrote a pair of number one songs for Connie Francis, 'Everybody's Somebody's Fool' and 'My Heart Has A Mind Of Its Own.' On his only attempt to write a song with Carole King, they produced The Everly Brothers' 'Crying In The Rain,' and with Helen Miller he wrote The Shirelles' top ten hit 'Foolish Little Girl,' and 'It Hurts To Be In Love' for Gene Pitney.

Since the early 60s, Greenfield's life partner had been Tory Damon, a very handsome and personable cabaret singer. They were so easygoing together that they just fit in as part of the crowd. Jack Keller and his wife Robi often double-dated with Howie and Tory, as did Artie Kaplan and his wife, not to mention Neil and Leba Sedaka.

Keller especially found it easy to write with Greenfield. "He was a fabulous guy and a talented guy and a workaholic," he told me when I interviewed him in 2004. "It was great chemistry with us. I liked to create, and he was a pusher. He had no qualm about initiating a conversation with an artist to make appointments to listen to our songs. I had no problem sitting down and playing them our songs, but I wasn't comfortable initiating the calls."[24]

Keller and Greenfield also wrote TV themes for Screen Gems after Kirshner sold his company to the studio, among them *Bewitched* and *Gidget*. When the Kellers moved out to California in the late 60s, Howie and Tory soon followed. And with his royalties, Greenfield was able to maintain a beautiful home in Beverly Hills as well as an apartment in San Francisco.

By the late 60s, however, Greenfield had grown depressed at how difficult it had become to write a hit song. When Keller wrote 'When Somebody Loves You' for Frank Sinatra in 1965, Howie wrote most of the lyrics, but Keller couldn't get him to finish it. Songstress Keely Smith ended up writing the final lyrics for the song, which appeared on the *Sinatra '65* album.

There's no doubt that two of Greenfield's very best songs were written in 1973 at the end of his writing relationship with Sedaka: 'Love Will Keep Us Together' and 'The Hungry Years.'

Connie Francis, meanwhile, remained one of Greenfield's closest friends to the end. She remembered calling him in "1983 or '84," asking him to write a song for her.

"I don't have anything," he replied, sounding depressed. "I'm empty."

"What do you mean you don't have anything?" Connie asked, trying to motivate him. "Write something."

"Tory's very sick," he told her, "and I'm not in the mood to write anything." After a pause, he said, "There's one song that we wrote a long time ago [that] you might want to record. It's called 'There's Still A Few Good Love Songs Left In Me.'"

"I love the title," Connie said. "Send it to me."

"I recorded the song," Francis told me, picking up the story, "but he couldn't do anything after that."

Tragically, by now both Greenfield and his partner had contracted AIDS. Howie didn't tell many people but he felt able to discuss it with Neil and Leba.

"He told us about it," said Sedaka. "He said it was a new disease, what they called a 'gay disease.' We couldn't believe it. They were a great couple. The four of us used to go on cruises together."

When Greenfield's illness became serious, Sedaka became his caretaker.

"He passed away just before his 50th birthday," Neil recalled. "He was sick for a year and half. We saw loss of memory. Leba and I hired a private nurse for his home in Beverly Hills, for both of them, because his partner Tory contracted it also. During that time, Howie asked me to drive him to Mexico. We did, and Howie went into a drugstore there. You didn't need a prescription. He was ordering a lot of pills and I asked him what they were for, and he said it was for his 'gay disease.' We'd visit them every week. It was so sad."

Howie Greenfield passed away March 4 1986, one of the first Americans to die from AIDS. Tory Damon died less than a month later. They are buried side by side at Forest Lawn in Los Angeles, the inscription on their tombstones reminiscent of the love shared by Abelard and Heloise. At the bottom of Howie's is the word 'Forever'; beneath Tory's it says 'Love Will Keep Us Together.'

"I was on a tour that finished on a ship in Bombay, India, when he died," Sedaka recalled, "and I couldn't get back in time for the funeral. It's sad, but his lyrics live on. Every time I sing them, he comes back to life. He was just 16 years old when he first knocked on my door."

After Greenfield's death, Sedaka approached his old friend Dick Asher, president of the PolyGram record label, to ask a favor. Asher had worked as lawyer for Don Kirshner and Al Nevins 25 years earlier, when Neil and Howie had first started.

"Neil asked me if I'd put out an album of Howie Greefield songs that he was dedicating to him," Asher told me when I reached him by phone. "He said the money would go to Howie's estate."

RCA had turned down Sedaka, but Asher said yes. The title of the album couldn't have been more apt. It was *My Friend*. Here is part of the dedication Neil wrote for the back cover:

> Howie's great talent was writing lyrics that were a perfect marriage to my melodies. His words were like novelettes, weaving a story from beginning to end. ... Although he has passed away, his spirit will live on through his wonderful lyrics, which have given and will continue to give great joy to millions all over the world. This album is dedicated to Howie Greenfield, my friend.[25]

Exactly five years later, Greenfield and Sedaka were inducted into the Songwriters Hall of Fame. Someday, hopefully, the Rock and Roll Hall of Fame will follow suit.

CHAPTER 19
SEDAKA: AN AMERICAN IDOL

Elton John's spending habits are now legendary. At his peak, if he saw something he liked—no matter how expensive it was—he bought it. He had stores like Tiffany & Co and Cartier close their doors so he could shop privately, and he referred to Van Cleef & Arpels, the famous jewelry store on the corner of 57th Street and 5th Avenue in Manhattan as "the candy store." He spent more on flowers than Forest Lawn Cemetery. He nearly went broke because of it all.

In Neil Sedaka's case, that generosity extended to a diamond Tiffany watch. Eventually, however, the tight bond between Neil and Elton had to break. There were too many people hanging around Elton for Neil to stay close, and once Neil's records started to slip down the charts, Elton's entourage had the perfect opportunity to put some distance between them. By the time Neil came to put together his third and final Rocket Records album, *Steppin' Out*, he felt a distinct lack of enthusiasm (and promotion) for the album.

"Elton had a lot of people around him," Neil told me. "It was the 70s, and they were always partying. When I signed with Rocket, I agreed to do three albums with them that were very successful. It was time to negotiate a new deal and I thought they'd make me an offer. I thought they'd offer me a raise, so to speak, but they didn't. They thought I should have been grateful for what they had done—and of course I was grateful to Elton. But Elektra offered me a great deal of money, [so] I left Rocket Records, and I think [Elton] was upset. I made the wrong choice. I owed it to Elton to stay with Rocket. It is a decision I have always regretted. What Elton did for me is something that could not be measured in dollars. For a while, it was a little chilly when we saw each other, but now we're very cordial."

In those days Elton was easily distracted. He was the biggest rock star in the world—everyone wanted a piece of him. He was a Neil Sedaka fan from the beginning, and there's no doubt that he loved Neil's music and was genuinely keen to resurrect his career. But the whole thing could have been a passing fancy, and once Elton saw that he had done what he set out to do—make Sedaka a star again—he could very easily have become bored of the whole enterprise. Whatever the reason, Neil and Elton's professional association had come to an end, but they never lost the respect they had for each other's music. Twenty-five years later, Elton would offer an incredible salute to Neil during a Lincoln Center celebration of Sedaka's 50 years in show business.

During the 80s and 90s, Neil continued to perform his hits all around the world. He published his autobiography, *Laughter In The Rain*, in 1982, the year before he was inducted into the Songwriters Hall of Fame by the National Academy of Popular Music. It was a tremendous honor.

In 1998, Neil was back on national television in the USA with an appearance on NBC's enormously popular *Today Show* Summer Concert series. In 1999, he received the ultimate tribute when the Madame Tussauds Las Vegas commissioned a waxwork of him.

In 2000, 'Breaking Up Is Hard To Do' reached the incredible landmark of five million plays on radio and television, according to BMI, and that same year the song made BMI's list of the 100 Top Songs of the Century.

All in all, Neil was settling into a very nice phase of his life and career as he reached his sixties. His children had grown into well-rounded adults, and he and Leba had lovely homes in New York and Los Angeles. Then, in 2003, the Sedakas were relaxing at home one evening watching the Fox network's hit new show, *American Idol*. Each week, the show would feature a celebrity guest tasked with helping the young performers hone their talents. Neil turned to his wife.

"I can do that," he said, as if there were nothing to it. "You know, Leba, this is a great show. I'm going to call them."

After making several calls to friends to get the right number, he dialed the *Idol* business office and was put through to Susan Slamer, the show's music supervisor.

"Hi," he began, "this is Neil Sedaka."

"Is this a joke?" she asked, clearly caught off guard. She was sure a friend was playing a joke on her.

"No," Neil replied. "I watch the show every week, and I'd love to be a guest judge."

"Don't move," Slamer told Neil, her excitement palpable. "I'm going into a meeting. I'll call you back in two hours."

Two hours later, Slamer did just that and arranged to fly Neil and Leba to Los Angeles so that he could mentor the final five contestants on the show, among them eventual winner Ruben Studdard and runner-up Clay Aiken. Unbeknown to Neil, there would also be a reunion of sorts with producer Nigel Lythgoe, who had worked with Sedaka 25 years earlier, on the BBC TV show *They Sold A Million*.

"You'd have to go back to the early '60s for the date when I first fell in love with Neil Sedaka's music," Lythgoe told me when I reached him by phone during the summer of 2012. "I auditioned for a show in Liverpool in 1960 or '61, and the first song I sang was 'Hey Little Devil.' The second song I sang was 'Happy Birthday, Sweet Sixteen.'

"I hadn't [yet] gotten to see him perform in concert then. I had only seen his pictures and heard his records. Years later, when I was a helping produce *They Sold A Million*, we had Neil on the program. Everyone on [the show] had sold a million records. And while I was thrilled to meet Neil, I wasn't about to tell him that I used his songs to audition with in '61."

Now, on *Idol*, the idea was for each of the five remaining contestants to sing one of Sedaka's most famous hit songs. During the show, Neil came bounding out in jeans and a suede jacket over a purple T-shirt. "What I'm most excited about is the fact that these songs were written before [the contestants] were born," Neil told host Ryan Seacrest, reminding the audience of the staying power of his songs.

Studdard, Aiken, and the others were given a list of Sedaka's hits early in the week and told to choose carefully. Aiken immediately knew which song he wanted to sing and hoped no one else would choose it.

I tried for several months without success to reach Clay Aiken until, finally, Rob Cotto from Neil Sedaka's office was able to track down the proper contact information. Clay was only too happy to cooperate.

"When I found out it was Neil Sedaka week and I saw the list of songs,

I knew right away that I wanted to do 'Solitaire,'" he told me. "In high school, our chorus teacher introduced us to the Carpenters, and I loved their version of the song. Karen Carpenter's voice was just haunting. In fact, at that time, I didn't even know that Neil Sedaka wrote it.

"I always loved 'Solitaire,' but I wasn't sure what it was about, so I made a few calls and actually got Neil on the phone to ask him. The show was only in its second season, and I wasn't sure if that was allowed, so I remember huddling in my room when nobody was around and the door was locked, so I could ask him about the song."

However, instead of telling Aiken what Phil Cody had had in mind when he wrote the words, Neil offered some wise advice. "It's your interpretation," he told Clay. "What do *you* think it means? However it moves you is how you should sing it."

First up on the night was the eventual winner, Studdard, who sang a slow, soulful version of 'Breaking Up Is Hard To Do,' which head judge Simon Cowell described as "absolutely sensational." Then, after Trenyce sang 'Love Will Keep Us Together' and Josh Gracin performed 'Bad Blood,' Kimberley Locke pulled off a great rendition of 'Where The Boys Are.' "You've gone beyond the bar," Cowell told her.

Last up was Aiken, who took to the stage dressed all in black. He stood alone under a spotlight, backed only by piano and the occasional tapping of a drum.

"Nobody else asked to do 'Solitaire,'" Aiken told me. "It was early in the show's history, and they weren't doing that much with production at that time. It was even a big deal to ask for a stool. I went to the producer and asked if he could give me just a bare stage and minimal [backing] music. I said, I want all the lights off, and I want you to light me from the back. I didn't know if it was allowed, but there was no harm asking. He said OK. It was a sad, powerful song, and I wanted to try and do something different."

Aiken's performance brought down the house. Neil was overjoyed. "Bravo Clay," he said. "I've lost the song forever to you. From now on, it will always be a Clay Aiken song."

Aiken was stunned. "That was pretty incredible," he told me. "Listen, you cling to every single compliment you get when you're on that show. You kind of can tell when something's genuine. And when he said that, it was clear to me—*holy crap*, he really meant it. It wasn't that he thought I did a wonderful job on the song, He really, really meant that. And that meant a lot to me. This was his product. I'm not a songwriter, but I imagine when you have ownership of something like that, and someone young records it, you're going to be a little more critical because it's yours."

After the show, Neil gave each of the contestants a surprise gift: a framed copy of the sheet music for the songs each of them had sung, with a personal note inscribed on each one.

"My mother was a huge Neil Sedaka fan as a teenager," Aiken continued. "When I built my house in Raleigh, my mom decorated the downstairs like a throwback diner. She took Neil's framed gift of 'Solitaire' and put it on the wall next to all of her old Neil Sedaka album covers. I love that wall."

While Ruben Studdard would eventually be named the winner of the 2003 season of *Idol*, it was Aiken who went on to more enduring success. When Sedaka got back to New York, meanwhile, he felt like it was 1975 all over again. Everywhere he went he was stopped and asked for his autograph. A new generation of music fans had been introduced to his songs, all at once. The official viewing figures indicated that 38 million people had tuned in to *Idol* that night. Thirty-eight million!

"I couldn't walk on the street after that," Sedaka told me. "I couldn't go to the cleaners. I couldn't go to the grocery store. Thirteen-year-olds stopped me for autographs."

And he loved every minute of it.

On October 26 2007, Neil was honored with a tribute show at the Avery Fisher Hall in New York's Lincoln Center. The show was entitled *Neil Sedaka: 50 Years Of Hits*, with proceeds going to the Elton John AIDS Foundation. The evening celebrated the five decades Neil had spent writing hit songs for himself and others. Many of those grateful recipients took part in the show, among them Connie Francis, The Captain & Tennille, Dion, Paul Shaffer, Natalie Cole, and Clay Aiken. The evening was co-hosted by Neil's former neighbor, the world famous oldies DJ Bruce 'Cousin Brucie' Morrow, and the great David Foster. Barry Manilow sent along a video tribute in which he hailed 'The Hungry Years' as one of the greatest pop songs ever written.

The program began with Foster introducing his protégé, Renee Olstead, who performed a touching version of 'Should've Never Let You Go' with Foster accompanying her on piano. The Captain & Tennille then sang their classic hit, 'Love Will Keep Us Together,' sounding every bit as great as the original. "Without Neil," Toni Tennille told the cheering crowd, "there would be no Captain & Tennille."

Dion was next, thrilling the audience with his version of 'Calendar Girl,' followed by Clay Aiken, who brought the house down with his version of 'Solitaire.' Next, Natalie Cole sang a beautiful and soulful rendition of 'Breaking Up Is Hard To Do,' and then Connie Francis performed one of the biggest hits Neil had written for her, 'Where The Boys Are.'

One of the highlights of the evening was Elton John's video tribute, recorded the day before during a break from his long-running show at Caesar's Palace in Las Vegas. The video opened with Elton sitting behind his famous red piano on a bare stage with just a black curtain behind him, his voice a bluesy rasp:

Don't take your love away from me
Please don't leave my heart in misery
If you go then I'll be blue
'Cos breaking up is hard to do ...

It was the slow version of 'Breaking Up Is Hard To Do,' but like no one had ever heard it before. Before anybody could get too comfortable, however, Elton had switched to an equally bluesy take on 'Laughter In The Rain':

Ooh, I hear laughter in the rain
Walking hand in hand with the one I love
Ooh, how I love the rainy days and the happy way I feel inside ...

Then, just as audience began to settle into the song, he dissolved into a version of 'Calendar Girl,' sung once again like it had never been sung before:

I love, I love, I love my little calendar girl

Oh, my calendar girl
Yeah, I love, I love, I love my little calendar girl
Each and every day of the week …

Finally, and once again without warning, he switched back to 'Laughter In The Rain.' It was a Sedaka medley like nobody had ever heard. And then Elton began to speak:

"Well, you must be feeling very happy tonight, Neil, because you're celebrating 50 incredible years in this torrid and very fickle business," he began. "You managed to last the distance—and then some. I wish I could be there for you tonight, but you can see I'm stuck in Las Vegas behind my red piano.

"We go back a long way. We had so much success, together, which makes me so happy. When 'Laughter In The Rain' was your number one single in America after a long time away from the charts, you became—and I became—extremely happy.

"That's what I wanted for you to have—the recognition in America, after you'd had tremendous success in Britain [in the early 70s] and all over the world. And if I played some small part of that with Rocket Records, then I'm very happy for you, because you're a fantastic songwriter.

"I just played three songs, no they were snippets of three songs and I could have been here another 45 minutes. And I'm very grateful for your generosity here tonight too, to donate the proceeds [from the show] to the Elton John AIDS Foundation. It defines you as a human being as well as a great musician.

"I send love to you and Leba and I hope you have the most fantastic night. And of course, there will be many more years to come. You ain't finished yet, buddy. Love you."

After that, Elton turned back to the piano and began softly singing the refrain from 'Laughter In The Rain' one last time:

Ooh, I hear laughter in the rain
Walking hand in hand with the one I love
Ooh, how I love the rainy days and the happy way I feel inside ...

Then, suddenly, he yelled out: "Go Neil!"

After Elton John's video tribute ended, Paul Shaffer took the stage and explained what a huge influence Sedaka had been on his life, before suddenly breaking into an impromptu version of 'Next Door To An Angel.' He then brought Neil onstage to a standing ovation and the fun continued. Neil sang a medley of 'The Diary,' 'Oh! Carol,' and 'The Hungry Years,' followed by a series of duets with his guests, including 'Happy Birthday, Sweet Sixteen' with Shaffer, and 'Stupid Cupid' with Connie Francis. It was the first song he had ever written for her, back in 1958, but they sang it as if it were yesterday.

Shaffer and David Foster then returned to the stage to accompany Neil on 'Bad Blood,' with Foster playing the electric piano—just as he did on the original recording in 1975—and Shaffer singing the backing vocal made famous by Elton John. Even without Elton, it sounded like a carbon copy of the original.

Neil was then joined onstage again by The Captain & Tennille for a version of 'Lonely Night (Angel Face),' a huge hit for the duo in 1976, before the entire group completed the evening singing together 'Laughter In The Rain' and 'That's When The Music Takes Me.'

It was a night Sedaka truly deserved—and one he'll never forget.

CHAPTER 20
THE SECRET SAUCE

Neil Sedaka began writing songs at the age of 13, when Harry Truman was completing his first term as President of the United States of America, and Winston Churchill was in the midst of his second spell as Prime Minister of the United Kingdom. He had his first chart success when Dwight Eisenhower was in office, and he had written a hit song during every presidency through 1980.

In order to stay connected to the music, Sedaka navigated through decades of change. When he began, he could only hope to one day be as popular as Johnny Cash, Buddy Holly, or Elvis Presley. In the beginning, he was writing doo-wop, then R&B, while country and folk music also had a heavy influence on rock'n'roll at that time. He watched the styles go from the girls wearing long skirts, bobby socks, and saddle shoes to mini-skirts that left little to the imagination.

Neil wrote during periods where dance revolutions ruled the charts, from the jitterbug and the lindy to the stroll, the twist, the bump, the frug, the mashed potato, the jerk, the watusi, the hustle, and probably a hundred more. Even though he fell out of favor as a performer during the later 60s and early 70s, his music never did. His songs successfully found a home during periods when the flavor of the day went from doo-wop and rhythm & blues to country and folk-rock, from blues-rock and punk-jazz to singer-songwriters and heavy metal, from hip-hop and Britpop right through to the alt.rock and bubblegum pop of the present day.

In 2005, Tony Christie's original 1970 recording of Sedaka & Greenfield's 'Is This The Way To Amarillo' was rereleased in the UK as part of the biannual Comic Relief telethon. The song caught fire all over again, but this time it didn't stop selling until it reached number one, becoming the biggest-selling single of the decade in the UK.

In the 50-plus years since Sedaka's first hit, so many of the world's top singers have lined up to cover his songs. Here's a short list of some of them: Frank Sinatra, Elvis Presley, Elton John, Carole King, Shirley Bassey, Cher, Abba, Rosemary Clooney, The Fifth Dimension, Tom Jones, Clay Aiken, Tony Christie, Petula Clark, Johnny Mathis, Frankie Valli, Sheryl Crow, the Carpenters, The Captain & Tennille, Patsy Cline, and Neil Diamond. Why is this, and why does it continue to happen?

'Breaking Up Is Hard To Do' was released 51 years ago, in 1962, yet we, our children, and our children's children will go on singing both the fast and slow versions of the song for at least another 50 years. The same goes for Sedaka classics such as 'Love Will Keep Us Together,' 'Laughter In The Rain,' 'Calendar Girl,' 'Where The Boys Are,' and 'The Hungry Years.'

Researching the history of Sedaka's music, I sought to learn the reason for the longevity of its success, and why we all keep going back to it. In effect, I wanted to know: what is in his secret sauce? What is the secret to his success? And to find the answer, I reached out to some of the biggest names in the business.

Sir Elton John was only too glad to offer his opinion when I reached him by phone early in 2013. "The secret of a great song is you have to give it your own little stamp," he began, "and Neil's songs lend themselves to that. You can sing them different ways because of the way Neil writes. You couldn't sing 'Wooly Bully' slow, but Neil's songs, the way they're written melodically and with his chord structures—you can. He knows, because he's a piano player. Piano players write different songs than guitar players. So you're able to make it bluesy because of the intelligent way it's written. He's an intelligent writer and a great classical pianist."

Asked whether he felt Sedaka's songs would still be sung 50 or 100 years from now, he replied, "Yes, of course. A great song never goes away."

When they were first getting started in Australia, The Bee Gees were heavily influenced by Neil Sedaka's songwriting and records. Earlier in this book, **Barry Gibb** spoke about the tremendous influence of 'Breaking Up Is Hard To Do.' "There are many artists that really have to work at what they do," he said, "and there are artists that have a gift from childhood. That's Neil Sedaka. He's a perennial. There are people who just never go away. There is no such thing as a comeback for Neil Sedaka. That's ridiculous. He's always been there. He's always in your heart; he's always in your mind, musically. Even when you're making records, you think, let's make a Neil Sedaka record."

For legendary producer and executive **Clive Davis**, "The essence of a great copyright is that it does become a part of the culture. Neil's songs have become part of the Great American Songbook, and they will be rediscovered for generations to come."

Award-winning producer **David Foster** first worked with Sedaka in 1974 on 'Laughter In The Rain.' "A lot of people write songs that the whole world knows," Foster said. "Neil is one those rare birds that writes songs that the whole world sings. He was all about melody. I

211

don't think that one lyricist was the key to his success. It didn't matter who wrote the lyrics—those melodies were just flawlessly perfect. And the arc of the song in just two-and-a-half minutes—he built this great arc with a beautiful bridge and the chorus and key changes. He was ahead of his time."

"Neil writes classic melodies," **Carole Bayer Sager** told me. "They're melodies that are produced in various different changing ways. Often it's not the song that loses its relevance, it could be the production that's dated. Neil's melodies were classically great. And Neil's songs with Howie and through his comeback [with Phil Cody] were great. He knew how to find the right writing partners. He was primarily a melodist and his melodies are timeless. History will show he's been one of the great songwriters of our time and one of the great melodists."

And this from **Burt Bacharach**, via email: "Neil has always struck me as a well-schooled musician/pianist. Certainly his melodies are very accessible and I have great appreciation of what he did."

Paul Shaffer was first affected by Sedaka's music in the early 60s, when he first heard 'Breaking Up Is Hard To Do.' "When Neil's songs grabbed us," he said, "they created a feeling within us that was so strong that we're still trying to get back to that. He is the alchemist, not us. He is the one who knows it."

Jay Siegel has known Neil since they met in chorus class at Abraham Lincoln High School in 1954. Although they went their separate ways, musically, after singing together in The Linc-Tones and The Tokens, they have remained close ever since. "Neil is one of the greatest songwriters to come out of any generation," Siegel told me. "From songs like 'I Go Ape' to 'Laughter In The Rain,' it's all about his ability to connect musically and to get the right lyricist that any generation can identify with. It's not just hip-hop and rap out there. There are still people like an Adele out there—it's about connecting a great song with a great songwriter and a great artist. Neil is all three. That's how he's stayed connected."

Nigel Lythgoe grew up singing Neil Sedaka songs in England, and many years later got to work with him on *American Idol* in the USA. "Neil just writes songs that people fall in love with their melodies," he said. "Music is timeless. We would never think that hip-hop or rap would last this long, but it has its audience. There always will be an audience for a Neil Sedaka song, and his performances as well. It will never be old or stale. [The secret is] a word that's been forgotten in recent years, except possibly in the case of Adele. The word is 'melody.' In all of his songs, the melody stands out."

Marilyn McCoo, who had hits with Sedaka's 'Workin' On A Groovy Thing' and 'Puppet Man' as part of The Fifth Dimension during the late 60s, had her own theory about his success. "Neil's melodies are so haunting," she said. "You find yourself singing them—it's another reason his songs keep coming back. One of the important things about Neil's music is that it has a timelessness about it." Or, as her husband, **Billy Davis Jr**, put it, "Neil's music is about love."

Producer and A&R man **Kip Cohen** was the one who had insisted back in the mid 70s that The Captain & Tennille record 'Love Will Keep Us Together.' He approached the question of Neil's 'special sauce' from a more technical perspective. "Neil's Julliard background allowed him to come from a position that understood the construction of songwriting in a very strict sense," Cohen told me. "He knew how to package a Tin Pan Alley song, going back to Irving Berlin. He wrote about things that were understandable to a very a wide range of people."

Connie Francis has known Neil since he was 19 years old and has recorded hit versions of a number of his songs. "First of all, he wrote popular music just to be a star," she said. "He had the ability to change with the times, and he was one of the few people who wrote their own hits, like Paul Anka and Bobby Darin. He adapted with the times, and of course when he hooked up with Elton John, that was the beginning of another arc to his career. He's never remained stagnant. And Elton recognized that genius in him."

Another longtime Sedaka admirer was been **Dion DiMucci**, who first met Neil at Annette Funicello's 16th birthday party in 1958. "Neil has always been a pop music genius," he said. "By genius, I mean you look at the distance between where he is and where everyone else is. His mind is sharp. He sees roads that aren't paved ahead of him and knows which one to take. He always takes his old fans with him, but he's managed to make new fans from recent generations."

Pop culture expert and rock'n'roll historian **Laura Pinto** felt the secret to Neil's success was the timelessness of his songs. "Regardless of the decade in which they were written, they never go out of style," she wrote to me in an email in late 2012. "They are fun, playful, touching, sad, heart-wrenching, and romantic. None are cynical, negative, violent, or crude. The lyrics of Mr Sedaka's songs, whether penned by Howard Greenfield, Phil Cody, or Sedaka himself, represent the thoughts and feelings of everyman (and woman).

"Sedaka has always had his piano-playing fingers firmly on the pulse of our collective consciousness," she continued. "And, to coin a word, his songs are wonderfully *singalongable*! It helps that Sedaka's own diction is so flawless, and that the words match the melodies perfectly without being rendered unrecognizable by the altering of their pronunciation or syllabic emphasis. Neil Sedaka is the Cole Porter of our generation, with a bit of George Gershwin and Stephen Foster tossed in as seasoning."

For veteran journalist, author, and *Billboard* writer **Fred Bronson**, "His songs have irresistible hooks. Listen to 'Breaking Up Is Hard To Do' or 'Laughter In The Rain.' He has the best hooks to his songs. How can you resist them? What Neil accomplished with having number one songs 13 years apart is one of those very rare occurrences in the business. And he sounds as good today—or better—than he did in 1975."

Phil Cody was an unknown singer-songwriter when Neil Sedaka asked him to write lyrics for his new songs in 1971. "I think writers sometimes get lost in the process and lose sight of the emotional connection our songs help make for people," Cody said. "Most folks can't easily articulate their emotions the way a good Sedaka melody can, and as long as that connection is available, people are going to keep coming back to it to mitigate their sorrows and celebrate their joys."

Cody picked out a quote from Mary Elizabeth Williams, a blogger for salon.com, that pretty much nails it:

We apply our most magical thinking to our favorite songs, playing them in endless loops and singing along as if in prayer. We believe them, because somehow a message with a melody becomes a kind of holy truth. Our truth. Our love. Our heartbreak. Our fear. And our fearlessness.

Why did 'We Are Never Ever Getting Back Together' rocket to the top of the iTunes chart the day it was released? Not because Taylor Swift is so cute. It's because a million people heard it and immediately thought, that girl is singing my life. It's because sometimes our deepest truths are buried in our pop songs.[26]

"And that," said Cody, is the relationship that a number of generations of people have with Neil's music and that's why those songs are going to be around for a long, long time." He then pointed out that 'Solitaire' has been recorded by 47 different artists, adding, "Neil is a true genius of the genre, and artists would not have lined up in droves to sing and play his wonderful melodies if it were not so."

According to critic and broadcaster **Paul Gambaccini**, Neil's classical background meant he was "familiar with some of the greatest melodists of all time—and I don't mean Burt Bacharach and Paul McCartney. I mean Chopin and Shubert. He was familiar with the most important composers who ever lived. He could compose without realizing he was using lessons learned from the greatest of all time.

"Even when he did the slow version of 'Breaking Up,' he prefaced it with a new bit, which was the type of recitative, which the great writers of the Great American Songbook would do. Some of the great copyrights of all time had little introductions, which are not often sung with the song. 'Over The Rainbow' had one, 'White Christmas' had one, and 'Breaking Up Is Hard To Do,' the second time, had one."

Tony Orlando first met Neil Sedaka as a 15-year-old at Don Kirshner's office at Aldon Music. He has achieved enduring success as a songwriter, producer, and singer of several number one hits, and like Gambaccini felt that Neil's classical background was a key ingredient in his success. "He has an understanding of melody that is really unique," Orlando said. "If you study Neil's melodies, he always coupled his melodies. It didn't matter if his songs were up-tempo, doo-wop-style, or a straight ballad—they hold up because the melodies were constructed so well. Then when you coupled that with Howie Greenfield or Phil Cody's lyrics, you have magic. Neil was always able to couple great melody, and great chord progressions, with an understanding of how important a lyric was.

"He is one of the very few that, if he were born 25 years earlier, he would have been Cole Porter or Irving Berlin. He would have been those guys. He understood the contemporary sound and he went with it with the same fervor, talent, and insight to writing that they did—and look how long their songs have lasted. They're standards, and so are Neil's."

Michael Feinstein first became known as the young man who helped Ira Gershwin catalogue all of his music, therefore preserving decades of treasures in the Great American Songbook. He has since gone on to become one the world's great cabaret performers, producers, and entrepreneurs as owner of the wonderful Feinstein's club in New York City. He has known and greatly admired Sedaka's work for years and had a unique perspective from which to compare it. For months I tried to catch up with this busy man. Finally, in late 2012, I did.

"Neil is so iconic to me," Feinstein said. "For me, Neil has always been one of the bridges from classic American popular song to contemporary music. He knows and loves the works of the classic songwriters—the Gershwins, the Ellingtons, the Kerns, and such—then started writing in the pop style in his youth and incorporated elements into his writing that were influences of the traditional writers.

"He has the ability to understand what makes a popular song popular. That is what makes him iconic, in my view. The greatest creators of song have instinctive ability that cannot be taught. And that's one of the things that strikes me about Neil. Anyone that sees him perform sees this incredible enthusiasm and joy—that he is loving the process as much as we do. He loves performing the songs because there's still a certain part of him that says, in the most charming way, gee, listen to this. Isn't this something? I wrote this."

Feinstein sees the whole picture of American songwriters, from Stephen Foster to the present day, and he knows exactly where Neil Sedaka fits in. "We can look back and say what Neil Sedaka did in the arc of his career," he continued. "He's not just another pop performer, because he has written songs that are part of the Great American Songbook. There are lots of gems in his catalog that aren't as well known as 'Solitaire,' 'The Hungry Years,' 'Breaking Up Is Hard To Do,' or 'Alone At Last.' The thing that makes a song last are the multiple recordings. And with a song like 'The Hungry Years,' it's been sung by more and more people. Sinatra sang it, Rosemary Clooney sang it, I recorded it. A song like that will grow in importance throughout the years. It doesn't have to just be performed by Neil to be acknowledged as a great song. Neil has a gift for understanding how to find a riff or a hook that will bring the listener in. He has a gift for coming up with something fresh.

"The thing that makes a song last is the melody, the lyric, and the harmonic structure. Neil feels that melody is the most important part of the song, and he has the ability to come up with melodies that are comparable to the classic songwriters. He can write in different pop styles that mirror the popular tastes of the moment, but his essence is that of a great melodist and someone who has great sophistication in his harmonic pallet.

"If Neil had worked 30 years earlier, in what we now consider to be that golden era, he would have been as successful [as Gershwin, Porter, Rodgers, Hart] and held his own with the best of them."

218

CHAPTER 21
WAKING UP IS HARD TO DO

I n the 90s, Neil Sedaka worked primarily as a performing artist, but amazingly, during the last decade—and while in his sixties and seventies—he returned to the recording studio and became very creative in the process. Through it all, he has always found a way to stay connected to the music.

Sometimes you just have to wonder where Neil gets his energy. It's hard to believe that a man of his age might wake up one day and say, "Hey, what a great day. I think I'll put together a new album." But in 2003, he decided to do exactly that with the release of *Brighton Beach Memoirs: Neil Sedaka Sings Yiddish*.

In 2004, the Actor's Fund of America/NYSAE honored Neil with *Broadway Sings Sedaka*, while 14-year-old Renee Olstead, star of the CBS comedy *Still Standing*, recorded a duet of 'Breaking Up Is Hard To Do' with jazz pianist and singer Peter Cincotti. The LP from which it was taken debuted at number four on the *Billboard* Jazz Album chart.

In 2006, Neil released *The Very Best Of Neil Sedaka: The Show Goes On* in the UK. It debuted at number 20 on the charts and was certified gold by the BPI three weeks later. Then, in 2007, just 68 years young, he decided it was time to write his first classical symphony. *Joie De Vivre* was first performed that year by the Kansas City Orchestra, with Lee Holdridge conducting. Neil was there for the event, which took place just one month prior to the sensational tribute to his *50 Years Of Hits* at Lincoln Center.

One day the following year, Neil decided to widen his audience further still by putting out an album for children, *Waking Up Is Hard To Do*. Neil and his son Marc rewrote the lyrics to many of the great Sedaka & Greenfield hits so they would appeal to kids. 'Love Will Keep Us Together' became 'Lunch Will Keep Us Together'; "I love, I love, I love my calendar girl" became "I love, I love, I love my dinosaur pet." The inspiration was simple: grandchildren.

Neil has maintained a close friendship with the oldies DJ Bruce 'Cousin Brucie' Morrow since the 50s. Morrow has always been more than just a pal who spins Sedaka's records: he helped Neil and Leba find an apartment when they returned from their honeymoon in 1962, and later became their neighbor in the close-knit Merriewold Park community. And now, more than 50 years after they first met, he helped Neil get into the children's book business by introducing him to publisher Charles Nurnberg.

"Neil started singing when he was about 16," Nurnberg told me when I reached him by phone, "and I started listening shortly after that. I've been a fan ever since. Neil was a good friend of Cousin Brucie, and so was I, so it was natural for Bruce to put us together."

Prior to working with Neil, Nurnberg had published a series of children's songbooks, including *Puff The Magic Dragon* with Peter Yarrow of Peter Paul & Mary and *Over The Rainbow* with Judy Collins.

"We chose *Waking Up Is Hard to Do* as the first book [of the series] to do with Neil," Nurnberg continued. "Then we did *Dinosaur Pet*, which was the old music from 'Calendar Girl.' *Waking Up* was quite a successful book, and *Dinosaur Pet* just became a phenomenon. People just loved it. Neil appeared on TV with his grandchildren talking about the book, and it really struck the public's fancy."

Each of the books came with a three-track CD of songs featured in the text. On May 27 2012, *Dinosaur Pet* debuted at number five on the *New York Times* bestsellers list. That night, Neil was interviewed at length at the 92nd Street Y before signing books for what seemed like a mile-long line of admirers (myself included).

"I think Neil Sedaka is one the most talented people I've ever seen," his proud publisher said. "There doesn't seem to be anything he can't do."

In connection with the debut of the book, Sedaka conducted a revealing interview with the *Huffington Post*:

I've spent a good majority of these last 50 years on the road, but I was never far away from my family. When Leba and I had children, we took them all over the world, moving to London in the early 70s ...

Performing with my grandchildren, 30 years later, was a dream I never knew I had, yet it was one that was realized effortlessly. The release of my second children's book, *Dinosaur Pet*, marked the occasion where my twin granddaughters, Amanda and Charlotte, and my grandson, Michael, joined me on [TV] as backup vocalists on the title song.

I'm a child at heart. I love taking my grandchildren to children's concerts and the amusement parks. I try to convince them to join Papa on the rollercoaster, but they're the one's that have to convince me to stay off them. I'm very proud attending their art shows and their recitals. Sitting in the audience, surrounded by all the other doting grandparents, I'm no longer singer/songwriter Neil Sedaka. I'm just Papa Neil. And that's when I'm the happiest.

When I first interviewed Neil at his home in New York, it was right after *Dinosaur Pet* had made its amazing debut on the bestseller lists. (After entering the *New York Times* chart at number five, it would rise, a week later, to number three.) Sedaka was jubilant.

"I'd like to be the next Raffi or Mr Rodgers, playing to two-to-seven-year-olds," he told me. "I'm going to take it to the stage. I'm going to have a children's show in the afternoon for the mothers and the grandmothers and the little ones. I want to reach them all. I've gone from the baby boomers to the babies."

In 2010, 40 years after the failure of his *Emergence* album, Neil received a call from the album's producer, Lee Holdridge. A great classical producer and arranger, Holdridge had remained friends with Sedaka over the years despite the failure of their joint effort.

"I saw him do a Chopin piece in his show," Holdridge told me, "and the audience just loved it. They just melted on the spot. I told Neil, you know, you should do something of your own with piano and orchestra."

That's all the encouragement Sedaka needed. Before long, he had written *Manhattan Intermezzo* for piano and orchestra. "It's a fairly elaborate piece—about 15 or 20 minutes," Holdridge explained. "We recorded it with the Philharmonia Orchestra in London. It's a terrific piece. The audiences just love it."

Manhattan Intermezzo is Sedaka's salute to his hometown. "It's a great page in his book—a nice side to him," Holdridge continued. "It shows his versatility. *Manhattan Intermezzo* is a lot of fun because he covers a lot of different styles in it, and he's able to perform his piano solos against the orchestra. So I think it's quite a showcase."

Sedaka felt that writing a classical piece gave him much greater freedom. "It's very rewarding," he revealed at the time of the first performance. "When you write classical, you have much more creative freedom, harmonically, rhythmically. Being from Manhattan, I wanted to catch the spirit of New York, the ethnic groups, the Latin, the Asian, the Russian. I wanted people to almost hear the honking of the taxis. I'm very proud of it."[27]

Holdridge is proud too that Sedaka is still singing 'Superbird' and 'Cardboard California' from *Emergence*. "It's his way of saying there were good songs in that album," Holdridge said. "If you listen to that album, and then his earlier [tra-la, dooby-doo] songs, you'll ask, is this the same guy? Now, live in concert, I see people of all ages at his shows. It tells me he's reaching all generations. When the dust settles on the 20th century, we'll see who remains standing. And Neil Sedaka will definitely be among the few."

CHAPTER 22
THE REAL NEIL

Have you ever gone to a concert and enjoyed the music but wished the performer had spent a little more time between songs telling you how they came to be? The link between an artist and his audience is already so personal; anything the audience can latch onto will bring the two closer.

In 2012, at the age of 73, Neil Sedaka released his 75th album, *The Real Neil*. It is by far the most intimate recording of his career. For one thing, it's acoustic—just Neil and his piano. For another, it was recorded as if Neil were playing a small cabaret show, talking softly in between songs and explaining their origins.

"Everything you hear today is so overproduced—and loud," he told British critic Philip Norman in 2012. "I wanted something more personal and intimate. In between songs, I talk about how each one came to be written."[28]

The Real Neil features two doo-wop songs written with Howie Greenfield back in the 50s but never released at the time: 'Everybody Knows' and 'Queen Of Hearts.' There are also reworked versions of classics like 'Laughter In The Rain,' 'You,' and 'Breaking Up Is Hard To Do,' as well as several freshly written tunes that have received some very flattering reviews. The final track is a surprise: Neil's 18-minute classical piece, *Manhattan Intermezzo*.

Sedaka begins the CD by talking directly to his audience. "Hi, this is Neil, welcome to my world of music. This is how my songs come to life, right here at the piano. This is the pure form of the song, the way I wrote them. I hope you enjoy *The Real Neil*." He goes on to describe the process of songwriting in the liner notes:

> The most challenging task for a songwriter is to write a simple tune but still bring an emotional feeling to it. After 60 years of writing, I am very proud of these new songs. This is my first acoustic album. Piano and voice, the pure form of the song, just the way I write them. The songs are very personal and come from my soul. It's the culmination of all the years of writing. No frills. No production gimmicks.[29]

That last line is telling. Have you ever listened to someone's record and then gone to see them in person? Often, when you listen to someone's record and then go to see them perform live, it sounds like a totally different singer, because they can't match the sound manufactured in the studio. Neil Sedaka, however, is the exact same voice you hear on record, which in this day and age is pretty amazing.

Writing for the Arts Desk, British music journalist Kieron Tyler was clearly impressed: "It's amazing that Sedaka still has it," he wrote. "At 73, he is still composing songs that sound like instant classics. Here, 'Broken Street Of Dreams' and 'Heart Of Stone' leap out ... These are as good as anything—and better than most—by writers from multiple recent generations: reflective, emotive, melodically tricky yet instantly memorable, and with lyrics that get straight to the point."[30]

On allmusic.com, critic Stephen Thomas Erlewine described the new songs on *The Real Neil* as having "a casual charm that's appealing. At his heart, Sedaka remains a showman, doing anything to get a smile out of his audience even if they're sitting alone at home, and that showmanship will indeed bring a smile to your face."

Among the new songs, the highlights include 'Heart Of Stone,' 'Beginning To Breathe Again,' and 'Broken Street Of Dreams.' In 'Sweet Music,' he takes a shot at the loud music of recent times, asking, "What happened to the harmony, what happened to the melody?" He has since explained the meaning behind that line:

> I was raised in an era when you could understand the lyrics. My heroes were George Gershwin, Richard Rodgers, Irving Berlin, Johnny Mercer, Frank Loesser. I can understand some of the new stuff, but it's more production and sound, rather than song. Whatever happened to the sweet melodies that we can sing? Being from the Brill Building, we were taught to write sing-able, memorable songs. And I think that's the basis of my success.[31]

Neil's 2012 UK tour included stops at ten different cities, including Glasgow's Clyde Auditorium, Bridgewater Hall in Manchester, the Symphony Hall in Birmingham, the Royal Concert Hall in Nottingham, the Liverpool Philharmonic Hall, and of course the Royal Albert Hall in London—the place where his comeback took flight 40 years earlier. It had to be an exhausting tour for a man of 73, but you'd never know it from the reception he got. It was quite a different story when he first toured Britain in 1958, when he followed wild-man Jerry Lee Lewis into most of the venues. Lewis, who had just married his 13-year-old cousin, often set fire to his piano during his act. As Philip Norman noted in his 2012 piece for the *Sunday Times*, Sedaka's appearance would have come as something of a relief:

Imagine the relief as the 19-year-old Sedaka walked onto the London Palladium stage, immaculately dressed and barbered, with a beaming smile in place of Jerry Lee's superciliously curled lip. Before pitching into his pop repertoire, the Juilliard-trained pianist gave a virtuoso performance of Chopin's 'Fantasie Impromptu.'

A chambermaid at the Dorchester hotel, where he was staying, expressed the general feeling. "Nice to see a bit of class," she told him, "after all the rubbish they've been sending over."[32]

When asked on the tour how long he'd been performing, Sedaka replied, "55 years as a performer—even longer than that as a songwriter." Then he put it all in perspective. "Billy Joel thinks I'm like something from the old American frontier—the Davy Crockett of pop."

The reviews from the UK tour were unanimous in their praise. *Listed* magazine raved about his show at the Bournemouth International Centre, calling it "a master class in how to write and perform numbers so catchy that they still have people singing along, a half a century after they were first released. ... Sedaka is a matinee idol tenor who can convey drama, heartbreak, and joy with deceptive ease and a sizable dash of rock'n'roll showmanship. It's a compelling combination."

During the tour, Neil played an entertaining 1961 video of his 21-year-old self singing 'Calendar Girl.' In the video, he is surrounded by beautiful girls, each representing a month of the year, and bounces from one to the other. After the video finished, he told the audience that he had recently met Miss January again in a restaurant. "She was a very, very old woman," he said with a smirk, and then pointed to his younger self on the screen. "Of course, I'm just the same."

In 1983, the National Academy of Popular Music inducted Neil Sedaka into the Songwriters Hall of Fame. It was a glorious honor, and indeed the highest achievement he could have been awarded, since at the time the Rock and Roll Hall of Fame did not yet exist.

Twenty-one years later, in 2004, the Songwriters Hall of Fame gave Neil the Sammy Cahn Lifetime Achievement Award, and a few years later he was given an honorary Ivor Novello award. Along the way, Neil has also been saluted by the Friars Club, presented with a star on the Hollywood Walk of Fame, and honored by the Hit Parade Hall of Fame. He's received just about every award imaginable—except one.

In 1985, four businessmen started a club to promote the things they loved most: making music and money. They were Atlantic Records founder Ahmet Ertegun, *Rolling Stone* founder Jann Wenner, record executive Seymour Stein, and Alan Grubman, perhaps the most powerful lawyer in the entertainment industry. They named their club The Rock and Roll Hall of Fame, and just like any club, its founders had the right to invite to join anyone they cared. The first induction ceremony took place on January 23 1986, and the inductees that year were hard to argue with: Elvis Presley, Chuck Berry, Buddy Holly, Little Richard, James Brown, Ray Charles, The Everly Brothers, Sam Cooke, Fats Domino, and Jerry Lee Lewis.

Sedaka, like others who had achieved tremendous success in the 50s, 60s, and 70s, longed to be invited. It didn't take long, however, for nepotism to start creeping in. In 1987, when The Coasters—a group most famous for recording novelty songs like 'Charlie Brown' and 'Yakety Yak' were voted in, many began to point fingers at Ertegun, since the group had recorded for his Atlantic label. That same year, Ertegun himself and his partner Jerry Wexler were voted into the Hall, too, alongside great acts like Ricky Nelson, Smokey

Robinson, and Roy Orbison. In fact, until Ertegun passed away 20 years later, there appeared to be a pronounced bias toward Atlantic acts like Laverne Baker and Ruth Brown, plus rhythm & blues—the genre with which Atlantic was most closely associated—in general.

In 2004, I interviewed Ertegun for my book about Don Kirshner. I asked him why two of the legendary songwriting teams Kirshner employed—Sedaka & Greenfield and Mann & Weil—hadn't been inducted into the Hall of Fame. (Goffin & King had been allowed in, but only in the 'non-performer' category—as if Carole King didn't qualify as a performer.)

Ertegun told me he found their work too "bubblegum-ish" to deserve inclusion in his club. He felt the same about Sedaka (despite the fact that he had written one of Laverne Baker's biggest R&B hits, 'I Waited Too Long,' in 1959).

In 2010, four years after Ertegun's death, Mann & Weil were finally given a belated induction into the Hall of Fame, while the following year even Kirshner got in through the back door (at Carole King's insistence). But there was no room for Neil Sedaka. The king of the dooby-doos and tra-la-las had become too closely associated with his early successes in the 50s to be recognized as someone who had also had huge success writing for everyone else. But if Neil's songs were really too "bubblegum-ish," greats like Elton John, Frank Sinatra, and Elvis Presley wouldn't have covered them.

Sir Elton, for one, is a staunch supporter of the idea of Sedaka being inducted into the Hall of Fame. "Absolutely yes!" he told me. "Neil should be in the Rock and Roll Hall of Fame for his body of work in the rock'n'roll era. He's been a classic performer and songwriter. Those people who did the groundwork—the people that paved the way for people like myself—deserve to be [there]."

Paul Gambaccini, a longtime member of the Rock and Roll Hall of Fame voting committee, had a theory that might explain Sedaka's absence. "I think the Rock & Roll Hall of Fame started out as a frame of mind," he said, "and I speak as a voter—not a nominator—from the beginning. There have always been arguments whether certain artists fit a type of music."

By way of explanation, Gambaccini pointed to the way radio works in the USA. A rock station won't play country or R&B, for example, and vice versa. In Britain, by contrast, pop radio stations have always played anything that's popular.

"Neil's indulgences remain unknown," Gambaccini continued. "By that I mean that Neil Sedaka does not present himself as a rock'n'roller. Consider that the Rock and Roll Hall of Fame was born out of the 60s. Neil is not a guy the public thinks of as living on the edge. He's not someone who has lived the sex and drugs and rock'n'roll lifestyle.

"Jerry Lee Lewis was inducted that first year, basically on the strength of one big hit, because he embodied the spirit of rebellion which rock'n'roll flatters itself into thinking it has to have. Sedaka's not in, in my estimation, because he doesn't fit their mold. No one doubts his popularity, but look how long it took Neil Diamond and Donna Summer to get in. No one doubts that these people were popular or great, but they didn't fit into the rock'n'roll stereotype. Neil Sedaka is almost pre-rock'n'roll."

That said, Gambaccini thinks there's still hope for Sedaka and others who don't "fit the mold" voters are looking for. "A challenge now faces the Rock and Roll Hall of Fame," he noted. "Just about everyone that fit that stereotype are now in, so they have to expand [their criteria]."

In the summer of 2012, I asked Seymour Stein, one of the Hall's four founding fathers, how it could be possible that Neil Sedaka had not yet been inducted. "I think it will eventually happen," he told me. "I think he has a better chance [to get in] as a songwriter. Two of Donnie Kirshner's three super songwriting teams have been inducted. Neil Sedaka and Howard Greenfield are up there with the best of them. I would certainly support their being inducted."

Stein then made an important point about Sedaka's early songs, like 'Calendar Girl,' which some might dismiss as bubblegum. "Back then, bubblegum *WAS* rock'n'roll," he said. "White rock'n'roll, but rock'n'roll."

Another of the founders of the Hall of Fame, Alan Grubman, pleaded no contest when I reached him by phone on the subject late in 2012. "I have enormous admiration for Neil and when I think of him it's very nostalgic for me," he said. "But my roll is on the business side of the Rock and Roll Hall of Fame as a lawyer. I have never had any involvement on the induction side. There's a formal process for getting into the Hall of Fame."

That process centers on a nominating committee. Once these powerful few nominators decide who is worthy of nomination, ballots go out to more than 500 music historians, journalists, executives, and musicians around the world to vote in the 'performer' category. Selections for the 'non-performer' and 'sideman' categories are made by a much smaller panel, which doesn't allow the overwhelming majority of voters to have a voice.

The fourth and final founding member of the Rock and Roll Hall of Fame, Jann Wenner, is perhaps the most influential. Several people I spoke with while researching this book—including one of the other founding members—told me that Wenner has the only vote that counts. I had heard that he wasn't a Neil Sedaka fan, and I wanted to verify it. I tried to reach him at his New York office to discuss Sedaka and the Hall of Fame, but he wasn't biting. Eventually, I got this response via email from his assistant, Ashley:

Hi Richard, (8-21-12)
Thank you for thinking of Jann, unfortunately he doesn't feel knowledgeable enough about Neil Sedaka to make a comment. He does however love 'Calendar Girl' and 'Oh Carol.'
All best, Ashley

There are, however, hundreds of thousands of fans who do feel Sedaka worthy of such an accolade. In fact, more than 15,000 of them have signed an online petition to have Sedaka inducted. When I mentioned this to Seymour Stein, he pointed out that supporters of The Moody Blues have assembled an even larger petition, and they are still not in the Hall of Fame.

One of the biggest supporters of Sedaka's induction is producer David Foster. "He was a victim of his own success—the dooby-doos and tra-la-las," he told me. "But thank god he had more in him and thank god he was able to expose it to the world and get it out there."

Paul Shaffer, who conducts the Hall of Fame band each year during the inductees' performances, is confident that Sedaka will get in eventually. "It's an honor that's long overdue," he said. Dion DiMucci, who was himself inducted in 1993, told me, "Neil's songs are a great legacy. He should be in the Hall of Fame."

Another who found it hard to believe that he still hadn't been inducted was Carole Bayer Sager. "I don't see why he's not in," she said. "There are a lot of people who should be in that aren't because they differentiate pop from rock." She pointed out that another deserving songwriter is her ex-husband Burt Bacharach, who wrote a string of pop hits as long as any.

Pop culture historian Laura Pinto felt that Sedaka's absence was a "puzzlement" that should be rectified sooner rather than later, "preferably during Mr Sedaka's lifetime," while entertainer Kathie Lee Gifford, a longtime friend and admirer, noted, "There isn't a person in the world who doesn't know a Neil Sedaka song. He deserves his place."

Neil's former bandmate Jay Siegel became very upset when I brought up the subject. "Neil is one of the greatest songwriters to come out of any generation," he said. "He should have been in the Hall of Fame years ago. Just look at the songs he's written. He's been one of the greatest musical influences of our lives. Everybody says it's very political. It can't have anything to do with talent. The man is still performing today doing 50, 60 shows a year. He's influenced so many artists and songwriters. How could he not be in the Hall of Fame? I can't figure it out."

For arranger and producer Artie Butler, Sedaka's continuing absence seemed nothing short of criminal. He had tried himself to rectify matters, he said, but "I can't send another email. They'll think I'm working for Neil. Do you have to have ten feet of hair and a nail sticking out of your nose to get in there? I don't get it. Not having Neil Sedaka in the Hall of Fame is like leaving George Washington off a list of US presidents."

In 2001, Fox News published a story criticizing the Rock and Roll Hall of Fame, quoting from an anonymous letter written by a journalist and former voter. In it, the author noted how artists were sometimes chosen "because of their affiliations with the directors of the hall," and how others were "shot down without so much as a moment of consideration simply because some people in that room didn't like them personally." The author went on to note how he had brought up the petition signed by thousands of Moody Blues fans at one such nomination meeting:

> I plunked it down on the conference table to a great roar of laughter from the assembled big shots ... On the other hand, I saw how Atlantic Records artists were routinely placed into nomination with no discussion at all, due to the large concentration of Atlantic executives on the committee. I saw how so-called critical favorites were placed into nomination, while artists that were massively popular in their time were brushed off. I saw how certain pioneering artists of the 50s and early 60s were shunned because there needed to be more name power on the list, resulting in 70s superstars getting in before the people who made it possible for them. Some of those pioneers still aren't in today ... I was finally kicked off the committee after writing a guest editorial for *Billboard* in which I criticized the Hall for its insider ways. Almost ten years later, nothing has changed."

Donna Summer is another great example of a performer who totally dominated her time and her genre, but who was overlooked year after year by the Hall and only inducted after her death in 2012, despite having recorded 13 top ten hits (including four number ones). Supporters of Bon Jovi, Chicago, Kiss, The E-Street Band, and The Guess Who all have their complaints.

In 2011, *Billboard* asked Kiss lead singer Gene Simmons if he'd accept an invitation to be inducted if one was tendered. "It's become a joke," he told them. "We've been thinking about it, and the answer is we'll just buy it and fire everybody."

What it all really comes down to is that the Rock and Roll Hall of Fame is a private club that has the right to include or exclude anyone it wishes to. Yes, it sounds a lot like a high school clique at times, but it's grown so big and important that it's time it became open to more diverse nominations. If there's room for rap there should be room for the pioneers like Sedaka and Connie Francis, who laid the groundwork for the stars of the last 40 years.

EPILOGUE

At least 40 years have passed since the majority of the events in this book took place. Time has been good to some of the main characters, unkind to others, and of course several have passed away. Here's a brief update on what happened next to the key players.

The last hit songs **Phil Cody** wrote with Neil Sedaka were 'Love In The Shadows' (1976) and 'Should've Never Let You Go' (1980). After writing together for almost a decade, he and Sedaka drifted apart when Cody moved to Southern California. While still with Don Kirshner in the 70s, he wrote the lyrics to ABBA's hit song 'Ring Ring,' and a few years later he wrote 'Doing It All For My Baby,' a number six hit for Huey Lewis & The News, taking inspiration from how he felt about his girlfriend of the time (and now wife), Barbara.

In recent years, Cody has turned his attention to teaching, which he loves. "The one thing that I keep trying to tell my students is that unless you are working to keep your ass fed and clothed and housed—unless you're writing with that goal in mind—you're not a writer," he told songfacts.com. "You learn how to do things when it's on the line, when having to eat is at stake."

Cody still performs his own music on occasion in the Los Angeles area, and he's started writing songs again—for his own voice, this time. "I don't want to stop," he said. "There's a lot to do. If nothing else, teaching has shown me how much can be done. As a songwriter,

I have material that I want to present if I'm lucky enough to find that niche audience that will listen to what I have to say. I have something important to impart as a songwriter, still. And that's what I'm going for. I don't know if I'll succeed. But I'm sure having a lot of fun trying to get there."[33]

Neil's lifelong pal **Freddie Gershon** is currently the CEO and chairman of Music International Theater (MTI). Since 1994, he has worked on the development of MTI's Broadway Junior program, designed to bring art, theater, dance, and music to children. He is also co-chairman of SECAC, a 75-year-old performing rights organization. He lives in New York City with his wife, Myrna.

At the time of writing, **Graham Gouldman** and his group 10cc have just completed a 30-city European tour—including a stop in Russia—to celebrate their 40th anniversary. He has also recently completed a trek to the ancient site of Machu Picchu in Peru to raise money for the Teenage Cancer Trust. And he's still writing music.

Connie Francis has performed on and off for the last few decades and was onstage at the Hilton Hotel in Las Vegas as late as 2011. Her hits like 'Who's Sorry Now,' 'Stupid Cupid,' and 'Lipstick On Your Collar' continue to sell, and she has recorded albums in nine different languages. She still regrets allowing her father to break off her love affair with Bobby Darin and regards not marrying Darin as "the biggest mistake I ever made."

Connie battled depression in the early 80s, and has since become an advocate for returning veterans suffering from the mental and emotional scars of battle. In recognition of this work, and in particular for her support for the South Florida State Psychiatric Hospital For Vets, she was named Woman of the Year by Broward County, Florida, in 2013.

Don Kirshner passed away unexpectedly from heart failure at the age of 76 in 2011. He posthumously attained his lifelong dream of being inducted into the Rock and Roll Hall of Fame in 2012. He and Sedaka patched up their differences and remained good friends until his death, with Don and his wife Sheila attending Neil's concerts every time he played in South Florida.

Howie Greenfield was one of the first Americans to die from AIDS in 1985. (For more, see the chapter devoted to his life and legacy, Saying Goodbye To Howie.)

Maurice Gibb of The Bee Gees, died unexpectedly from cardiac arrest at the age of 53 while waiting to have surgery for a twisted intestine in 2003. Neil, a close friend to the end, was left devastated by the news.

The Captain & Tennille continued to perform together well into the 21st century, although in recent years Daryl 'The Captain' Dragon has been slowed by a neurological condition. Toni Tennille still sounds as great as ever.

Mac Sedaka was a simple man with an easygoing attitude who died much too soon, after suffering with colon cancer, on June 6 1981. He was 68. Neil, Leba, Marc, and Dara were at his bedside at the end. Mac's wife **Eleanor** lived a comfortable life in South Florida before passing away in March 1992 aged 90.

Neil's sister, **Ronnie Sedaka Grossman** was 18 months older than her brother, who adored her, and with whom she was always close. She was a cheerleader at Abraham Lincoln High and went on to become a teacher before settling down to marry Edward Grossman. Among her students was Senator Chuck Schumer. She had two children, Gary and Barry, and five grandchildren. Sadly, she died in 1995, aged 57, after being diagnosed with pancreatic cancer.

"I remember [Edward] called me and said Ronnie had just six weeks to live," Neil recalled. "Exactly six weeks later, she was gone." Ronnie's granddaughter, Holly, 21, an aspiring actress, will play the part of her grandmother when the musical *Laughter In The Rain* opens on Broadway.

Nobody knows what happened to **Ben Sutter** after Neil told him his services as manager were no longer required. The music world stopped paying attention to him, and Eleanor Sedaka eventually broke off her relationship with him. Some have suggested that he moved to Las Vegas, but nobody I spoke to for this book knew for sure.

At the age of 66, **Sir Elton John** is still going strong. He recently completed a run of 241 performances behind his famous red piano at Caesar's Palace. A winner of countless awards for his music, he is also known for his charity work, notably with the Elton John AIDS Foundation, which has raised nearly $300 million since its formation. He was knighted Sir Elton Hercules John by Queen Elizabeth II for services to music and charitable services." As well as making numerous million-selling records, he is also the composer of the Broadway and West End shows *The Lion King*, *Aida*, and *Billy Elliot*. He was inducted into the Rock and Roll Hall of Fame in 1994, and we will always remember him for reuniting the USA with Neil Sedaka.

Neil and Leba Sedaka are still going strong. They celebrated their 50th wedding anniversary on September 11 2012. She is his rock, and they form an incredible team.

The future, it seems, holds more of everything for Neil Sedaka. In 2013, famed producer Bill Kenwright plans to mount a musical based on Neil's life and songs on London's West End entitled *Laughter In The Rain*. There are also other CDs and children's books in the works.

When I asked why he decided to take on some of his later projects, Neil was unequivocal. "I did everything I always wanted to do," he told me. "I didn't care about commercialism. I did a Yiddish album. I did a children's album. I did a classical album where I wrote lyrics to Puccini and Beethoven. I did original Christmas songs. I wanted to do things that were close to my heart."

About the Rock and Roll Hall of Fame, too, he is nothing if not positive. "It would be very nice, but it's out of our hands," he said. "I would like to live to see it—if not as a singer, then as a songwriter."

"There's one other thing I'd like," he told me.

"What's that?" I asked.

"Just one more number one song before I'm through."

THE TRA-LA DAYS
AN AFTERWORD BY PHILIP CODY

L ooking back, we were just two guys, having a good time writing songs. Like two kids playing games with a piano, Neil would play a line of melody and I'd respond with the appropriate words to match the mood and the meter. We'd finish a line and move on to the next, and so on and so on, until we had a complete song. I occasionally experienced a little bit of retroactive guilt that my work with Sedaka was so easy and so much fun—mostly because I wasn't an easy or fun person, back then.

I was a child of the 60s, an eyewitness to the assassination of heroes and to the ascendancy of tricky villains. I watched men of the American military establishment fire upon American college students and watched cops go on the rampage against their fellow citizens on the streets of Chicago. It was not a fun time for a whole lot of people, me included.

And then there was this Sedaka person, bursting through my office door and assaulting my consciousness, like a ray of polyester sunshine, looking like he'd just escaped from center court at some important tennis tournament. I honestly didn't know what to make of the guy. Of course, I knew who he was, but I wasn't particularly a fan of his music. So, I accepted his invitation to write songs together with more than a small dollop of skepticism.

You know, 99.999 percent of the time, a guy like me takes an impetuous leap from a curb in New York City and gets killed by a bus. Rarely, very rarely—almost never—is there a golden chariot waiting at the other end of that leap—and rarely, very rarely, does that golden chariot transport one to a land of wealth, fame, and happiness.

And so, in a fit of uncharacteristic impetuosity, I took the leap and found myself camped out at the right elbow of Neil Sedaka, who was sitting at a baby grand in the 28th-floor office of our mutual musical Godfather, Don Kirshner, looking down upon the ants marching along Sixth Avenue and Central Park South. It was the occasion of our first song together, immediately followed by another and, right after that, another. Oh, by the way, the three titles we just happened to knock off that afternoon were 'Trying To Say Goodbye,' 'Don't Let It Mess Your Mind,' and a little number called 'Solitaire.'

I had no idea, not a clue, as to what was to come, or how my life and circumstances would be changed beyond that afternoon. Sitting there, listening to Sedaka put my words and feelings to music, left me feeling elevated and embraced by an optimism I hadn't known I was capable of. No matter what else was going on in the world or in my life at the time, that optimism always managed to find me every time I sat down with Neil to write a song.

A year or so later, Neil and Howard Greenfield wrote a song called 'Our Last Song Together.' There was a line in that song that went something like "The tra-la days are over," and I remember thinking at the time that while there were still Neil Sedaka songs in circulation, the tra-la days would never be over. For me, personally, the tra-la days were just beginning.

Thank you, Neil!

PHILIP CODY, Los Angeles, March 2013

SELECT DISCOGRAPHY
All releases US unless otherwise noted.

SINGLES

Laura Lee / Snowtime
Released 1957
Decca

Ring-A-Rockin' / Fly, Don't Fly On Me
Released 1958
Guyden Records

Oh, Delilah! / Neil's Twist
Released 1958
Pyramid

The Diary / No Vacancy
Released 1958
RCA #14

I Go Ape / Moon Of Gold
Released 1959
RCA #42

Crying My Heart Out For You / You Gotta Learn Your Rhythm And Blues
Released 1959
RCA #111

Stupid Cupid / As Long As I Live
Released 1959
RCA (Italy)

All I Need Is You / Fallin'
Released 1959
RCA (Italy)

Oh! Carol / One Way Ticket (To The Blues)
Released 1959
RCA #9

The Girl For Me / I Ain't Hurtin' No More
Released 1959
RCA

Stairway To Heaven / Forty Winks Away
Released 1960
RCA #9

You Mean Everything To Me / Run Samson Run
Released 1960
RCA #17 / 28 (double A-side)

**Calendar Girl / The Same Old
Fool**
Released 1961
RCA #4

Little Devil / I Must Be Dreaming
Released 1961
RCA #11

**Sweet Little You / I Found My
World In You**
Released 1961
RCA #59

**Happy Birthday, Sweet Sixteen /
Don't Lead Me On**
Released 1961
RCA #6

King Of Clowns / Walk With Me
Released 1962
RCA #45

**Breaking Up Is Hard To Do / As
Long As I Live**
Released 1962
RCA #1

**Next Door To An Angel / I
Belong To You**
Released 1962
RCA #5

Alice In Wonderland / Circulate
Released 1963
RCA #17

**Let's Go Steady Again / Waiting
For Never**
Released 1963
RCA #26

**The Dreamer / Look Inside Your
Heart**
Released 1963
RCA #33

**Bad Girl / Wait 'Til You See My
Baby**
Released 1963
RCA

**The Closest Thing To Heaven /
Without A Song**
Released 1964
RCA #107

Sunny / She'll Never Be You
Released 1964
RCA #86

**I Hope He Breaks Your Heart /
Too Late**
Released 1964
RCA #104

**Let People Talk / In The Chapel
With You**
Released 1964
RCA #107

**The World Through A Tear /
   High On A Mountain (Deep
   In A Valley)**
Released 1965
RCA #76

**The Answer To My Prayer / Blue
   Boy**
Released 1965
RCA #89

**The Answer Lies Within /
   Grown-Up Games**
Released 1966
RCA

**We Can Make It If We Try / Too
   Late**
Released 1966
RCA #121

**Star-Crossed Lovers / We Had A
   Good Thing Goin'**
Released 1969
SGC (Australia #1)

Rainy Jane / Jeannine
Released 1969
SGC

Ebony Angel / Puppet Man
Released 1969
MCA (UK)

**Wheeling, West Virginia / The
   Love Of A Woman**
Released 1969
Festival (Australia #20)

**My World Keeps Getting Smaller
   Every Day / Everything Is
   Beautiful**
Released 1971
RCA (Australia)

**I'm A Song (Sing Me) / Silent
   Movies**
Released 1971
Kirshner / RCA

Superbird / Rosemary Blue
Released 1971
RCA (UK)

**Beautiful You / Anywhere You're
   Gonna Be (Leba's Song)**
Released 1972
Kirshner / RCA (UK #43)

**That's When The Music Takes Me
   / Don't Let It Mess Your Mind**
Released 1972
RCA (UK #27)

**Dimbo Man / Trying To Say
   Goodbye**
Released 1972
RCA (UK)

Standing On The Inside / Let Daddy Know
Released 1973
MGM (UK #26)

Our Last Song Together / I Don't Know What I Like About You
Released 1973
MGM (UK #31)

Love Will Keep Us Together / Rock'n'roll Wedding Day
Released 1973
Polydor (UK)

A Little Lovin' / Lightning Ridge
Released 1974
Polydor (UK)

Going Nowhere / Brighton
Released 1974
Polydor (UK)

Laughter In The Rain / Kiddio
Released 1974
Polydor (UK #14)

Laughter In The Rain / Endlessly
Released 1974
Rocket #1

That's When The Music Takes Me / Standing On The Inside
Released 1974
Rocket #27

The Immigrant / Your Favorite Entertainer
Released 1975
Polydor (UK)

The Immigrant / Hey Mister Sunshine
Released 1975
Rocket #22

The Queen Of 1964 / Solitaire (Live)
Released 1975
Polydor (UK)

Bad Blood / Your Favorite Entertainer
Released 1975
Rocket #1

Bad Blood / Hey Mister Sunshine
Released 1975
Polydor (UK)

New York City Blues / Baby Blue
Released 1975
Polydor (UK)

Breaking Up Is Hard To Do / Nana's Song
Released 1975
Rocket #8

**Breaking Up Is Hard To Do /
  Lonely Night (Angel Face)**
Released 1975
Polydor (UK)

**Love In The Shadows / Baby
  Don't Let It Mess Your Mind**
Released 1976
Rocket #16

**Love In The Shadows / Nana's
  Song**
Released 1976
Polydor (UK)

**Steppin' Out / I Let You Walk
  Away**
Released 1976
Rocket / Polydor #36

**No. 1 With A Heartache / Good
  Times, Good Music, Good
  Friends**
Released 1976
Polydor (UK)

**You Gotta Make Your Own
  Sunshine / Perfect Strangers**
Released 1976
Rocket / Polydor #52

Amarillo / The Leaving Game
Released 1977
Elektra / Polydor #44

Alone At Last / Sleazy Love
Released 1977
Elektra / Polydor #104

All You Need Is The Music
Released 1978
Elektra

**Sad, Sad Story / Love Keeps
  Getting Stronger Every Day**
Released 1978
Elektra / Polydor

**Letting Go / It's Good To Be
  Alive Again**
Released 1980
Elektra / Polydor #107

**Should've Never Let You Go
  (with Dara Sedaka) / You're So
  Good For Me**
Released 1980
Elektra / Polydor #19

**My World Keeps Slipping Away /
  Love Is Spreading Over The
  World**
Released 1981
Elektra / Polydor

Losing You / On The Road Again
Released 1981
Elektra / Polydor

You're Precious Love (with Dara Sedaka) / Searchin'
Released 1983
Curb / MCA

Rhythm Of The Rain / New Orleans
Released 1983
Curb / MCA

Love Made Me Feel That Way
Released 1985
Curb

ALBUMS

Neil Sedaka & The Tokens
Released 1958
Guest Star G-1448
I Love My Baby / Come Back Joe / Taste Of A Tear // While I Dream / Don't Go / Never Til Now

Neil Sedaka & The Tokens & Coins
Released 1958
Crown Records CST-641
While I Dream / Taste Of A Tear / Come Back Joe / Don't Take Me For Granted / Mary G // I Love My Baby / Never Til Now / Born To Be A Loser / Lay Some Kisses On Me / Run Don't Walk

Neil Sedaka (aka Rock With Sedaka)
Released 1959
RCA Victor LPM-2035

You're Knocking Me Out / The Diary / I Ain't Hurtin' No More / Stupid Cupid / All I Need Is You / I Waited Too Long // Fallin' / Another Sleepless Night / I Go Ape / I Belong To You / As Long As I Live / Moon Of Gold

Circulate
Released 1961
RCA Victor LSP-2317
Circulate / Smile / Nothing Ever Changes / All The Way / We Kiss In A Shadow / Bess You Is My Woman // Look To The Rainbow / Everything Happens To Me / Felicidade / I Found My World In You / You Took Advantage Of Me

Neil Sedaka Sings Little Devil & His Other Hits
Released 1961
RCA Victor LPM-2421
Little Devil / Oh! Carol / You Mean

Everything To Me / Run Samson Run / The Girl For Me / Stairway To Heaven // Calendar Girl / I Must Be Dreaming / Going Home To Mary Lou / The Diary / What Am I Gonna Do / One Way Ticket

Three Great Guys (with Paul Anka and Sam Cooke)
Released 1963
RCA Victor LPM-2720
Neil's songs: This Endless Night / Too Late // Without Your Love / Another Day, Another Heartache

Neil Sedaka En Español
Released 1964
RCA Victor MKL-1566
Mi Vecinita / Maria Elena / Alicia / Mi Dicha Lejana / Besame Otra Vez / Mas // Chica Mala / Divina Ilusion / Ire Por Ti / Creo Estar Soñando / El Reloj / El Soñador

Neil Sedaka: Italiano
Released 1964
RCA LSP-10140
I Tuoi Capricci / Quando Sorridi Cosi / La Terza Luna / Adesso No / Finche Vivro / Il Cielo Ti Ha Creata Per Me // Tu Non Lo Sai / Non Cercare Un'Altra Bocca / Il Re Dei Pagliacci / L'Ultimo Appuntamento / A 16 Anni Tu Vuoi Amare / Se C'e Un Paradiso

Workin' On A Groovy Thing
Released 1969
Festival SFL-933616
Puppet Man (Pull My String) / Johnny Walker / Ebony Angel / Wheeling, West Virginia / You With Darkness On Your Mind / The Love Of A Woman // Workin' On A Groovy Thing / The World I Threw Away / Don't Look Over Your Shoulder / Cellophane Disguise / The Girl I Left Behind / Summer Symphony

Oh! Carol—Neil Sedaka With Stan Applebaum & Orchestra
Released 1970
RCA International INTS-1131
Oh! Carol / Next Door To An Angel / King Of Clowns / Happy Birthday, Sweet Sixteen / Stairway To Heaven / Breaking Up Is Hard To Do // One Way Ticket / Calendar Girl / Little Devil / Sweet Little You / Run Samson Run / You Mean Everything To Me

Emergence
Released 1971
RCA APL1-1789
I'm A Song (Sing Me) / Gone With The Morning / Superbird / Silent Movies / Little Song / Cardboard California // One More Mountain To Climb/ God Bless Joanna / Is Anybody Gonna Miss You / What

Have They Done To The Moon /
Rosemary Blue / Wish I Was A
Carousel / I'm A Song (Reprise)

Solitaire
Released 1972
RCA AP1-1790
That's When The Music Takes Me /
Beautiful You / Express Yourself /
Anywhere You're Gonna Be
(Leba's Song) / Home / Adventures
Of A Boy Child Wonder // Better
Days Are Coming / Dimbo Man /
Trying To Say Goodbye / Solitaire /
Don't Let It Mess Your Mind

The Tra-La Days Are Over
Released 1973
MGM 2315-248
Little Brother / Standing On The
Inside / Alone In New York In The
Rain / Caribbean Rainbow / Let
Daddy Know / Suspicions // Love
Will Keep Us Together / The
Other Side Of Me / Rock'n'roll
Wedding Day / For Peace And
Love / Our Last Song Together

Laughter In The Rain
Released 1974
Polydor 2383-265
The Immigrant / A Little Lovin' / Sad
Eyes / Flame / Laughter In The
Rain / For The Good Of The
Cause // The Way I Am / Going

Nowhere / Love Ain't An Easy
Thing / Betty Grable / Endlessly

Sedaka's Back
Released 1974
Rocket Records MCA-463
Standing On The Inside / That's
Where The Music Takes Me /
Laughter In The Rain / Sad Eyes /
Solitaire / Little Brother // Love
Will Keep Us Together / The
Immigrant / The Way I Am / The
Other Side Of Me / A Little Lovin'
/ Our Last Song Together

Neil Sedaka Live At The Royal Festival Hall
Released 1974
Polydor 2383-299
I'm A Song (Sing Me) / The Other
Side Of Me / Solitaire / For The
Good Of The Cause / Laughter In
The Rain // Our Last Song Together
/ Medley / Going Nowhere / That's
When The Music Takes Me

Overnight Success
Released 1975
Polydor 2442-131
Crossroads / Lonely Nights / Stephen /
Bad Blood / Goodman Goodbye /
Baby Blue // The Queen Of 1964 /
New York City Blues / When You
Were Lovin' Me / The Hungry
Years / Breaking Up Is Hard To Do

The Hungry Years
Released 1976
Rocket Records PIG-2157
Crossroads / Lonely Nights (Angel Face) / Stephen / Bad Blood / Your Favorite Entertainer / Baby Blue // Tit For Tat / New York City Blues / When You Were Lovin' Me / The Hungry Years / Breaking Up Is Hard To Do

Steppin' Out
Released 1976
Rocket Records PIG-2195
Sing Me / You Gotta Make Your Own Sunshine / #1 With A Heartache / Steppin' Out / Love In The Shadows / Cardboard California // Here We Are Falling In Love Again / I Let You Walk Away / Good Times, Good Music, Good Friends / Perfect Strangers / Bad & Beautiful / Summer Nights

On Stage
Released 1976
RCA INTS-1486
Sugar Sugar / Everything Is Beautiful / Bridge Over Troubled Water— Danny Boy / Oh! Carol—Happy Birthday, Sweet Sixteen—Star Crossed Lovers—Little Devil— Breaking Up Is Hard To Do— Calendar Girl / The Father Of Girls / Polonaise In A-flat // Proud Mary / Bye Bye Blackbird—I Don't Know Why—I Can't Give You Anything But Love / My World Keeps Getting Smaller Every Day / Scapriciatiello / The History Of Rock & Roll (Medley)

Neil Sedaka & His Songs—A Solo Concert
Released 1977
Polydor 2LP 2672-036
Fantasie Impromptu / My Life's Devotion / I Waited Too Long / Stupid Cupid / Where The Boys Are / I Go Ape / The Diary / Oh! Carol / Stairway To Heaven / Run Samson Run / Calendar Girl / Happy Birthday, Sweet Sixteen / Next Door To An Angel / Breaking Up Is Hard To Do / Amarillo // One More Ride On The Merry-Go-Round / Gone With The Morning / Sing Me / Solitaire / Our Last Song Together / Love Will Keep Us Together / Laughter In The Rain // The Immigrant / Leba's Song / Standing On The Inside / The Hungry Years / The Queen Of 1964 / Stephen / Let Daddy Know // Superbird / Betty Grable / Brighton / The Other Side Of Me / Cardboard California / That's When The Music Takes Me / Breaking Up Is Hard To Do

251

A Song
Released 1977
Elektra 6E-102
Produced by George Martin
A Song / Never Done It Like That /
    The Leaving Game / Amarillo /
    Alone At Last / Hollywood Lady //
    I've Never Really Been In Love
    Before / One Night Stand / Hot &
    Sultry Nights / Sleazy Love / Tin
    Pan Alley / A Song (Reprise)

All You Need Is The Music
Released 1978
Elektra 6E-161
All You Need Is The Music / Candy
    Kisses / Should've Never Let Her
    Go / Sad, Sad Story / Tillie The
    Twirler // Love Keeps Getting
    Stronger / Born To Be Bad / What
    A Surprise / You Can Hear The
    Love / City Boy

In The Pocket
Released 1980
Elektra 6E-259
Do It Like You Done It When You
    Meant It / Junkie For Your Love /
    Letting Go / You Better Leave
    That Girl Alone / My Friend // It's
    Good To Be Alive Again / You /
    Should've Never Let You Go /
    You're So Good For Me / What A
    Difference A Day Makes

Neil Sedaka: Now
Released 1981
Elektra 6E-348
Losing You / What Have They Done
    To My Town / Pictures From The
    Past / Since You've Been Gone /
    On The Road Again //
    Summertime Madness / My World
    Keeps Slipping Away / Love Is
    Spreading Over The World / Bring
    Me Down Slow / The Big Parade

Come See About Me
Released 1984
MCA/Curb MCA-5466
Produced by Dan Hartman
Come See About Me/ Your Precious
    Love / Rhythm Of The Rain /
    Tears On My Pillow / It's All In
    The Game // New Orleans /
    Searchin' / Earth Angel / Cathy's
    Clown / Stagger Lee

The Good Times
Released 1986
Polygram Australia 826824-1
Love Made Me Feel This Way / Sweet
    Dreams Of You / Rosarita / The
    Hungry Years / Wonderful World
    Of Love // The Good Times / Let
    Me Walk With You Again / Paint
    Me Again / Tomorrow Never Came

Classically Sedaka
Released 1995
Vision VISMC-5
Prologue / A Moscow Night / Turning
 Back The Hands Of Time / The
 Keeper Of My Heart / Never-
 ending Serenade / Steel Blue Eyes
 / Santiago / I'm Always Chasing
 Rainbows / There Is A Place / Clair
 De Lune / I'll Sing You A Song /
 Honey Of My Life / As Gentle As
 A Summer's Day / Goodnight, My
 Love, Goodnight

Tales Of Love
Released 1998
Artful Records IN43
I'll Be Seeing You / Good Time Man /
 The Very Thought Of You / I Let
 You Walk Away / Alone At Last /
 Goodbye / You Go To My Head /
 Time Marches On / Inseparable /
 One More Ride / My Funny
 Valentine / Swept Away / Pray For
 Rain / I Found My World In You /
 Moonlight In Vermont / When
 You're Gone / Tied To Each Other
 / Turning Back The Hands Of
 Time

The Show Goes On
Released 2003
NSM S6CD01
When I'm Close To You / Shake A Hand
 / Laughter In The Rain / You / Been

There, Done That / Letters From
 The Road / Lovely Leba / Ship
 Without A Sail / Stuck In The Middle
 / I Feel In Love With A Dream /
 The Show Goes On / Solo Tu

Brighton Beach Memories—Neil
 Sedaka Sings Yiddish
Released 2003
NSM S6CD05
Vi Ahin Zol Ich Geyn / Shein Vi Di
 L'Vone / My Yiddishe Momme /
 Eishes Chayil / Bei Mir Bist Du
 Shein / Mein Shtetele Belz /
 Tumbalalaliko / Sunrise, Sunset /
 Ochichoniyo (Dark Eyes) / Exodus
 / Ich Hob Dich Tzufillieb /
 Anniversary Song / Tzena Tzena
 Tzena

The Miracle Of Christmas
Released 2005
NSM 2CD S6CD06
A Lonely Christmas In New York / A
 Christmas Prayer / A Christmas
 Miracle / Love Is Spreading Over
 The World / Baby's First Christmas
 Lullaby / Happy New Year Baby /
 Christmas Round The World /
 Razzle Dazzle Christmas / What A
 Lousy, Rotten Christmas /
 Christmas Time Is Not The Same /
 Without You / Where Is God? / A
 Christmas Melody // Let It Snow,
 Let It Snow, Let It Snow / Silent

253

Night / Winter Wonderland / O Holy Night / White Christmas / What Child Is This? / Have Yourself A Merry Little Christmas / The First Noel / The Christmas Song / O Come All Ye Faithful

Waking Up Is Hard To Do
Released 2009
Razor & Tie AM05
Waking Up Is Hard To Do / Dinosaur Pet / Where The Toys Are / Lunch Will Keep Us Together / Happy Birthday, Number Three / Laughter In The Rain / Rubber Duckie / Is This The Way To Cross The Street / Little Devil / I Go Ape / Baby's First Christmas Lullaby

The Music Of My Life
Released 2010
Razor & Tie
Do You Remember??/ A Fool In Love?/ Living In A Fantasy?/ Right Or

Wrong?/ I Got To Believe In Me Again?/ The Music Of My Life?/ I Keep Searching?/ Waiting?/ Won't You Share This Dream Of Mine?/ How Can I Change Your Mind?/ Bringing Me Back To Life?/ You

The Real Neil
Released 2012
Music Infinity (UK) / NSM S6CD11
Produced by Neil Sedaka & Robert Cotto
Intro / Beginning To Breathe Again / You'll Be There / You / Breaking Up Is Hard To Do / Laughter In The Rain / Amarillo / Broken Street Of Dreams / Heart Of Stone / It's Hard To Say Goodbye / Queen Of Hearts / Everybody Knows / Captured By Your Love / Runaway Lover / Mi Amor / Sweet Music / Manhattan Intermezzo

COMPILATIONS

The Neil Sedaka Collection
Released 1974
RCA International PJL2-8011

24 Rock'n'roll Hits
Released 1975
RCA Starcall HY-1005

Oh! Carol & Other Big Hits
Released 1975
RCA ANL1-0879

Neil Sedaka Sings His Greatest Hits
Released 1975
RCA APL1-0928

Neil Sedaka Original Hits
Released 1976
RCA 2LP DPL2-0149

Let's Go Steady Again
Released 1976
RCA Camden CDS-1151

Stupid Cupid
Released 1976
RCA Camden CDS-1147

*Breaking Up Is Hard To Do (The
    Original Hit)*
Released 1976
Pickwick ACL-7006

Pure Gold
Released 1976
RCA ANL1-1314

*Laughter & Tears: The Best Of
    Neil Sedaka*
Released 1976
Polydor 2383-399

Neil Sedaka's Greatest Hits
Released 1977
Rocket Records PIG-2297

Sedaka: The 50s & The 60s
Released 1977
RCA APL1-2254(E)

Sounds Of Sedaka
Released 1977
MCA MCF-2780

The Many Sides Of Neil Sedaka
Released 1978
RCA AFL1-2524

The Best Of Neil Sedaka
Released 1983
Polydor 2383-660

*My Friend (Dedicated To The
    Memory Of Howard Greenfield)*
Released 1986
Polydor 831-235-Y-2

*Timeless—The Very Best Of Neil
    Sedaka*
Released 1991
Polygram TV-511-442-2

*Neil Sedaka: Love Will Keep Us
    Together*
Released 1993
Polygram TV-517 351-2

Neil Sedaka Anthology
Released 1999
BMG Australia 2CD

The Very Best Of Neil Sedaka
Released 1999
Universal Music UK 2CD

Neil Sedaka Sings The Hits
Released 1999
BMG 2CD

The Definitive Collection
Released 2007
Razor & Tie

Tune Weaver (Classic Hits &
Hidden Gems Revisited)
Released 2002
Sanctuary Records 2CD SELCD621

Laughter In The Rain
Released 2010
Universal Music UK

The Very Best Of Neil Sedaka: The
Show Goes On
Released 2005
Universal Music UK 2CD 9837951

SELECT LIVE APPEARANCES, 1958-78

What follows is not a comprehensive list of concert performances by Neil Sedaka—that would require a book in itself—but is indicative of the places he performed during the first three decades of his career.

1958	Esther Manor, the Catskills, NY
1958	Smart Spot, Haddonfield, NJ
1959	Three Rivers Inn, Syracuse, NY
1959	Tour of Brazil
1960	Holiday House, Pittsburgh, PA
1960	Palumbo's, Philadelphia, PA
1961	Blinstrub's, Boston, MA
1961	Paramount Theater, Brooklyn, NY
1962	Eden Roc, Miami Beach, FL
1962	Copacabana, New York, NY

1963	Tours of Argentina and Italy
1963	Le Barrel Ouitre, Quebec, Canada
1963	Fairmont Hotel, Downtown Las Vegas, NV
1963–66	Grossinger's, the Catskills, NY (various dates)
1963–66	Concord, the Catskills, NY (various dates)
1963–66	Stevensville Hotel, the Catskills, NY (various dates)
1963–66	Shady Nook Hotel, the Catskills, NY (various dates)
1963–66	Nevele Grand Hotel, the Catskills, NY (various dates)
1963–66	Homowack Lodge, the Catskills, NY (various dates)
1963–66	Raleigh Hotel, the Catskills, NY (various dates)
1963–66	Lillian Lodge, the Catskills, NY (various dates)
1963–66	Esther Manor, the Catskills, NY (various dates)
1967	Six-week tour of workingmen's clubs in Australia
1971	Bitter End, New York, NY
1971	Quiet Nights, Chicago, IL
1971	Marvelous Marv's, Denver, CO
1972–73	Fiesta Club, Sheffield, England (various dates)
1972–73	Wooky Hollow, Liverpool, England (various dates)
1972–73	Golden Garter, Manchester, England (various dates)
1972–73	Batley Variety Club, Leeds, England (various dates)
1972–73	Cutlery, Sheffield, England (various dates)
1973	Royal Albert Hall, London, England
1974	Royal Festival Hall, London, England
1974	Palladium, London, England
1974	Talk of the Town, London, England
1975	Oakdale Music Theatre, Wallingford, CT (opening for the Carpenters)
1975	Garden State Arts Center, Holmdel, NJ (opening for the Carpenters)
1975	Pine Nob Music Theater, Detroit, MI (opening for the Carpenters)

1975	Ravinia Music Festival, Highland Park, IL (opening for the Carpenters)
1975	Riviera Hotel, Las Vegas, NV (opening for the Carpenters)
1975	Riviera Hotel, Las Vegas, NV (first time headlining on the Strip)
1976	Lincoln Center, New York, NY
1976	Edmonton Symphony, Edmonton, Canada
1976	UK tour
1976	Summer tour of the USA
1976	Universal Amphitheater, Los Angeles, CA
1976–78	Riviera Hotel, Las Vegas, NV (various dates)
1976–78	Harrah's, Reno, NV (various dates)
1976–78	Harrah's, Lake Tahoe, NV (various dates)

TV SHOWS

1958–62	*American Bandstand*, Philadelphia, PA (various appearances)
1961	*The Ed Sullivan Show*, New York, NY
1973	*Top Of The Pops*, London, England
1975	*The Tonight Show With Johnny Carson*, Burbank, CA
1975	*Dinah!*, Los Angeles, CA
1976	*The Merv Griffin Show*, Los Angeles, CA
1976	*The Mike Douglas Show*, Philadelphia, PA
1976	*The Sonny & Cher Comedy Hour*, Los Angeles, CA
1976	*The Tony Orlando & Dawn Show*, Los Angeles, CA
1976	*Midnight Special*, New York, NY

ENDNOTES

1 Jeff Marcus, *Goldmine*, February 15 2012

2 Myrna Katz Frommer and Harvey Frommer, *It Happened In The Catskills*

3 Myrna Katz Frommer and Harvey Frommer, *It Happened In The Catskills*

4 Neil Sedaka, *Laughter In The Rain*

5 Michael Turner, *Appreciating Neil Sedaka*

6 Joe Smith, *Off The Record*

7 Paul Baratta, *Songwriter Magazine*, November 1976

8 Neil Sedaka, *Laughter In The Rain*

9 wythenshawe.btck.co.uk/ GoldenGarterNightclub

10 Michael Turner, *Appreciating Neil Sedaka*

11 Paul Gambaccini, interview for *The Very Best Of Neil Sedaka: The Show Goes On* (Universal 2006)

12 Simon Barber and Brian O'Connor, sodajerker.com podcast episode 25, October 2012

13 Simon Barber and Brian O'Connor, sodajerker.com podcast episode 25, October 2012

14 Neil Sedaka, *Laughter In The Rain*

15 Neil Sedaka, *Laughter In The Rain*

16 Ken Barnes, *Rolling Stone*, January 2 1975

17 allmusic.com

18 Stephen Holden, *Rolling Stone*, November 20 1975

19 Tom Nolan, *Rolling Stone*, December 1975

20 Tom Nolan, *Rolling Stone*, December 1975

21 Neil Sedaka, *Laughter In The Rain*

22 *Elton John: The Story Of Pop Special* (Phoebus Publishing 1975)

23 Neil Sedaka, *Laughter In The Rain*

24 Rich Podolsky, *Don Kirshner*

25 Don Charles Hampton, popculturecantina.blogspot.com, July 27 2006

26 Neil Sedaka, liner notes to *My Friend* (PolyGram 1986)

27 Mary Elizabeth Williams, salon.com, September 2 2012

28 Simon Barber and Brian O'Connor, sodajerker.com podcast episode 25, October 2012

29 Philip Norman, *Sunday Times*, October 7 2012

30 Neil Sedaka, liner notes to *The Real Neil* (Music Infinity 2012)

31 Kieron Tyler, theartsdesk.com, October 1 2012

32 Simon Barber and Brian O'Connor, sodajerker.com podcast episode 25, October 2012

33 Philip Norman, *Sunday Times*, October 7 2012

34 Carl Wiser, songfacts.com, September 13 2011

BIBLIOGRAPHY & SOURCES

Unless otherwise stated, all quoted material is from the author's own interviews.

BOOKS
Francis, Connie *Who's Sorry Now?* (St Martin Press, 1984)
Frommer, Myrna Katz, and Harvey Frommer, *It Happened In The Catskills: An Oral History In The Words Of Busboys, Bellhops, Guests, Proprietors, Comedians, Agents, And Others Who Lived It* (Mariner Books, 1996)
Podolsky, Rich, *Don Kirshner: The Man With The Golden Ear* (Hal Leonard, 2012)
Sedaka, Neil *Laughter In The Rain—My Own Story* (Putnam, 1982)
Smith, Joe *Off The Record: An Oral History of Pop Music* (Warner Books, 1988)
Turner, Michael *Appreciating Neil Sedaka* (College Press, 2012)
Whitburn, Joel *Joel Whitburn's Top Pop Singles, 1955–2002* (Record Research, 2003)

ARTICLES
Baratta, Paul, 'Neil Sedaka, Home At Last' *Songwriter Magazine*, November 1976
Frazier, Jenni, 'Neil Sedaka: The Kosher Carol Singer' *The Jewish Chronicle*, March 23 2006
Marcus, Jeff, 'A Tale of Two Idols: Fabian and Neil Sedaka' *Goldmine*, February 15 2012
Nolan, Tom, 'Neil Sedaka: Second Stairway To Heaven' *Rolling Stone*, December 1975
Sager, Jeanne, 'Neil Sedaka Never Forgot His Roots' *Sullivan County Democrat*, February 14 2006
Wiser, Carl, Philip Cody Interview, songfacts.com, September 13 2011

LYRIC PERMISSIONS
'Star-Crossed Lovers'
Words and Music by Neil Sedaka and Howard Greenfield
Copyright (c) 1968 (Renewed 1996) SCREEN GEMS-EMI MUSIC INC.
All Rights Reserved International Copyright Secured Used by Permission
Reprinted by Permission of Hal Leonard Corporation

'Solitaire'
Words and Music by Neil Sedaka and Phil Cody
(c) 1972 (Renewed 2000) EMI SOSAHA MUSIC INC., EMI JEMAXAL MUSIC
INC., SONGS OF SJLRSL MUSIC CO., SJL-RSL SONGS COMPANY and
SONY/ATV MUSIC PUBLISHING LLC All Rights on behalf of SONY/ATV
MUSIC PUBLISHING LLC Administered by SONY/ATV MUSIC
PUBLISHING LLC, 8 Music Square West, Nashville, TN 37203 All Rights
Reserved International Copyright Secured Used by Permission
Reprinted by Permission of Hal Leonard Corporation

'That's When The Music Takes Me'
Words and Music by Neil Sedaka
(c) 1972 (Renewed 2000) EMI SOSAHA MUSIC INC., SONGS OF SJL-RSL
MUSIC CO. and SONY/ATV MUSIC PUBLISHING LLC
All Rights on behalf of SONY/ATV MUSIC PUBLISHING LLC Administered
by SONY/ATV MUSIC PUBLISHING LLC, 8 Music Square West, Nashville, TN
37203
All Rights Reserved International Copyright Secured Used by Permission
Reprinted by Permission of Hal Leonard Corporation

'The Hungry Years'
Words and Music by Neil Sedaka and Howard Greenfield
(c) 1974 (Renewed 2002) EMI SOSAHA MUSIC INC., SONGS OF SJL-RSL
MUSIC CO. and UNIVERSAL MUSIC - CAREERS
All Rights Reserved International Copyright Secured Used by Permission
Reprinted by Permission of Hal Leonard Corporation

'Standing On The Inside'
Words and Music by Neil Sedaka
(c) 1973 (Renewed 2001) EMI SOSAHA MUSIC INC. and SONGS OF SJL-RSL
MUSIC COMPANY All Rights Reserved International Copyright Secured Used
by Permission
Reprinted by Permission of Hal Leonard Corporation

'Laughter In The Rain'
Words and Music by Neil Sedaka and Phil Cody
© 1974, 1975 (Renewed 2002, 2003) EMI SOSAHA MUSIC INC., EMI
JEMAXAL MUSIC INC., SONGS OF SJL-RSL MUSIC CO., SJL-RSL SONGS
COMPANY and SONY/ATV MUSIC PUBLISHING LLC All Rights on behalf of
SONY/ATV MUSIC PUBLISHING LLC Administered by SONY/ATV MUSIC
PUBLISHING LLC, 8 Music Square West, Nashville, TN 37203 All Rights
Reserved International Copyright Secured Used by Permission Reprinted by
Permission of Hal Leonard Corporation

'Breaking Up Is Hard To Do'
Words and Music by Howard Greenfield and Neil Sedaka
© 1962 (Renewed 1990) SCREEN GEMS-EMI MUSIC INC. and UNIVERSAL
MUSIC – CAREERS All Rights Reserved International Copyright Secured Used
by Permission
Reprinted by Permission of Hal Leonard Corporation

'Calendar Girl'
Words and Music by Howard Greenfield and Neil Sedaka
© 1961 (Renewed 1989) SCREEN GEMS-EMI MUSIC INC. and UNIVERSAL
MUSIC – CAREERS All Rights Reserved International Copyright Secured Used
by Permission
Reprinted by Permission of Hal Leonard Corporation

'Our Last Song Together'
Words and Music by Neil Sedaka and Howard Greenfield
© 1973 (Renewed 2001) EMI SOSAHA MUSIC INC., SONGS OF SJL-RSL
MUSIC CO. and UNIVERSAL MUSIC – CAREERS All Rights Reserved
International Copyright Secured Used by Permission Reprinted by Permission
of Hal Leonard Corporation

INDEX

Unless otherwise noted, words in *italics* are albums; words in 'quotes' are songs. Numbers in **bold** refer to illustrations.

ABBA, 236
Abbott, George, 59, 60
Academy Awards, 95
Adler, Lou, 39, 71
Aiken, Clay, 97, 201, 202, 203–4, 205, 210
Aldon Music (publisher), 24–5, 45, 51, 70–1, 216
All You Need Is The Music, 189
Allen, Peter, 62
Allen, Woody, 75, 194
'Alice In Wonderland,' 40, 44
'Alone At Last,' 218
Alpert, Herb, 148, 179
A&M Records (label), 148, 166, 167, 168, 179
American Bandstand (TV show), 11, 34, 107
American Idol (TV show), 97, 201–5, 213
American Top 40 (radio show), 162–3
Animals, The, 64, 160
Anka, Paul, 17, 32, 165, 214
Appere, Robert, 148–9, 152, 153, 154, 162, 165, 171, 175, 176
Armstrong, Louis, 150
Ashburn, Richie, 10
Asher, Dick, 197–8
'At The Hop,' 49
Atkins, Roger, 64, 88
Atlantic Records (label), 24, 228, 229, 234
Avalon, Frankie, 17, 32
Average White Band, The, 149

Bacharach, Burt, 62, 63, 179, 212, 216, 233
'Baby Don't Go,' 108
'Bad Blood,' 13, 15, 107, 163, 170–1, 185, 186, 188, 203, 208

'Bad Girl,' 40
Baker, Laverne, 228
Barbis, John, 126
Barnes, Ken, 164–5
Barry, Jeff, 150
Bass, David, 28, **131**
Batley Variety Club, 85, 86, 87, 98
Bayer, Carole, *see* Sager, Carole Bayer
Beach Boys, The, 168
Beatles, The, 8, 17, 18, 39, 40, 41–4, 47, 67, 68, 72, 117, 165, 174, 18, 194
'Beautiful You,' 116–17, 122
Bee Gees, The, 55, 84, 97, 98, 211, 238
Bee, Molly, 51
'Beginning To Breathe Again,' 226
Bennett, Rony, 49
Berlin, Irving, 226
Bewitched (TV show), 195
Bitter End (club), 74–6
Block, Martin, 49
BNB, 178, 185
Bono, Sonny, 108
Braxton, Toni, 153
'Breaking Up Is Hard To Do,' 8, 12, 13, 26, 34, 76, 107, 153, 172–5, 176, 177, 194, 201, 203, 206, 210, 211, 212, 215, 216, 218, 219, 224
Brighton Beach Memoirs (play), 19
Brighton Beach Memoirs. Neil Sedaka Sings Yiddish, 219
Brill Building, 7, 25, 72, 89, 150, 151, 226
British Invasion, 12, 17
'Broken Street Of Dreams,' 225
Bronson, Fred, 215
Brown, James, 171
Browne, Jackson, 149
Burnely, Annette, 86
Burnely, Jimmy, 86
Burnett, Jonny, 35
Butler, Artie, 111, 150, 152, 155, 182, 184, 233
'Buttons And Bows,' 21

'Calendar Girl,' 7, 12, 16, 26, 39, 76, 85, 100, 107, 194, 205, 206–7, 210, 220, 227, 231, 232

Campbell, Glen, 181
'Candle In The Wind,' 127
Cantor, Eddie, 67
Captain & Tennille, The, 13, **143**, 166–9, 193, 205, 208, 210, 213, 238
'Cardboard California,' 73, 74, 128, 223
Carpenter, Karen, 178, 182, 183
Carpenter, Richard, 178, 181, 182, 183
Carpenters, the, 95, 97, 128, 148, 176, 178–84
Carr, Alan, 182
Carson, Johnny, 162
Caruso, Enrico, 92
Cash, Johnny, 209
Cassidy, David, 176
Cassotto, Walden Robert, 89
Charles, Dick, 45–6, 151
Charles, Ray, 35, 172, 220
Chase, Chevy, 185
Cher, 108
Chicago Cubs, 10
Chopin, Frédéric, 39, 216, 222, 227
Christie, Tony, 193, 210
Chubby Checker, 35
Churchill, Winston, 209
Cincotti, Peter, 219
Clanton, Jimmy, 193
Clapton, Eric, 55
Clark, Dick, **141**, 181
Cliburn, Van, 174
Clooney, Rosemary, 49, 175, 210, 218
Coasters, The, 35, 228
Cocker, Joe, 148, 150
Cody, Phil, 88–96, 103, 106, 107, 111, 114, 116, 118, 119, 120, 121, 122, **141**, 148, 155, 165, 166, 170, 176, 189, 191, 203, 212, 214, 215–16, 217, 236, 241–2
Cohen, Kip, 167, 168, 213
Colby, Paul, 74–5, 76
Cole, Clay, 35
Cole, Nat 'King,' 190
Cole, Natalie, 153, 190, 205, 206
Columbia Screen Gems, 40, 48, 61, 62, 63, 89, 195
Concord Hotel, 30, 32, 33, 61
Cookies, The, 172

Copacabana, 14, 35, 37, 38, 51, 61, 81, 83, 179
Corrigan, James and Betty, 86
Cosby, Bill, 75
Cosby, Bob, & The Bobcats, 167
Cowell, Simon, 203
Creatore, Luigi, 46
Creme, Lol, 113
Croce, Jim, 178
'Crocodile Rock,' 118
Crosby Stills & Nash, 149
Cross, Christopher, 62
'Crying In The Chapel,' 17
'Crying In The Rain,' 45, 195
Crystals, The, 47, 94
Curb, Carol, 123
Curb, Mike, 122–3, 124

Damon, Tory, 46, 106, 110, 195, 197
Danny & The Juniors, 49
Darin, Bobby, 35, 37, 40, 53, 89, 110, 214, 237
Dave Clark Five, 117
David, Hal, 179
Davis Jr, Billy, 64, 65, 213
Davis, Clive, 96–7, 211
De Mille, Agnes, 59, 60
Diamond, Neil, 62, 73–4, 123, 150, 162, 210, 230
Diamonds, The, 94, 107
'Diary, The,' 11, 12, 15, 25, 26, 32, 34, 50, 107, 195, 208
Diddley, Bo, 35, 36
DiMucci, Dion, 32, 35, 205, 214, 232
Dinosaur Pet, 220–1, 222
Dion *see* DiMucci, Dion
Dion, Celine, 153
Doerge, Craig, 149
'Doing It All For My Baby,' 236
Domino, Fats, 66, 228
Don Kirshner: The Man With The Golden Ear (book), 12–13, 15, 72
Don Kirshner's Rock Concert, 161
'Donna,' 114–15
'Don't Let It Mess Your Mind,' 92, 103, 114, 242
Douglas, Mike, 162
Dragon, Daryl, **142**, **143**, 166, 167, 168, 169, 238

'Dreamer, The,' 40
Drifters, The, 35, 84
Dudgeon, Gus, 146, 155
Dylan, Bob, 75

Earth Wind & Fire, 149
Ed Sullivan Show, The (TV show), 34, 39, 40, 42–3, 44, 174
Edwards, Tommy, 11
Eisenhower, Dwight, 192, 209
Elegants, The, 11
Elektra Records (label), 189, 200
'Embraceable You,' 83
Emergence, 74, 76, 78, 88, 90, 101, 117, 128, 222, 223
End Records (label), 25
Epstein, Brian, 41–3
Ertegun, Ahmet, 228, 229
Estefan, Gloria, 176
Esther Manor, 28–9, 31, 33, 49, 65
Everly Brothers, The, 11, 40, 45, 107, 193, 195, 228
'Everybody Knows,' 224
'Everybody's Somebody's Fool,' 45

Fabares, Shelley, 176
Feliciano, Jose, 90
Feliciotto, Philip, *see* Cody, Phil
Fifth Dimension, The, 64, 65, 88, 210, 213
'First Time Ever I Saw Your Face, The,' 93
Fitzgerald, Ella, 167, 175
Flack, Roberta, 93
Ford, Mary, 174
Foster, David, 153–5, 162, 171, 172–3, 205, 208, 211, 232
Foster, Stephen, 215, 218
Four Seasons, The, 176
Fox, Dick, 74, 79, 81, 182
Francis, Connie, 12, 17, 24, 25, 31, 37, 40, 45, 49–50, 53, 71, 110, **134**, 193, 195, 196, 205, 206, 208, 214, 235, 237
Franklin, Aretha, 159, 191
Freed, Alan, 23, 35
Fremont Hotel & Casino, 50–1
'Foolish Little Girl,' 45, 195
Funicello, Annette, 32, 214

Gambaccini, Paul, 110, 146, 177, 194, 216, 230
Georgy Girl (musical), 88
Gerard, Donny, 149
Gershon, Freddie, 20, 21, 54, 55–7, 99, 128, 145, 146, 158, 182, 190, 237
Gershwin, George, 91, 215, 217, 226
Gershwin, Ira, 218
Gibb, Andy, **142**
Gibb, Barry, 65, 172, 211
Gibb, Maurice, 65, 84, 97–8, 100, **142**, 187, 238
Gidget (TV show), 195
Goday, Happy, 24
Godley, Kevin, 113
Goffin, Gerry, 46, 62, 71, 89, 150, 229
Gold, Wally, 91, 94
Golden Garter (club), 84, 98, 113
Goldner, George, 25, 47
Gouldman, Graham, 82, 113, 114, 237
Gracin, Josh, 203
Greenfield, Ella, 22–3
Greenfield, Howard 'Howie,' 11, 22, 24–5, 44, 45, 64, 67, 69, 71, 73, 88, 89–90, 91, 100, 106, 107–8, 109, 110, 111–12, 119, **134**, **138**, 150, 155, 166, 167, 175, 176, 193, 194, 195–8, 210, 214, 217, 220, 224, 229, 231, 238, 242
Griffin, Merv, 162
'Groovy Kind Of Love,' 46, 61–2, 64, 69, 88, 148, 213
Grossinger's, 30, 61
Grubman, Alan, 228, 231
Guettel, Mary Rodgers, *see* Rodgers, Mary

Hammerstein, Oscar, 77–8
Haness, Abigail, 149, 162
'Happy Birthday, Sweet Sixteen,' 7, 16, 26, 85, 107, 163, 172, 194, 202, 208
Harrison, George, 41, 44
Harrison, Rex, 128
Hart, Lorenz, 77, 193–4, 218
'Heart Of Stone,' 225, 226
'Hello Mary Lou,' 47

'He's A Rebel,' 47
Hitchcock, Alfred, 103
Holden, Stephen, 176
Holdridge, Lee, 73, 74, 76, 219,
    222–3
Hollies, The, 84, 117
Holly, Buddy, 209, 228
Hope, Bob, 21
Hot Legs, 113
Howe, Bones, 64
Huey Lewis & The News, 236
Hugo & Luigi, 46
'Hungry Years, The,' 15, 107,
    109–11, 177, 194, 196, 208,
    218
Hungry Years, The, 176–7
Hyland, Brian, 35

'I Go Ape,' 85, 212
'I Got You Babe,' 108
'I Saw Mommy Kissing Santa
    Claus,' 51
'I Want To Hold Your Hand,' 43,
    117
'I'm A Song (Sing Me),' 73, 128
'I'm Not In Love,' 113
'Immigrant, The,' 13, 158, 165–7,
    175
'Is This The Way To Amarillo,' 113,
    210
'It Hurts To Be In Love,' 45, 47,
    101, 117, 195
'It's Too Late,' 71, 73

Joel, Billy, 122, 227
John, Elton, 7–9, 16, 18, 98–9,
    118, 125–7, 128, **140**, **141**,
    143, 145, 146–7, 152, 155,
    157–9, 161–2, 164, 171, 172,
    176, 179, 185, 186, 188, 192,
    194, 199–200, 205, 206–8,
    214, 229, 239
Joie De Vivre, 219
Jones, Tom, 64, 66, 113, 176,
    181, 193, 210

Kaplan, Artie, 51, 172, 195
Kasem, Casey, 162–3
Keller, Jack, 45, 71, 195–6
Kennedy, John F., 43
Kenwright, Bill, 239
King, Carole, 13, 14, 16, 23–4, 45,

62, 71–2, 73, 107, 126, **131**,
    176, 195, 210, 229
King, Jonathan, 114–15
Kingston Trio, The, 11
Kirshner, 13, 24–5, 33, 37, 39, 40,
    42, 45, 47, 48, 51, 61, 62, 63,
    64, 70, 71, 73, 89–90, 92, 94,
    101, 110, 113, 114, 115, 116,
    122–3, **131**, 161–2, 194, 195,
    197, 229, 231, 236, 238, 242
Kiss, 234–5
Kitchen, Gary, 81, 85
Klein, Carol, *see* King, Carole
Knight, Gladys, 150
Koppelman, Charles, 69–70
Kortchmar, Danny, 149
Kunkel, Russ, 149, 162

*Late Show With David Letterman,
    The* (TV show), 173
Laughing Sandwich, 90
'Laughter In The Rain,' 8, 12–13,
    15, 18, 120–2, 146, 147, 148,
    149, 152, 153, 154–6, 157,
    158, 159, 160, 161–2, 163,
    164, 165, 170, 171, 178, 185,
    186, 191, 206, 207–8, 210,
    211, 212, 215, 224
Laughter In The Rain (album), 157,
    162, 171
Laughter In The Rain (book), 14,
    32–3, 125–6, 200
Laughter In The Rain (musical),
    237
Lawrence, Vicki, 150
Lee, Brenda, 35, 193
Lee, Peggy, 49
Leiber, Jerry, 150, 151
Lennon, John, 98, 165–6
'Let's Go Steady Again,' 40
Levy, Morris, 57
Lewis, Jerry Lee, 26, 226, 228,
    230
Lightfoot, Gordon, 107
Linc-Tones, The, 23–4, 91, **130**,
    212
'Lion Sleeps Tonight, The,' 23, 46
'Lipstick On Your Collar,' 237
Listberg, Harvey, 113
Little Anthony & The Imperials, 25,
    35, 88
'Little Brother,' 119, 158, 165

'Little Darlin','. 94, 107
'Little Devil,' 26, 194, 202
Little Eva, 176
'Little Lovin', A,' 146, 165
Little Richard, 26, 228
Lloyd Price, 107
Locke, Kimberley, 203
'Locomotion, The,' 46
Loesser, Frank, 226
'Lonely Night (Angel Face),' 169,
    208
'Love Will Keep us Together,' 13,
    113, 119, 120, 128, 158, 163,
    166–7, 168–9, 185, 186, 194,
    196, 197, 203, 205, 210, 213,
    220
Lucy In The Sky, 146
Lulu, 84, 98
'Lunch Will Keep Us Together,'
    220
Lythgoe, Nigel, 201–2, 213

'MacArthur Park,' 74
Macey, Charlie, 172
Madame Tussauds, 200
Maitland, Mike, 160
Make Believe Ballroom (radio
    show), 23, 49
Man Who Knew Too Much, The
    (film), 103
'Man Who Shot Liberty Valance,
    The' 47
Manchester, Melissa, 62
Mancini, Henry, 95
Manhattan Intermezzo, 222–3,
    224
Manilow, Barry, 205
Mann, Barry, 64, 71, 94, 160
Margo, Mitch, 90
Margo, Phil, 90
Martin, George, 42
McCartney, Paul, 13, 127, 128,
    155, 216
McCoo, Marilyn, 64, 65, 213
McDermott, Paul, 82, 84
Medress, Hank, 23–4, **130**
Melba Records (label), 24, 73
Mercer, Johnny, 95, 226
Merchant, Larry, 10
Merriewold Park, 59, 60, 77, 79,
    100, 118, 120, 160, 186, 220
MGM Records (label), 122–3

Midnight Special, The (TV show), 164
Mike Douglas Show, The (TV show), 191
Miller, Helen, 45, 195
Monkees, The, 18, 61, 63–4, 89
Moody Blues, 234
'Moon River,' 95
More Of The Monkees, 63
Morrow, Bruce 'Cousin Brucie,' 35, 59, 67, 163, 205, 220
Moses, Mary, 66, 80
Most, Mickey, 64
'Moving Out,' 122
Murray, Jan, 37, 179
My Friend, 197–8
'My Heart Has A Mind Of Its Own,' 45, 195
'My Yiddishe Momma,' 38, 39

National Academy of Popular Music, 200, 228
Neil Sedaka: 50 Years Of Hits (show), 200, 205–8, 220
Nelson, Ricky, 11, 17, 40, 47, 228
'Never Again,' 175
Nevins, Al, 24–5, 34, 36–7, 39, 48, 51–2, **131**, 197
'Next Door To An Angel,' 13, 26, 39, 44, 194, 208
Nixon, Richard, 128, 166, 185
Nolan, Tom, 180, 181
Nordanelles, The, 28–31, **131**
Norman, Philip, 224, 226
Nurnberg, Charles, 220

Ocean's Eleven (film), 180
'Oh! Carol,' 7, 12, 26, 85, 107, 116–17, 118, 122, 131, 145, 146, 194, 195, 208, 232
'Oh Neil,' 131
Olstead, Renee, 205, 219
'Only Love Can Break A Heart,' 47
Orbison, Roy, 229
'Our Last Song Together,' 112–13, 119, 146, 158, 165, 242

Page, Patti, 49, 175
Paleface (film), 21
Partridge Family, The, 176
Paul, Les, 174
Perry, Richard, 95, 96

'Personality,' 107
Peter Paul & Mary, 75, 220
Philadelphia Phillies, 10
Pinky Lee (TV show), 51
Pinto, Laura, 214, 233
Pitney, Gene, 47, 84, 193, 195
'Please Mr Postman,' 179
Please, Please Me, 42
Pleshette, Eugene, 36
Polydor (label), 116, 118
PolyGram (label), 197
'Por Amor Viviremos,' 169
Presley, Elvis, 16, 17, 25, 26, 44, 66, 147, 209, 210, 228, 229
'Puppet Man,' 64, 65, 213

'Queen Of Hearts,' 224

Rabkin, Eddie, 23, **130**
Raelettes, The, 172
Rapp, Charlie, 29
RCA (label), 7, 12, 25, 34, 45–7, 48, 50, 51–2, 73, 90, 95, 101, 116, 117, 120, 198
Reagan, Ronald, 192
Real Neil, The, 224
Reid, John, 128, 145, 146, 159, 160, 164
Rickles, Don, 51
Righteous Brothers, The, 108
'Ring Ring,' 236
Rivers, Joan, 75
Riviera Hotel, 179–81, 183, 184, 186
Road To Nowhere, 71
Roberts, Lea, 159, 160
Robinson, Smokey, 229
Rock and Roll Hall of Fame, 198, 228–33, 235, 238–9, 240
Rock'n'roll Christmas Show, 35
'Rock'n'roll Wedding Day,' 119
Rocket Records (label), 18, 145, 146–7, 155, 157, 159, 175, 187, 199–200, 207
Rodgers, Mary, 60, 77, 78
Rodgers, Richard, 60, 77, 78, 194, 226
Rogers, Bob, 68–9
Rolling Stones, The, 117
Ronettes, The, 108
Royal Albert Hall, 15, 18, 102–4, 117, 226

Royal Festival Hall, 127–8
Royal Philharmonic Orchestra, 15, 98, 222
Rubin, Don, 69–70
Russell, Brenda, 149, 162
Russell, Brian, 149
Russell, Leon, 148
Ruth, Babe, 105
Rydell, Bobby, 17, 35

'Sad Eyes,' 158
Sager, Carole Bayer, 18, 46, 61, 62–3, 75, 88, 101, 212
Saturday Night Fever (film), 82, 190
Saturday Night Live (TV show), 185
Schreibman, Marc, 59
Section, The, 149
Sedaka, Dara, 13, 40, 52, 61, 78, 79, 98, **142**, **144**, 157, 186, 188, 189–92, 238
Sedaka, Eleanor, 19–21, 25, 26–8, 33–4, 36, 37–8, 52, 53–4, 55, 58, **129**, **132**, 186, 238, 239
Sedaka, Leba, 15, 22, 30–2, 33–4, 35–6, 46, 52, 53–4, 56, 58, 59, 60, 62, 66–7, 71, 79, 80, 83, 86, 97, 98, 101, 104, 107, 110, 112, 117–18, 123, 126, 127, 128, **138**, **142**, 146, 160, 161, 162–3, 178, 181–2, 185–6, 195, 197, 201, 207, 220, 221, 224, 238, 239
Sedaka, Mac, 19–20, 21, 27–8, **129**, **132**, 186, 238
Sedaka, Marc, 61, 72, 79, 125–6, 161, 186, 220
Sedaka, Ronnie, 19, 20, 27–8, **129**, 238–9
Sedaka's Back, 158, 159, 162, 164, 167, 168, 188
Shaffer, Paul, 172, 173–4, 205, 208, 212, 232
Sharp, Dee Dee, 176
Shirelles, The, 35, 45, 195
Shoals, Steve, 25, 46, **131**
Shore, Dinah, 21, 162, 191
'Should've Never Let You Go,' 13, 190–2, 205, 236
Siegel, Jay, 23–4, 90, 91, 212, 233

Simmons, Gene, 234–5
Simon, Carly, 62, 149, 162
Simon, Neil, 19
Sinatra, Frank, 13, 16, 37, 154, 164, 180, 190, 196, 210, 218, 229
Sinatra, Nancy, 190
'Since I Fell For You,' 175
Sklar, Leland, 149, 162
Slammer, Susan, 201
Smith, Keely, 196
Smith, William, 149
'Solitaire,' 15, 18, 93–7, 101, 103–4, 111, 114, 116, 127, 128, 159, 162, 165, 179, 186, 203, 204, 206, 216, 218, 242
Solitaire, 7, 114–15, 116, 157, 158
'Someone Saved My Life Tonight,' 194
'Somethin' Stupid,' 190
Sonny & Cher, 108–9
Sonny & Cher Show (TV show), 108–9
South Sydney Leagues Clubs, 66
Spector, Phil, 11, 94, 108
Spizz, Norman, 28, 30, **131**
'Splish Splash,' 37, 89
Springfield, Dusty, 117
'Stairway To Heaven,' 12, 26, 194
'Standing On The Inside,' 110 20, 123, 128, 146, 158, 165
'Star-Crossed Lovers,' 67–8, 69, 88, 101, 117
Stein, Seymour, 128, 145, 228, 231, 232
Steinberg, Jerry, 38, 53, 56–7, 59
'Steppin' Out,' 188
Steppin' Out, 188, 199
Stewart, Eric, 113, 115
Stewart, Rod, 127
Stigwood, Robert, 55, 182, 190
Still Standing (TV show), 219
Stoller, Mike, 150, 151
Strassberg, Esther, 28–9, 30, 31, 33, 38
Strassberg, Leba, *see* Sedaka, Leba
Studdard, Ruben, 201, 202, 203, 204
'Stupid Cupid,' 12, 25, 37, 49, 73, 194, 208, 237

Stylistics, The, 106–7
Styne, Jule, 77
Sullivan, Ed, 39, 42, 43, **137**, *see also Ed Sullivan Show, The*
Summer, Donna, 234
'Sundown,' 107
'Sunny,' 48
'Superbird,' 73, 74, 78, 128, 223
'Superstar,' 179
'Suspicions,' 119
Sutter, Ben, 26–7, 33, 37–8, 39, 40, 50, 51–2, 53, 54–8, 59, 60, 178, 179, 239
Swinging Blue Jeans, 117

'Take Good Care Of My Baby,' 107
Tapestry, 14, 71–2, 73
Taupin, Bernie, 194
Taylor, James, 71, 148, 149, 162
'Tears On My Pillow,' 25, 107
Teddy Bears, The, 11
10cc, 7, 18, 82, 113, 114–15, 119, 120, 128, 237
Tennille, Toni, **142**, **143**, **144**, 166, 169, 238
Thatcher, Margaret, 189
'That's When The Music Takes Me,' 13, 101–2, 114, 127, 128, 146, 158, 188, 208
'There's Still A Few Good Love Songs Left In Me,' 196
They Sold A Million (TV show), 201, 202
'Things We Do For Love, The,' 113
Thompkins Jr, Russell, 106–7
Three Suns, The, 25
Tin Pan Alley, 24, 213
Tischler, Howard, 28, **131**
'To Know Him Is To Love Him,' 11
Today Show (TV show), 200
Tokens, The, 24, 25, 46, 73, 90, 91, 212
Tonight Show, The (TV show), 95, 191
'Top Of The World,' 179
'Town Without Pity,' 47
Tra-La Days Are Over, The, 7, 119, 122, 126, 157–8, 167
Trenyce, 203
Truman, Harry, 209
'Trying To Say Goodbye,' 92, 103, 114, 242

Turner, Michael, 47, 84
Twitty, Conway, 11

UK (label), 114
'Unforgettable,' 190
'Uptown,' 94

Vee, Bobby, 35, 107
Vinton, Bobby, 35, 165

Waking Up Is Hard To Do, 220
Warwick, Dionne, 193
Washington, Dinah, 100, 175
'Way I Want To Touch You, The,' 168
'We Gotta Get Out Of This Place,' 64, 160
Webb, Jimmy, 74
Weil, Cynthia, 71, 89, 94, 229
Welch, Lenny, 174–5
Wenner, Jann, 228, 231
'We've Only Just Begun,' 179
Wexler, Jerry, 24, 228
'When Love Comes Knockin' At Your Door,' 18, 61, 63
'When Somebody Loves You,' 196
'Where The Boys Are,' 194, 203, 206, 210
'Who Put The Bomp,' 64
'Will You Still Love Me Tomorrow,' 73
William Morris Agency, 74
Williams, Andy, 95, 97, 162, 176
Wilson, Mary, 84
Wine, Toni, 45, 46, 47, 62
Wooky Hollow (club), 82, 83, 87, 98
'Wooly Bully,' 211
Workin' On A Groovy Thing, 69

'Yesterday Once More,' 179
'You Never Done It Like That,' 170
Young, Kenny, 148

Zolotin, Cynthia, 23, **130**

ACHNOWLEDGEMENTS

AUTHOR'S THANKS

Without the full cooperation of Neil and Leba Sedaka and their children, Dara and Marc, this wouldn't be possible. Nothing was off limits. They not only opened their doors to me, they opened their lives. I also have to thank Rob Cotto, Neil's assistant and co-producer of *The Real Neil*, for his enormous help on this, along with Neil's longtime assistant Lui Marquez.

To be able to connect with more than 50 songwriters, musicians, music executives, and disc jockeys, one needs a lot of help. And, to put it all down and shape into an interesting and exciting read, one needs great editors. Sari Botton once again performed magic on my early drafts. I can't thank her enough. Many thanks also go out to Tom Seabrook, who edited the book for Jawbones Press, for his patience, great eye, and expertise. A wonderful writer in his own right (*Bowie In Berlin*), Tom was a joy to work with. I'd also like to thank John Cerullo for his early thoughts on the structure of the book.

A key to the story was Elton John. From the first day, I knew he would be difficult to interview. My thanks go out to Fran Curtis of Rogers & Cowan for her efforts on my behalf, and especially to John Barbis, the head of Elton's North American management company, who made my interview possible.

While Sir Elton made Neil's comeback possible, it couldn't have happened without all the great new songs Sedaka wrote with Phil Cody. I can't thank Phil enough for his openness in retelling how he met Neil, and how the lyrics to these songs came about from his perspective.

I also need to thank the following songwriters, producers, and performers who took time to discuss the great success they had recording Mr Sedaka's songs or their relationships with him. They include Barry Gibb of The Bee Gees, Dion, Toni Tennille, Kip Cohen, Graham Gouldman of 10cc, Marilyn McCoo and Billy Davis Jr of The

Fifth Dimension, Clay Aiken, Seymour Stein, Clive Davis, Richard Perry, John Reid, Paul Shaffer, Connie Francis, Jay Siegel of The Tokens, Nigel Lythgoe of *American Idol*, Carole Bayer Sager, Burt Bacharach, Tony Orlando, Mary Rodgers, Toni Wine, Dick Fox, Robert Appere, Artie Butler, Artie Kaplan, Lee Holdridge, Bill Kenwright, Laurie Mansfield, Alan Grubman, Kathie Lee Gifford, Bruce 'Cousin Brucie' Morrow, Phillip Norman, and Paul Gambaccini.

Special thanks also go out to Mr Sedaka's boyhood friend Freddie Gershon, who recounted those early days, to record exec Colin Finkelstein, to Michael Feinstein, and to David Foster.

My gratitude also goes out to Emily Churchill, archivist for the Royal Festival Hall, to rock'n'roll historian Laura Pinto, to Michael Jurick for his digital photography assistance, to UK podcasters Simon Barber and Brian O'Connor, and to Stuart Marland and Glenn Rosenblum for their expertise. Last but not least, I want to thank my wife Diana and my children Sarah and Daniel for their patience during all the calls and the time this book took me away from them.

PUBLISHER'S THANKS

All of the photographs used in this book are from Neil Sedaka's personal archives, and we are grateful for his help. Thanks also to Robert Cotto and Lui Marquez for their help with sourcing the images and compiling the discography.

MILLION DOLLAR
BASH: BOB DYLAN,
THE BAND, AND THE
BASEMENT TAPES
by Sid Griffin

ISBN 978-1-906002-05-3

HOT BURRITOS:
THE TRUE STORY OF
THE FLYING BURRITO
BROTHERS
by John Einarson with
Chris Hillman

ISBN 978-1-906002-16-9

BOWIE IN BERLIN:
A NEW CAREER IN A
NEW TOWN
by Thomas Jerome
Seabrook

ISBN 978-1-906002-08-4

TO LIVE IS TO DIE:
THE LIFE AND DEATH
OF METALLICA'S
CLIFF BURTON
by Joel McIver

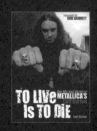

ISBN 978-1-906002-24-4

MILLION DOLLAR
LES PAUL: IN SEARCH
OF THE MOST
VALUABLE GUITAR IN
THE WORLD
by Tony Bacon

ISBN 978-1-906002-14-5

THE IMPOSSIBLE
DREAM: THE STORY
OF SCOTT WALKER
AND THE WALKER
BROTHERS
by Anthony Reynolds

ISBN 978-1-906002-25-1

JACK BRUCE:
COMPOSING
HIMSELF: THE
AUTHORISED
BIOGRAPHY
by Harry Shapiro

ISBN 978-1-906002-26-8

FOREVER CHANGES:
ARTHUR LEE AND THE
BOOK OF LOVE
by John Einarson

ISBN 978-1-906002-31-2

RETURN OF THE
KING: ELVIS PRESLEY'S
GREAT COMEBACK
by Gillian G. Gaar

ISBN 978-1-906002-28-2

A WIZARD, A TRUE
STAR: TODD
RUNDGREN IN THE
STUDIO
by Paul Myers

ISBN 978-1-906002-33-6

SEASONS THEY
CHANGE: THE STORY
OF ACID AND
PSYCHEDELIC FOLK
by Jeanette Leech

ISBN 978-1-906002-32-9

WON'T GET FOOLED
AGAIN: THE WHO
FROM LIFEHOUSE TO
QUADROPHENIA
by Richie Unterberger

ISBN 978-1-906002-35-0

THE
RESURRECTION OF
JOHNNY CASH:
HURT, REDEMPTION,
AND AMERICAN
RECORDINGS
by Graeme Thomson

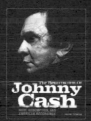

ISBN 978-1-906002 36-7

CRAZY TRAIN: THE
HIGH LIFE AND
TRAGIC DEATH OF
RANDY RHOADS
by Joel McIver

ISBN 978-1-906002-37-4

JUST CAN'T GET
ENOUGH:
THE MAKING OF
DEPECHE MODE
by Simon Spence

ISBN 978-1-906002-56-5

GLENN HUGHES:
FROM DEEP PURPLE
TO BLACK COUNTRY
COMMUNION
by Glenn Hughes

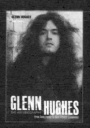

ISBN 978-1-906002-92-3

ENTERTAIN US:
THE RISE OF NIRVANA
by Gillian G. Gaar

ISBN 978-1-906002-89-3

MIKE SCOTT:
ADVENTURES OF A
WATERBOY
by Mike Scott

ISBN 978-1-908279-24-8

SHE BOP: THE
DEFINITIVE HISTORY
OF WOMEN IN
POPULAR MUSIC
by Lucy O'Brien
Revised Third Edition

ISBN 978-1-908279-27-9

SOLID
FOUNDATION: AN
ORAL HISTORY OF
REGGAE
by David Katz
Revised and Expanded
Edition

ISBN 978-1-908279-30-9

READ & BURN:
A BOOK ABOUT WIRE
by Wilson Neate

ISBN 978-1-908279-33-0

BIG STAR: THE STORY
OF ROCK'S
FORGOTTEN BAND
by Rob Jovanovic
Revised & Updated
Edition

ISBN 978-1-908279-36-1

RECOMBO DNA: THE
STORY OF DEVO: OR
HOW THE 60s BECAME
THE 80s
by Kevin C. Smith

ISBN 978-1-908279-39-2

TOUCHED BY
GRACE: MY TIME
WITH JEFF BUCKLEY
by Gary Lucas

ISBN 978-1-908279-45-3